Secrets and Power in Myanmar

The **ISEAS – Yusof Ishak Institute** (formerly Institute of Southeast Asian Studies) is an autonomous organization established in 1968. It is a regional centre dedicated to the study of socio-political, security, and economic trends and developments in Southeast Asia and its wider geostrategic and economic environment. The Institute's research programmes are grouped under Regional Economic Studies (RES), Regional Strategic and Political Studies (RSPS), and Regional Social and Cultural Studies (RSCS). The Institute is also home to the ASEAN Studies Centre (ASC), the Temasek History Research Centre (THRC), and the Singapore APEC Study Centre.

ISEAS Publishing, an established academic press, has issued more than 2,000 books and journals. It is the largest scholarly publisher of research about Southeast Asia from within the region. ISEAS Publishing works with many other academic and trade publishers and distributors to disseminate important research and analyses from and about Southeast Asia to the rest of the world.

Secrets and Power in Myanmar

Intelligence and the Fall of General Khin Nyunt

ANDREW SELTH

 YUSOF ISHAK INSTITUTE

First published in Singapore in 2019 by
ISEAS Publishing
30 Heng Mui Keng Terrace
Singapore 119614

E-mail: publish@iseas.edu.sg
Website: <http://bookshop.iseas.edu.sg>

All rights reserved. No part of this publication may be reproduced, stored in a retrieval system, or transmitted in any form or by any means, electronic, mechanical, photocopying, recording or otherwise, without the prior permission of the ISEAS – Yusof Ishak Institute.

© 2019 ISEAS – Yusof Ishak Institute, Singapore

The responsibility for facts and opinions in this publication rests exclusively with the author and his interpretations do not necessarily reflect the views or the policy of the publisher or its supporters.

ISEAS Library Cataloguing-in-Publication Data

Name: Selth, Andrew.
Title: Secrets and Power in Myanmar : Intelligence and the Fall of General Khin Nyunt / by Andrew Selth.
Description: Singapore : ISEAS – Yusof Ishak Institute, 2019. | Includes index.
Identifiers: ISBN 978-981-4843-77-5 (paperback) | ISBN 978-981-4843-79-9 (pdf)
Subjects: LCSH: Military intelligence--Myanmar. | Myanmar--Armed forces.
Classification: LCC UB251 B9S46

Cover photo credit: AP Photo/Apichart Weerawong.

Typeset by International Typesetters Pte Ltd

Deep in Burmese thinking is the belief that to have secrets is to be on the side of power.

> Lucian W. Pye
> *The Spirit of Burmese Politics* (1959)*

---

* Lucian W. Pye, *The Spirit of Burmese Politics: A Preliminary Survey of a Politics of Fear and Charisma* (Cambridge: Centre for International Studies, Massachusetts Institute of Technology, 1959), p. 14.

CONTENTS

Executive Summary   ix

Preface   xii

Acronyms and Abbreviations   xxiii

1. Introduction   1

2. Myanmar's Intelligence Apparatus Before 2004   8
   The Military Intelligence Organization
   Other Intelligence Agencies
   Related Organizations and Laws

3. The Fall of General Khin Nyunt   56
   Five Theories
   Personalized Power

4. Power Shifts and Structural Changes   82
   Out With The Old
   In With The New

5. Intelligence Developments Since 2011   113
   Organizational Changes
   Behavioural Changes

6. Intelligence Failures　151
   Operational Failures
   Analytical Failures

7. Foreign Relationships　170
   Foreign Operations
   Counterespionage Concerns
   Cooperative Arrangements

8. Questions of Accountability　197

9. Conclusion　205

Select Bibliography　211

Index　233

About the Author　248

EXECUTIVE SUMMARY

In 2003, Myanmar was described as one of the most tightly controlled dictatorships in the world. The main instrument used by the military regime to maintain this status was the country's extensive intelligence apparatus, which was dominated by the Office of the Chief of Military Intelligence (OCMI), known before 2001 as the Directorate of Defence Services Intelligence (DDSI). It not only performed all the usual intelligence functions, but played a major role in Myanmar's political, economic and social life. It was also an important factor in its international relations. Since 1983, this apparatus had been managed by General Khin Nyunt.

During this period, five features marked the intelligence state. First, the apparatus was dominated by the armed forces. Second, the main focus of the national intelligence effort was on domestic security. Third, the intelligence apparatus was characterized by a total commitment to unity, stability and sovereignty, as perceived by the ruling military council. Fourth, all security agencies relied on human intelligence, much more than on technical sources. Fifth, there was a tension between the imperative to have a single person or organization directing the entire intelligence apparatus, and the wish to spread power between multiple agencies under independent managers.

The power and behaviour of DDSI/OCMI exacerbated tensions between Khin Nyunt and other members of Myanmar's military leadership, leading to his downfall in 2004. OCMI was comprehensively purged and replaced by the Office of the Chief of Military Security Affairs (OCMSA). Primary responsibility for internal security shifted to the Myanmar Police Force's Special Branch. However, Myanmar's intelligence capabilities had been severely weakened. Since 2004, considerable efforts have been made to recover these capabilities, but they have still not been fully restored, contributing to a number of notable intelligence failures.

Since the advent of Thein Sein's quasi-civilian government in 2011, and the election of Aung San Suu Kyi's National League for Democracy administration in 2015, there appear to have been few significant structural changes to Myanmar's intelligence apparatus. The organizations and practices that characterized military rule appear to have survived, although the authorities now seem to be relying more on technical sources, and semi-legal rather than extra-legal means, to exercise controls. Some recent developments, however, including a series of attacks by militant groups in Rakhine State, could prompt greater attention to intelligence issues.

Since the political opening in 2011, Myanmar's security forces have reached out to their foreign counterparts, both in the region and further afield. New defence links have been forged. However, Naypyidaw is now facing the prospect of a return to international isolation and punitive sanctions, as the government and armed forces face charges of ethnic cleansing—even genocide—against the Muslim Rohingyas in Rakhine State. Relationships with Myanmar's neighbours and some others will survive, but one casualty of its renewed pariah status may be any developing intelligence contacts with Western countries.

Even as Myanmar faces new external pressures, it is unlikely that the focus on internal security will change. Both Aung San Suu Kyi's government and the armed forces know that their survival—and, in their view, the country's survival—are threatened more by disunity and domestic instability than by any international developments. This will ensure that the national intelligence apparatus will continue to be given a high priority, will still be internally focused and will effectively remain under the control of the country's armed forces.

PREFACE

NOMENCLATURE

After Myanmar's armed forces crushed a nation-wide pro-democracy uprising in September 1988, the country's official name (in English) was changed from its post–1974 form, the "Socialist Republic of the Union of Burma", back to the "Union of Burma", which had been adopted when Myanmar regained its independence from the United Kingdom (UK) in January 1948. In July 1989, the new military government changed the country's name once again, this time to the "Union of Myanmar", which had long been the vernacular version (in the literary register, at least). In the formal declaration of the country's independence from the UK in 1948, for example, it was called the Union of Burma in the English version and the Union of Myanmar (or "Myanma") in the Burmese version. Also in July 1989, a number of other place names were changed to conform more closely to their original pronunciation in the Burmese language. In 2011, after formal promulgation of the 2008 national constitution, the country's official name was changed yet again, this time to the "Republic of the Union of Myanmar".

The new names have been accepted by most countries, the United Nations and other major international organizations. A few governments, activist groups and news media outlets, however, still cling to the old forms, apparently as a protest against the former military regime's refusal to put the question of a name change to the people of Myanmar.[1] The old names were also believed to be the preference of then opposition leader Aung San Suu Kyi, who was held under virtual house arrest by the military regime for almost fifteen years. Questioned about the official name of the country soon after her party took office in 2016, Aung San Suu Kyi stated her continuing preference for the colonial-era term "Burma", but said that both names were acceptable.[2] In this book, the official change of names has been observed, although "Burma" and "Burmese" have been retained for formal titles used before 1989 and for the citation of works using that name. "Burmese" is also used to describe the dominant language of the country. Such usage does not carry any political connotations.

The armed forces have effectively ruled Myanmar ever since General Ne Win's military coup in March 1962 but, from 1974 to 1988, they exercised power through an ostensibly elected "civilian" parliament dominated by the Burma Socialist Programme Party, the country's only legal political organization. On taking back direct control in September 1988, the armed forces created the State Law and Order Restoration Council (SLORC), which ruled by decree. In November 1997, apparently on the advice of a United States-based public relations firm, the regime changed its name to the State Peace and Development Council (SPDC), but continued to rule through executive fiat.[3] In May 2008, it held a constitutional referendum, with predictable results.[4] This was followed by carefully managed elections on 7 November 2010. The resulting national parliament, consisting of 75 per cent elected officials and 25 per cent non-elected military officers, met in January 2011. A new government was installed under President Thein Sein in March that year.

Continuing this process, by-elections were staged on 1 April 2012 to fill 48 seats left vacant after recently-elected Members of Parliament (MPs) had resigned to take up ministerial appointments, or had died. The opposition National League for Democracy (NLD), which was re-registered for the elections in December 2011, claimed that fraud and rules violations were widespread, but the party still won 43 of the 45 seats available on the day. One successful candidate was the party's leader, Aung San Suu Kyi.

On 8 November 2015, a new general election was held which, by most accounts, was reasonably free and fair.[5] The NLD received about 65.6 per cent of all votes cast, while the pro-military Union Solidarity Development Party received 27.5 per cent. Under Myanmar's "first-past-the-post" electoral system, this gave the NLD 79.4 per cent of all the available seats.[6] It secured 255 in the 440-seat lower house (*Pyitthu Hluttaw* or House of Representatives), and 135 in the 224-seat upper house (*Amyotha Hluttaw* or House of Nationalities), a total of 390 of the 491 seats contested at the Union level.[7] The armed forces were allocated 25 per cent of the seats in both houses, but this gave the NLD a clear majority in the combined Union Assembly (*Pyidaungsu Hluttaw*). As a result, it was able to elect a new president in 2016 and pass a law creating the position of State Counsellor for Aung San Suu Kyi (who under the 2008 constitution is unable to become president).[8] The national charter clearly states that the president "takes precedence over all other persons" in Myanmar but, even before the elections, Aung San Suu Kyi had made it clear that she intended to be "above the president" and act as the country's de facto leader.[9]

After the UK dispatched troops to the royal capital of Mandalay and completed its three-stage conquest of Burma (as it was then called) in December 1885, Yangon (then known as Rangoon) was confirmed as the administrative capital of the country. It remains the commercial capital, but in November 2005 the SPDC formally designated the newly-built city of Naypyidaw (or Nay Pyi Taw), 325 kilometres north of Yangon, as the seat of Myanmar's government. Where they appear in this book, the terms "Rangoon regime", "Yangon regime", or in some cases simply "Rangoon" or "Yangon", are used as shorthand terms for the central government, including the military government that was created in 1962 and re-invented in 1974, 1988 and 1997. The government after 2005 is referred to as the "Naypyidaw regime", or "Naypyidaw", to reflect the administrative change that took place that year.

Another term used in this book is *Tatmadaw*. It is usually translated as "royal force", but the honorific "daw" no longer refers to the monarchy. Since 1948, the name has been the vernacular term for Myanmar's tri-service (army, navy and air force) armed forces. In recent years, it has gained wide currency in English language publications on Myanmar. Sometimes, the Tatmadaw is referred to simply as "the army", reflecting that service arm's overwhelming size and influence, compared with the other two. While the term "Defence Services" usually refers only to the armed forces, it is sometimes used in a wider context to refer collectively to the armed forces, the Myanmar Police Force, the "people's militia" and sundry other state-endorsed paramilitary forces. On occasion, the Myanmar Fire Services Department and Myanmar Red Cross have also been included in this category. As the 2008 constitution decrees that "all the armed forces in the Union shall be under the command of the Defence Services", the formal title of the Tatmadaw's most senior officer is Commander-in-Chief of Defence Services.[10]

Over the years, some components of Myanmar's intelligence apparatus have changed their formal titles several times. The military intelligence organization, for example, has periodically been renamed, usually to coincide with structural changes in the armed forces. These adjustments have not always been known to, or recognized by, foreign observers. Also, Burmese language titles have been translated into English in different ways. The use of popular names has added another complication. For example, ever since 1948 the Tatmadaw's intelligence arm has been widely known as the Military Intelligence Service, or simply the "MI" ("em-eye"). Similarly, the Police Force's Special Intelligence Department (or, strictly translated, the "Information Police"), has long been known as the Special Branch, or "SB". All this has meant that in the literature some agencies have been called by several different names, and not always accurately.

SOURCES AND METHODS

The aim of this book is to update and complement an earlier study of Myanmar's intelligence apparatus, first published as a working paper by the Australian National University's Strategic and Defence Studies Centre (SDSC) in 1997.[11] The paper surveyed the development of Myanmar's intelligence system and capabilities over the half century from 1948, when the country first created independent intelligence agencies. An extract from this paper later appeared as "SLORC's 'IntelNet': Burma's Intelligence Apparatus" in the *Burma Debate*, a publication of The Burma Project of the Open Society Institute.[12] In 1998, a revised version of the SDSC working paper was published as an article titled "Burma's Intelligence Apparatus" in the academic journal *Intelligence and National Security*.[13]

This book is intended to reprise some of the historical background, establish a baseline for information, and take the story forward to the present day, using the downfall of General Khin Nyunt in 2004 to highlight a number of changes to Myanmar's intelligence system. It also briefly examines developments since the advent of a "discipline-flourishing democracy" under a mixed civilian-military government in 2011. A short introduction to the subject has already appeared in *Australian Outlook*, the blog of the Australian Institute of International Affairs.[14]

Despite the close attention paid to Myanmar's coercive apparatus since the 1988 pro-democracy uprising, little reliable information is available. Even now, after the political opening of 2011, hard data about the sizes, budgets and capabilities of the various security forces is still difficult to obtain.[15] The structure and internal workings of the country's intelligence agencies are even more opaque. It is unlikely that the civilian members of Aung San Suu Kyi's government—including the State Counsellor herself—are privy to all the relevant information. Particularly sensitive matters are probably known only to a small group of senior military officers. Indeed, secrecy has long been an obsession with those concerned with security issues, and harsh penalties are imposed on anyone believed to have betrayed state secrets, a term that has a very wide definition in Myanmar.[16] This has made most people in the country (and even outside it, if they wish to preserve their access and protect family members still resident there) wary of speaking about sensitive issues with researchers. Even foreign agencies with access to advanced technologies and privileged information consider the country's security forces, including the national intelligence apparatus, a black hole.[17]

Ironically, the lack of reliable information about Myanmar's intelligence agencies seems at times to be in inverse proportion to the number of people who have written about them, and commented on their organization, leadership and operations. Much of this product is based on anecdotal evidence, gossip and speculation. However, as Donald Emmerson once noted, "the plural of anecdote is not data".[18] Occasional glimpses behind the scenes have rarely, if ever, given observers the whole picture.[19] Also, Myanmar's security forces tend to arouse strong feelings on the part of some commentators, leading at times to biased and misleading reports. That said, over the years some useful contributions have been made to the public record by well-informed and objective reporters and analysts.[20] By carefully surveying all this material, weeding out improbabilities and trying to connect the dots, it is possible to make some broad observations about the historical development and current status of Myanmar's intelligence apparatus, its structure, activities and attitudes. Albeit based on incomplete data and informed guesswork, such an exercise can throw some light on the way that the apparatus functions and facilitate a greater understanding of its place in modern Myanmar.

It is acknowledged that this book relies heavily on works published in English. If they were able and prepared to speak frankly, much could be learned from members or former members of the Myanmar government and security forces. At the very least, they could correct or put into context reports that have appeared in the news media or online, the reliability of which must in many cases be considered suspect. Also, in recent years, a number of autobiographical and historical works have been published in Burmese by former military and intelligence officers, including by Khin Nyunt himself.[21] They tend to be rather self-serving, and are often couched in cautious language, but even so they offer personal and in some cases useful perspectives on the developments discussed in this book.[22] A number of interviews were conducted, and unofficial translations of some memoirs were consulted.[23] Where appropriate, they have been reflected in the text and endnotes. However, it has been left to researchers with a greater command of the Burmese language to follow up the matters raised below, and to make the public record more accurate and complete.

ACKNOWLEDGEMENTS

In researching and writing this book, I was assisted by a number of colleagues and fellow Myanmar-watchers, notably *Sayagyi* David Steinberg and Rhys Thompson. Michael Wesley and Ian Holliday were kind enough to read the manuscript and provide comments for the cover. For various reasons, others did not wish to be named, but I owe them all my thanks. I am also indebted to the three anonymous reviewers who made a number of helpful suggestions for additions and amendments. As always, the encouragement and support of my wife Pattie was invaluable. Needless to say, any errors of commission or omission are mine alone. Finally, for the record, my 1998 article on this subject drew only on open sources, represented my views alone and had no official status or endorsement. The same caveats apply to this book.

Notes

1. Andrew Selth and Adam Gallagher, "What's in a Name: Burma or Myanmar?", *The Olive Branch*, 21 June 2018, https://www.usip.org/blog/2018/06/whats-name-burma-or-myanmar.

2. Andrew Selth, "More Name Games in Burma/Myanmar", *The Interpreter*, 10 August 2016, https://www.lowyinstitute.org/the-interpreter/more-name-games-burmamyanmar.
3. David S. Mathieson, "The Burma Road to Nowhere: The Failure of the Developmental State in Myanmar", *Policy, Organisation and Society* 17, no. 7 (1999): 108. See also "A SLORC By Any Other Name", *Washington Post*, 6 March 1998, https://www.washingtonpost.com/archive/opinions/1998/03/06/a-slorc-by-any-other-name/84bdf222-1eb8-417c-97ee-032cd9535e91/?noredirect=on.
4. The SPDC claimed that 92.48 per cent of eligible voters endorsed the new constitution. *Constitution of the Republic of the Union of Myanmar (2008)* (Nay Pyi Taw: Ministry of Information, 2008), p. iv.
5. The Carter Centre, *Observing Myanmar's 2015 General Elections: Final Report* (Atlanta: Carter Centre, 2016), https://www.cartercenter.org/resources/pdfs/news/peace_publications/election_reports/myanmar-2015-final.pdf.
6. Kyaw Kyaw, "Analysis of Myanmar's NLD Landslide", *New Mandala*, 1 May 2012, http://www.newmandala.org/analysis-of-myanmars-nld-landslide/.
7. *The Myanmar Elections: Results and Implications*, Asia Briefing No. 147 (Yangon/Brussels: International Crisis Group, 9 December 2015).
8. "Myanmar's 2015 Landmark Elections Explained", *BBC News*, 3 December 2015, http://www.bbc.com/news/world-asia-33547036.
9. *Constitution of the Republic of the Union of Myanmar (2008)*, chapter 3, clause 58. See also "Myanmar Election: Aung San Suu Kyi will be 'Above President'", *BBC News*, 5 November 2015, http://www.bbc.com/news/av/world-asia-34729691/myanmar-election-aung-san-suu-kyi-will-be-above-president.
10. *Constitution of the Republic of the Union of Myanmar (2008)*, chapter 7, clause 338.
11. Andrew Selth, *Burma's Intelligence Apparatus*, Working Paper No. 308 (Canberra: Strategic and Defence Studies Centre, Australian National University, 1997).

12. Andrew Selth, "SLORC's 'Intel-Net': Burma's Intelligence Apparatus", *Burma Debate* 4, no. 4 (October 1997): 4–18.
13. Andrew Selth, "Burma's Intelligence Apparatus", *Intelligence and National Security* 13, no. 4 (Winter 1998): 33–70.
14. Andrew Selth, "Myanmar's Intelligence State", *Australian Outlook*, 20 September 2018, https://www.internationalaffairs.org.au/australianoutlook/myanmars-intelligence-state/.
15. Andrew Selth, "Known Knowns and Known Unknowns: Measuring Myanmar's Military Capabilities", *Contemporary Southeast Asia* 31, no. 2 (August 2009): 272–95.
16. See, for example, "Reuters Reporters Arrested in Yangon Under Official Secrets Act", *The Irrawaddy*, 13 December 2017, https://www.irrawaddy.com/news/burma/breaking-reuters-reporters-arrested-yangon-official-secrets-act.html.
17. Andrew Selth, "Myanmar's Coercive Apparatus: The Long Road to Reform", in *Myanmar: The Dynamics of an Evolving Polity*, edited by David I. Steinberg (Boulder: Lynne Rienner, 2015), pp. 13–36.
18. This comment was made at a workshop on Myanmar arranged by the Konrad Adenauer Foundation and the Brookings Institution, held in Washington D.C. in October 2009 and attended by the author.
19. For example, the autobiography of former Chief of Intelligence Khin Nyunt, titled *The Experiences of My Life* and published in Burmese in 2015, as well as a number of other works by him, are useful but cannot be taken at face value.
20. In 2010 and 2011, a large number of cables sent from the US Embassy in Yangon (called Rangoon by the US Government) to the State Department in Washington D.C. were obtained by the Wikileaks organization and released without official authorization. While several of these cables have been quoted in this book, it must be noted for the record that, as leaked documents, they cannot be verified as genuine, or accurate.
21. See, for example, Sean Gleeson, "Still Not Sorry: Neither Modesty nor Mea Culpa in Khin Nyunt Memoir", *The Irrawaddy*, 3 March

2015, https://www.irrawaddy.com/news/burma/still-not-sorry-neither-modesty-nor-mea-culpa-in-khin-nyunt-memoir.html; and "War and Politics, in Burmese", *New Mandala*, 17 November 2010, https://www.newmandala.org/war-and-politics-in-burmese/.

22. For example, a memoir by Nay Yi published in 2014 devotes an entire chapter to the fall of Khin Nyunt and the purge of the military intelligence apparatus in 2004. See Myo Lwin, "Book Review: Political Thoughts of a Former Military Intelligence Officer", *Myanmar Times*, 16 March 2015, https://www.mmtimes.com/national-news/13523-book-review-political-thoughts-of-a-former-military-intelligence-officer.html.

23. Several attempts were made to arrange an interview with former general Khin Nyunt in Yangon, but they were unsuccessful. Other interviews are noted by place, month and year only, to protect the identities of those involved.

ACRONYMS AND ABBREVIATIONS

In English

AA	Arakan Army
AIU	Air Force Intelligence Unit
AMIIM	ASEAN Military Intelligence Informal Meeting
ARF	ASEAN Regional Forum
ARSA	Arakan Rohingya Salvation Army
ASEAN	Association of Southeast Asian Nations
BGP	Border Guard Police
BSI	Bureau of Special Investigation
BSPP	Burma Socialist Programme Party
C-in-C	Commander-in-Chief
CEC	Central Executive Committee
CI	Chief of Intelligence
CIA	Central Intelligence Agency
CID	Criminal Investigation Department
COMINT	communications intelligence
CPB	Communist Party of Burma
DDSI	Directorate of Defence Services Intelligence
DKBA	Democratic Karen Buddhist Army
DSA	Defence Services Academy
DSIB	Defence Services Intelligence Bureau
DVB	*Democratic Voice of Burma*

EAG	ethnic armed groups
FBI	Federal Bureau of Investigation
GAD	General Administration Department
GCSB	Government Communications Security Bureau
GDR	German Democratic Republic
HIV/AIDS	human immuodeficiency virus infection and acquired immune deficiency syndrome
HQ	headquarters
HUMINT	human intelligence
IB	Intelligence Branch
IBMND	Intelligence Bureau of the Ministry of National Defence (*Ch'ing pao chu*)
ICG	International Crisis Group
IMINT	imagery intelligence
INSCOM	Intelligence and Security Command
IT	information technology
KIA	Kachin Independence Army
KNLA	Karen National Liberation Army
KNU	Karen National Union
LORC	Law and Order Restoration Council
LID	Light Infantry Division
MAS	Military Affairs Security
MFA	Ministry of Foreign Affairs
MFIU	Myanmar Financial Intelligence Unit
MI	Military Intelligence
MI5	(UK) Security Service
MI6	(UK) Secret Intelligence Service
MIS	Military Intelligence Service
MNDAA	Myanmar National Democratic Alliance Army

MOU	memorandum of understanding
MP	Member of Parliament
MPT	Ministry of Posts and Telecommunications
MPF	Myanmar Police Force
MRTV	Myanmar Radio and Television
MSA	Military Security Affairs
NCGUB	National Coalition Government of the Union of Burma
NCO	non-commissioned officer
NDSC	National Defence and Security Council
NGO	non-government organization
NIAS	Nordic Institute of Asian Studies
NIB	National Intelligence Bureau
NIU	Navy Intelligence Unit
NLD	National League for Democracy
NSA	National Security Agency
NUS	National University of Singapore
OCC	Operation Control Command
OCMAS	Office of the Chief of Military Affairs Security
OCMI	Office of the Chief of Military Intelligence
OCMSA	Office of the Chief of Military Security Affairs
OIC	Organisation of the Islamic Conference
OSINT	open source intelligence
OSS	Office of Strategic Studies
OTS	Officer Training School
P(4)	People's Property Protection Police
PDC	Peace and Development Council
PPF	People's Police Force
RAW (also R&AW)	Research and Analysis Wing
RCC	Regional Control Command

RMC	Regional Military Command
RRT	Refugee Review Tribunal
SB	Special Branch
SB2	Special Branch 2
SDSC	Strategic and Defence Studies Centre
SID	Special Intelligence Department
SIGINT	signals intelligence
SLORC	State Law and Order Restoration Council
SPDC	State Peace and Development Council
UAV	unmanned aerial vehicle
UK	United Kingdom
UN	United Nations
US	United States (of America)
USDA	Union Solidarity Development Association
USDP	Union Solidarity Development Party
UWSA	United Wa State Army

In Burmese

MaBaTha	Association for the Protection of Race and Religion
MaWaTa	Township Law and Order Restoration Council
MaYaKa	Township Peace and Development Council
NaAhPha	State Peace and Development Council
NaKaTha	Border Area Trade Directorate
NaSaKa	Border Area Immigration Control Command
NaSaYa	Border Supervisory Battalions
NaWaTa	State Law and Order Restoration Council
PaWaTa	Provincial Law and Order Restoration Council
SaSaSa	Bureau of Special Investigations

SaYaHpa	military intelligence organization
SaYaKha	Office of the Chief of Military Security Affairs
YaWaTa	Ward/Village Law and Order Restoration Council
YaYaKa	Ward/Village Peace and Development Council

Other Languages**

DGSE	*Direction Generale de la Securite Exterieure* (General Directorate for External Security)
Gestapo	*Geheime Staatspolizei* (Secret State Police)
GRU	*Glavnoye Razvedyvatelnoye Upravlenie* (Chief Intelligence Directorate of the Soviet General Staff)
IRASEC	*Institut de Recherche sur l'Asie du Sud-Est Contemporaine* (Research Institute on Contemporary Southeast Asia)
KGB	*Komitet Gosudarstvennoy Bezopasnosti* (Committee for State Security)
KMT	*Kuomintang* (Chinese National People's Party)
Mossad	*Ha Mossad le Modiyn ve le Tafkidim Mayuhadim* (Institute for Intelligence and Special Operations)
RSF	*Reporters Sans Frontieres* (Reporters Without Borders)
Shin Bet	*Sherut ha-Bitahon haKlali* (General Security Service)
Stasi	*Staatssicherheitsdienst* (Ministry for State Security)

** Diacritical marks have not been included.

Chapter 1

INTRODUCTION

> Rangoon is, during even normal times, a city of swirling rumours and wild speculation. The opacity of the regime's decision making, rare public forays and pronouncements by the SPDC's top generals, and extreme censorship all combine to create a void of factual information perhaps like no other country in the region. The result is incessant, and highly inconsistent, guesswork among local observers and Burmese citizens on the latest machinations of the secretive regime, often fuelled by international radio services (especially the Democratic Voice of Burma and Radio Free Asia) that frequently broadcast unconfirmed street rumours.
>
> "Is the Burmese Regime Coming Unglued?"
> Cable from the US Embassy, Rangoon, 28 January 2005[1]

In 2003, Myanmar was described by the United States (US) Council on Foreign Relations as "one of the most tightly controlled dictatorships in the world".[2] A number of factors contributed to this judgement, but the most obvious was the "pervasive intelligence apparatus" that had underpinned the ability of the armed forces (known as the *Tatmadaw*) to maintain a firm grip on the country for the previous forty years.[3] During this time, however, the intelligence system had evolved, changing not only in size and shape but also in its reach and influence. For the previous twenty years, it had been under the command of one man who, more than anyone else, was responsible for its development, power and impact on Myanmar society.

In 1983, after an extensive purge of its personnel, Myanmar's intelligence system had, in the words of a later president, "collapsed entirely".[4] One apparent result was that, in October that year, a team of three North Korean agents was able secretly to enter the country and stage a bomb attack in Yangon (then known as Rangoon) against the visiting South Korean president.[5] This incident deeply shocked and angered paramount leader General Ne Win, who decided to revamp the country's internal security agencies. He recalled the then relatively unknown Colonel Khin Nyunt from a posting to 44 Light Infantry Division (LID) and on 30 December 1983 appointed him Chief of Intelligence (CI).[6] Under Khin Nyunt's direction, the national intelligence apparatus was steadily rebuilt. Over the next two decades, it expanded in size, developed new capabilities and created new systems to manage information flows. As time passed, it extended its reach well beyond its traditional roles to embrace a wide range of important policy functions. In 1997, Thailand's National Security Council was told that Myanmar was spending 20 to 30 per cent of its "military development" budget on intelligence.[7]

Inside Myanmar, the military element of this apparatus collected and analysed strategic, operational and tactical intelligence. Assisted by a number of civilian agencies and investigative units, it rooted out dissidents in the public service and security forces, and conducted counter-espionage operations against suspected foreign agents.[8] Diplomatic missions were closely watched.[9] The civil population was monitored through an extensive and multi-faceted surveillance network, consisting of both professional agents and unpaid informers.[10] Agencies routinely intercepted radio traffic, listened to domestic and overseas telephone calls, recorded private conversations and opened mail.[11] From the mid-1990s, they kept a watchful eye on computer activity in Myanmar, monitored email and social media accounts, and engaged in information warfare. As far as their resources allowed, a few agencies exploited aerial photography of different kinds and, after it became available and affordable, commercial satellite imagery.[12]

Outside Myanmar, the government maintained a string of spies and informers, mainly in neighbouring countries.[13] Together with the diplomats and defence staff posted to Myanmar's embassies, agents and regime sympathizers reported on the activities of ethnic insurgents, black marketeers, narcotics and people traffickers, refugees and expatriates, including political activists and exile communities.[14] They also kept an eye on military developments in border areas that might affect Myanmar's security. The activities of international organizations like the United Nations (UN) and non-government organizations (NGOs) with an interest in Myanmar were monitored, as were the activities of selected foreign academics and journalists. A blacklist was maintained, identifying thousands of so-called "enemies of the state". The names of both foreigners and Myanmar citizens were included, ranging from genuine activists to people who had simply been critical of the regime.[15] At different levels, and in different ways, liaison relationships were developed with counterpart intelligence agencies in South Asia, China and the Association of Southeast Asian Nations (ASEAN).[16] There were also reported to be cooperative links with the security services of friendly countries, like Israel.[17]

As Myanmar's intelligence apparatus grew, so did its reputation. By the early 1990s, an experienced Myanmar-watcher could compare it to other official organizations in the country, and pronounce it "highly efficient".[18] A Thai observer described it in 1994 as "one of Asia's most efficient secret police forces".[19] In 1997, another went even further, calling Myanmar's "military intelligence network" the "fourth most efficient in the world", employing techniques used by services like Israel's *Mossad*, the United Kingdom's (UK) Secret Intelligence Service (known as MI6), the US's Central Intelligence Agency (CIA) and Federal Bureau of Investigation (FBI), and the Soviet Union's KGB.[20] This kind of hyperbole, added to the sensational stories that constantly circulated inside the country, helped give Myanmar's military intelligence organization (known to everyone as "the MI") a cachet that it did not always deserve. However, it remained the case that intelligence was one of the most powerful weapons in the military government's arsenal, helping to perpetuate its rule by crushing its opponents and performing a wide range of other functions.

By 2003, the intelligence apparatus was being described by both local and foreign observers as "an invisible government", a "state within the state".[21]

Notes

1. "Is the Burmese Regime Coming Unglued?", Cable from the US Embassy, Rangoon, 28 January 2005, *Public Library of US Diplomacy*, https://wikileaks.org/plusd/cables/05RANGOON121_a.html.
2. Mathea Falco, *Burma: Time for a Change: Report of an Independent Task Force Sponsored by the Council on Foreign Relations* (New York: Council on Foreign Relations Press, 2003), p. 1.
3. *Burma/Myanmar: How Strong is the Military Regime?*, Asia Report No. 11 (Bangkok/Brussels: International Crisis Group, 21 December 2000), pp. 11–12, https://www.files.ethz.ch/isn/28311/011_myanmar_military_regime.pdf.
4. Maung Maung, *The 1988 Uprising in Burma*, Monograph No. 49 (New Haven: Yale Southeast Asia Studies, 1999), p. 183.
5. Robert Trumbull, "A Political Purge May Have Led to Burma Security Lapses in Blast", *The New York Times*, 14 October 1983, https://www.nytimes.com/1983/10/14/world/a-political-purge-may-

have-led-to-burma-security-lapses-in-blast.html. See also Andrew Selth, "The Rangoon Bombing: A Historical Footnote", *The Interpreter*, 16 May 2012, https://archive.lowyinstitute.org/the-interpreter/rangoon-bombing-historical-footnote.

6. Khin Nyunt, *I, the Military Intelligence, SLORC and SPDC* (Yangon: Daw Maw Maw, 2017) (in Burmese), unofficial translation in the author's possession. General Tha Kha was initially appointed to the CI position but was dropped in favour of Khin Nyunt following the North Korean attack on President Chun Doo Hwan. See Robert H. Taylor, "'One Day, One Fathom, Bagan Won't Move': On the Myanmar Road to a Constitution", in *Myanmar's Long Road to National Reconciliation*, edited by Trevor Wilson (Singapore: Institute of Southeast Asian Studies, 2006), p. 27, note 30.

7. The claim was made by Lieutenant General Thanom Watcharaphut, commander of the Third Army Region, which includes northern and northwestern Thailand. It is not clear what he meant by Myanmar's "military development" budget, but in any case his estimate seems rather high. See Ekkarat Banleng, "Burma – 007 Spies on Thai Soil", *Bangkok Phuchatkan*, 3 March 1998 (in Thai), http://www.burmalibrary.org/reg.burma/archives/199803/msg00146.html. Mac McClelland has written that the general was "speculating" about the funds allocated to intelligence as a proportion of Myanmar's entire defence budget, but this is highly unlikely. Mac McClelland, *For Us Surrender is Out of the Question: A Story from Burma's Never-ending War* (Berkeley: Soft Skull Press, 2010), p. 163.

8. For example, according to Mary Callahan, in 1998 "three of the 23 DDSI intelligence detachments are responsible for surveillance of army, navy and air force personnel". Mary P. Callahan, "Junta Dreams or Nightmares? Observations of Burma's Military since 1988", *Bulletin of Concerned Asian Scholars* 31, no. 3 (1999): 56.

9. See, for example, Kyi Win Sein, *Me and the Generals of the Revolutionary Council: Memoirs of Turbulent Times in Myanmar* (Whitley Bay: Consilience Media, 2015), p. 488.

10. The US Government believed that, as early as 1973, DDSI "has plain clothes operations in every city and village". See US Army Intelligence and Security Command (INSCOM), "Directorate of Defence Services Intelligence (DDSI) Influence in Burma", 12 January 1973, released to the author under the Freedom of Information Act by the Defence Intelligence Agency, Washington D.C., 3 December 2003.
11. One knowledgeable observer wrote in 1996 that "telephone tapping by military intelligence is a major industry in Burma". Derek Brooke-Wavell, "Obituary: Leo Nichols", *The Independent*, 26 June 1996, https://www.independent.co.uk/news/people/obituaryleo-nichols-1338889.html. See also Pyinsa Yupa, "Surveillance of mail in Myanmar", April 2003, https://web.archive.org/web/20050319090437/http://www.bilston73.freeserve.co.uk/surveillance/surveill.htm.
12. On at least one occasion, Myanmar's lack of a developed imagery intelligence (IMINT) capability forced it to turn to China for help, to the extent of permitting a People's Liberation Army Air Force surveillance aircraft to photograph the entire Myanmar-India border. See Bahukutumbi Raman, *The Kaoboys of R&AW: Down Memory Lane* (New Delhi: Lancer Publications, 2007), pp. 18–19.
13. The number of agents sent abroad by Myanmar is unknown, and in any case must fluctuate, but in the late 1990s the Thai government was convinced that there were "thousands of MIS spies" in Thailand, scattered all around the country, in many different guises. See, for example, Ekkarat Banleng, "Burma – 007 Spies on Thai Soil".
14. One former Myanmar ambassador suggested to the author that the intelligence agencies did not need to infiltrate most expatriate communities, as there was always plenty of people prepared to act as unpaid informers, either out of "a sense of patriotism" or with a view to securing some personal advantage. Interview, Canberra, October 2013. See also Julien Moe, "The Military Elite Class: Embassies, Agents, Moles and Informers", *Online Burma Library*, 30 June 1999, http://www.burmalibrary.org/reg.burma/archives/199906/msg00633.html.

15. Some of those listed may have constituted a genuine threat to the regime, but many cannot have posed any real danger. Most people seem to have been denied visas to enter Myanmar simply because they had been critical of the military government. The list contained many errors.
16. See, for example, Bertil Lintner, "Velvet Glove", *Far Eastern Economic Review*, 7 May 1998, p. 19; and Aung Zaw, "Et Tu, General?", *The Irrawaddy*, 21 July 2011, http://www2.irrawaddy.com/article.php?art_id=21735&page=1.
17. Andrew Selth, *Burma's Secret Military Partners*, Canberra Papers on Strategy and Defence No. 136 (Canberra: Strategic and Defence Studies Centre, Australian National University, 2000), pp. 51–52.
18. Bertil Lintner, "Myanmar's Military Intelligence", *International Defence Review*, January 1991, p. 39.
19. "Spy Master's Rise to Power", *The Nation*, 2 September 1994, http://www.burmalibrary.org/reg.burma/archives/199409/msg00003.html.
20. Ekkarat Banleng, "Burma – 007 Spies on Thai Soil".
21. See, for example, Donald M. Seekins, "Burma in 1998: Little to Celebrate", *Asian Survey* 39, no. 1 (1999): 13; and Aung Zaw, "Khin Nyunt: Maybe Insein's the Right Place", *The Irrawaddy*, 13 June 2005, http://www2.irrawaddy.com/opinion_story.php?art_id=4710.

Chapter 2

MYANMAR'S INTELLIGENCE APPARATUS BEFORE 2004

> There are many reports on [the] Directorate of Defence Services Intelligence (DDSI) and none of them portray the all pervasive influence of this organisation on all segments of society in Burma ... No foreigner can ever know the complete organisation of DDSI because by its nature much of its activity is cloaked in secrecy.
>
> "Directorate of Defence Services Intelligence (DDSI) Influence in Burma"
> US Army Intelligence and Security Command (INSCOM), 12 January 1973[1]

This elevated status and all these activities were made possible by the development of a large, diverse and multi-layered system consisting of several different agencies and investigative units, located in the armed forces, police force and civil service. Dominating them all was the military intelligence organization.

THE MILITARY INTELLIGENCE ORGANIZATION

When Khin Nyunt was appointed CI in 1983, the lead agency was the Directorate of Defence Services Intelligence (DDSI), commonly known as the Military Intelligence Service (MIS).[2] It performed all the usual functions of military intelligence organizations but, after the 1988 pro-democracy uprising, dramatically increased in size, sophistication and territorial presence. It also took greater responsibility for protecting the military government. Reportedly managed by a committee of twenty-three mid-level officers personally loyal to Khin Nyunt, DDSI's headquarters (HQ) in Yangon was divided into nine departments or bureaux covering such subject areas as combat intelligence, counter-intelligence, foreign intelligence, counter-narcotics, the navy and the air force.[3] All statistics relating to Myanmar need to be treated with caution, but at its peak DDSI appears to have had an operational strength of about 2,000 men.[4] There were companies attached to the then twelve regional military commands (RMC), and (in 1998) about twenty-seven Military Intelligence Sections and Light Military Intelligence Sections scattered around the country.[5] Units at all levels were identified by numbers, as MI-1, MI-2, MI-3 and so on, although the number thirteen was apparently not used to designate a field unit as it was considered unlucky. Population centres like Yangon had small township-level offices.

The status of intelligence officers within the Tatmadaw's three service arms has never been entirely clear. In the case of the Myanmar Army (*Tatmadaw Kyi*), however, intelligence staffs were simply extensions of the DDSI. Suitable personnel were identified and transferred from other army units. After one or more courses at the DDSI's main training centre in Yangon, some were posted to intelligence battalions or companies to carry out "political" and counter-intelligence work, while others were sent to military commands or combat units to perform intelligence functions more closely related to operations. According to Tatmadaw training and staff manuals, during this period there were intelligence units attached to all RMCs (usually under majors). Regional Control Commands (RCC), the first of which was formed in 1992 to facilitate command and control functions, had intelligence sections. Major combat formations like Operation Control Commands (OCC), first created in 1995, and the ten LIDs, also had dedicated intelligence units, usually commanded by captains or lieutenants.[6] When fully staffed, the HQ of each infantry battalion and light infantry battalion had an intelligence section of up to ten men.[7] The lowest rank for enlisted men appears to have been corporal.

There were also a small number of intelligence units in the Myanmar Navy (*Tatmadaw Yay*) and the Myanmar Air Force (*Tatmadaw Lei*).[8] The navy had its main intelligence centre at Fleet HQ in Yangon, but personnel were also posted to the five regional naval commands. During this period, they seem to have been occupied mainly with tactical and operational level intelligence relating to the navy's surveillance and policing duties around the country's long coastline and in the Bay of Bengal and Andaman Sea. Air force intelligence officers were assigned to Mingaladon Airfield and other major air bases, like those at Meiktila/Shante. They too seem to have focused mainly on short term tasks, usually related to the air force's main mission at the time, which was to provide air support for ground operations against ethnic armed groups (EAGs) and the armies of narcotics warlords. It is assumed that air force intelligence officers also assisted with the interpretation of aerial photographs. Like the army units, both navy and air force intelligence units answered to DDSI, not to their respective service Chiefs of Staff. Also, before 1983 and after 1992, all out-posted service intelligence personnel reported directly back to DDSI HQ, bypassing the normal military chains of command.

One of the DDSI's highest priorities was surveillance of the opposition National League for Democracy (NLD), effectively led since its formation in 1988 by Nobel Peace Prize winner Aung San Suu Kyi.[9] The rest of the population was also monitored closely by both professional intelligence officers and a large network of paid and unpaid informers.[10] The number fluctuated over time, but it was estimated in 1991 that there was one "spy" for every twenty students at Myanmar's universities. In the armed forces, the ratio was reportedly one "spy" for every ten servicemen.[11] Most people lived in fear of being overheard speaking ill of the regime, or of being reported for minor infractions of the government's repressive laws.[12] Indeed, such was the suspicion generated by the state that, even if they were not being watched or recorded, most people in Myanmar assumed that they were, and behaved accordingly.[13] As Morten Pedersen has written:

> Although the surveillance may be broader than it is deep, the common perception among Burmese that "MI knows everything" creates an atmosphere and distrust in which people generally police themselves.[14]

Members of the ethnic minorities concentrated around the periphery of the country were perhaps even more fearful than the majority ethnic Burmans in the centre and south. As one observer familiar with Karen communities put it, "They saw spies everywhere, spies who would report to Rangoon and spies who would assassinate their leaders."[15]

Foreigners were also targeted. Resident diplomats who maintained contact with opposition groups and other critics of the regime were followed, their movements noted and, where possible, their conversations recorded. Even foreign language students were closely monitored.[16] Locally-engaged staff members at missions in Yangon and regional centres like Mandalay and Sittwe were forced to inform on their employers, fearing retribution against their families if they failed to do so.[17] Domestic servants too were obliged to report anything of interest to DDSI and the police force's Special Branch (SB).[18] Journalists visiting Myanmar, either openly or by pretending to be tourists, were often followed and their local contacts intimidated.[19] Describing how they managed to evade the regime's "spies" (real or imagined) always made good copy.[20] Visiting academics and tourists were also watched, although probably not as often as claimed. Indeed, it almost became *de rigueur* for foreigners visiting Myanmar during this period to return home with tales of being shadowed by intelligence operatives, or of having their bags searched in their hotel rooms by the ubiquitous "MI".[21] To some, being blacklisted seemed to grant bragging rights.[22]

Occasionally, foreign observers were given insights into the nature and extent of the military regime's surveillance operations. After the 1988 uprising, for example, DDSI published several books and documents intended to show the world that the armed forces had saved Myanmar from a disastrous takeover by "treasonous minions" and their "traitorous cohorts abroad".[23] In several ways, these publications were quite revealing. Also, in 1997 Khin Nyunt gave a press briefing in which he described in detail how certain individuals and unnamed Western powers were "aiding and abetting terrorism" in Myanmar.[24] It too hinted at intelligence sources and methods. In 2002, the US Embassy in Yangon was given a report about Rohingya contacts with international Islamist extremist groups that, despite its obvious underlying political purpose, demonstrated some of the concerns and capabilities of Myanmar's intelligence agencies.[25] In 2003, a microphone was found under a table in a room at Insein Gaol being used by a visiting UN official for confidential meetings with political prisoners.[26] In 2004, the Indonesian Government accused the then ruling State Peace and Development Council (SPDC) of tapping the telephone landlines used by Indonesia's diplomatic and defence staff in Yangon.[27]

As Rudyard Kipling wrote in his classic spy novel *Kim*, "The Game is so large that one sees but a little at a time."[28] In these and sundry other ways, however, observers could get glimpses into the enormous effort that was put into gathering information and compiling files on dissidents, insurgents, diplomats, foreign activists, journalists and their local contacts. Not all these efforts reflected well on the DDSI's capabilities. For example, Gustaaf Houtman has suggested that:

> It is well-known ... that especially in the 90s inexperienced intelligence staff made serious errors in identifying relations between family members. Since the policy in Burma is to repress family members directly or indirectly associated with dissidents, there have been many inappropriate arrests and suspicions as the result of perceived family continuities in names.[29]

Houtman speculated that the large size of Myanmar's intelligence apparatus may have been due in part to the difficulty of keeping track of a population that did not use surnames, could easily change their names and often used pseudonyms and nicknames.[30] Interestingly, a list of fifteen blacklisted Thai journalists drawn up by Myanmar intelligence agents in Bangkok in 2002 contained several errors, most related to their names.[31]

In strict legal terms, DDSI officers had no authority to conduct arrests, only to investigate suspected crimes. The regime maintained the fiction that the seizure and detention of people by military intelligence officers was merely part of the investigation process and they were later handed over to the Myanmar Police Force (MPF), which made the formal arrests. However, according to Amnesty International, "personnel from Military Intelligence (MI) branches conduct the vast majority of political arrests".[32] The legal basis offered for the DDSI's direct involvement in arrests was the National Intelligence Bureau Law of 1983, which created an umbrella organization to determine intelligence policy and coordinate operations. The other agency most involved in political arrests was the MPF's SB.[33] The Assistance Association for Political Prisoners (Burma) has estimated that between 1988 and 2004, while Khin Nyunt was CI, about 10,000 people in Myanmar were arrested for political offences of various kinds.[34] As the UN, Amnesty International and several other international agencies have recorded, many of those detained were tortured and subjected to sham trials, usually resulting in lengthy prison sentences, served under dreadful conditions.[35] Some died while in custody.

The brutal methods employed by the intelligence agencies, the "disappearance" of individual dissidents and the unexplained deaths of prominent activists and ethnic leaders inevitably gave rise to the belief that the DDSI assassinated perceived enemies of the state. This is not easy to prove, but there have been indications that "targeted killings" did occur.[36] For example, in 2011 a former intelligence officer stated that he and several of his colleagues then living in Australia had been members of a DDSI "hit squad". He told reporters that he had personally killed at least twenty-four regime opponents after the 1988 pro-democracy uprising and been involved in the deaths of up to 150 others.[37] In 2001, the Royal Thai Police was reported as saying that agents from Myanmar sometimes murdered "anti-Rangoon activists" in border towns like Mae Sot.[38] After the unexplained deaths of two prominent NLD members in China and Thailand, exile groups claimed that the regime employed assassins to eliminate its critics when they travelled abroad.[39] Such reports need to be considered carefully. Some cases cited may have been misinterpreted. The murder of Karen National Union (KNU) Secretary-General Padoh Mahn Shah in Mae Sot in 2008, for example, could have been part of an inter-Karen factional struggle, rather than a DDSI operation.[40] Also, it is unlikely that the regime had the resources, or the inclination, to send assassins very far beyond its borders to eliminate its critics.

In 1994, the then ruling State Law and Order Restoration Council (SLORC) created the Office of Strategic Studies (OSS) under Khin Nyunt, as its "Chief".[41] Creating an "Office" above a "Directorate" in the Tatmadaw's formal structure helped justify Khin Nyunt's promotion in 1993 to Lieutenant General (three star rank).[42] According to one senior OSS officer in 1996, the main (albeit unstated) reason for the creation of the Office was the need to manage Myanmar's increasing contacts with the outside world, something that it was felt could not be left to the Ministry of Foreign Affairs (MFA).[43] The Ministry had lost considerable power and influence under Ne Win, who adopted a strictly neutral foreign policy and severely restricted Myanmar's international relations. However, after the SLORC took power in 1988, it wanted to become more engaged with the international community. Before too long, the OSS was dictating foreign policy. It is widely believed, for example, that Myanmar's move to join ASEAN, beginning in 1994 and ending successfully in 1997, was an OSS initiative.[44] In 2001, the Brussels-based International Crisis Group (ICG) went so far as to state that "The OSS is directly responsible for Myanmar's international relations."[45] The Office's interests, however, soon went well beyond foreign affairs.

The members of the OSS were reportedly handpicked and, according to some observers, represented "a new generation" of Tatmadaw officers, "clearly more sophisticated and polished than their elders".[46] Unusually for the time, some had experience overseas and many spoke second languages. A number retained their DDSI positions, while working for the OSS. One Thai newspaper described them as "Burma's best and brightest".[47] By 2001, the OSS consisted of about fifty people, working in five departments covering domestic security, ethnic affairs, narcotics, international affairs and information technology (IT). The latter department also covered science and the environment.[48] The Office quickly developed a reputation for innovative thinking and pragmatism. For example, while the process was a complex one involving several other players, it was with the help of the DDSI/OSS that in the 1990s Khin Nyunt was able to arrange ceasefires with seventeen EAGs, removing a major security threat and lifting a burden from the SLORC's shoulders when it was under considerable external pressure.[49] He openly admitted that Myanmar faced a growing HIV/AIDS epidemic, previously a taboo subject, and helped initiate a plan to tackle the problem.[50] Increasingly, foreign missions began to bypass the civil service and seek the help of the OSS, which worked virtually twenty-four hours a day. It also seemed to be able to cut through Myanmar's notorious red tape, make firm decisions and achieve results, even on difficult issues.[51]

The creation of the OSS and its success helped highlight, and address, a number of major shortcomings in the military government at the time. As Mary Callahan argued in 1999:

OSS departments appear to have taken on responsibilities for coordinating and perhaps even initiating policies in areas as significant as the drug trade, the economy, ethnic affairs and foreign affairs. ... OSS's apparent consolidation of coordinating authority over everything from fossils to foreign affairs would never have occurred had the ad hoc nature of SLORC's earlier policies not been so seriously deficient in implementation. By the mid-1990s, it was clear that SLORC rule wasn't working, and as various members of the junta scrambled to find appropriate solutions, OSS materialised under the aegis of Gen Khin Nyunt.[52]

Describing the OSS a few years later, Christina Fink wrote:

> Seeking to institutionalise their power, Lt Gen Khin Nyunt and his intelligence colleagues have expanded their reach both geographically and vertically, delving into virtually every sphere of cultural and political life.[53]

Together with a number of like-minded officials outside the intelligence community, Khin Nyunt and the OSS constituted a "distinct and competent voice within the military hierarchy" with a prominent role in government affairs. According to Morten Pedersen, they represented "an emerging separation between the military-as-government and the military-as-institution, which held out the promise at least of better governance".[54] The OSS was not without its critics, both within the Tatmadaw and outside it, but it became enormously influential.[55] Indeed, it "evolved into an organisation that was credited with near omnipotence in Burma's political realm".[56] In 2000, the ICG called it the military regime's "new brain".[57] Bertil Lintner felt that "In effect, it is the government."[58]

As the OSS became more influential, so other parts of the military intelligence organization appear to have expanded, ventured into new fields and developed a range of new capabilities.

Probably with the help of the Myanmar Army's Signal Corps, DDSI monitored telecommunications in and around Myanmar.[59] As demonstrated by publications like *Skyful of Lies*, released soon after the 1988 uprising, DDSI could monitor and transcribe radio transmissions, although attempts to jam insurgent signals and commercial radio broadcasts appear to have been less successful.[60] Also, from 1994 DDSI took the lead in exploiting the rapid advances being made in IT. This was initially prompted by the need to counter use of the Internet by anti-regime activists, but it did not take long for Khin Nyunt to grasp IT's potential to achieve much more.[61] Several DDSI officers were sent to the United States for specialized IT training. By 1995, DDSI boasted "the largest computer facility in Burma", popularly known as the "Cyber War Centre".[62] This facility reportedly monitored and recorded a wide range of transmissions, including those made via satellite.[63] It also appears to have overseen both military and civilian interception activities and monitored the spread and use of computers and fax machines. Internet cafes were obliged to monitor their customers. The 1996 Computer Science Development Law, which was drafted with the help of DDSI/OSS, prohibited the use of computer networks or IT "for undermining State security, law and order, national unity, the national economy, or national culture".[64] It did not hurt that Khin Nyunt was Chairman of the Myanmar Computer Technology Development Council.

In 2000, DDSI founded the Internet service provider Bagan Cybertech. It later established close ties to Thaksin Shinawatra's telecommunications group Shin Corp, giving it access to a wide range of modern technologies.[65] The resulting intercept capabilities added greatly to DDSI's "coercive muscle".[66] According to the United States, by 2004 Myanmar had "fairly well developed

... technical surveillance capabilities focused primarily on the domestic political opposition and insurgent groups".[67] Once again, these capabilities might have been exaggerated in the public mind but, as one NGO noted, "The military government's stringent filtering regime fosters fear and self-censorship."[68] Also, DDSI was suspected of operating signals intelligence (SIGINT) collection stations in Myanmar's embassies in Thailand, Bangladesh and Vientiane, using equipment supplied by Israel, China and Singapore.[69] There were also rumours of a large SIGINT facility on Myanmar's Coco Islands in the Andaman Sea, operated in close cooperation with China. These suspicions were encouraged by credulous journalists and academics. Even the Indian foreign minister was inclined to believe such stories, to the point of repeating them in public.[70] However, on being thoroughly investigated they were found to have no basis in fact, something later admitted by the chief of the Indian armed forces.[71]

The DDSI/OSS became heavily engaged in information warfare. It developed interests in several local media outlets including, from 1999, the English-language newspaper *Myanmar Times*, which was said broadly to reflect the OSS's views.[72] The DDSI/OSS routinely placed propaganda articles in other news outlets, including the state-run English-language *Working People's Daily* and, after a name change in 1993, *Global New Light of Myanmar*.[73] The OSS staged "academic" seminars, to which selected foreigners were invited.[74] It published its own books, issued special news bulletins and in other ways promoted the regime's public image. For example, in 1997 it produced a booklet entitled *Political Situation of Myanmar and Its Role in the Region*, which eventually ran to over twenty-five editions.[75] It sought to answer a range of criticisms often levelled against the military government. In the late 1990s and early 2000s, the OSS also published *The Truth*, a series of English-language reports in which statements and other materials released by the NLD, activist news media groups and organizations like Amnesty International and the Karen Human Rights Group were analysed and rebutted.[76] In another foray into information warfare, the OSS sponsored the visit to Myanmar in 1996 of an American author who was writing a biography of Aung San Suu Kyi, apparently in the hope that she would be persuaded to present a more sympathetic account of the regime.[77]

DDSI/OSS also seems to have branched out into paramilitary operations. Around 1998, a special unit was created to carry out targeted killings among Karen communities in Eastern Myanmar. It seems to have operated along similar lines to the CIA-sponsored Phoenix Program in South Vietnam between 1965 and 1972.[78] This "death squad" was known by several names, including *Dam Byan Byaut Kya* ("Guerrilla Retaliation Unit") and *A'Htoo Ah Na Yah A'Pweh* ("Special Authority Group").[79] It was also called the *Sa Thon Lon* ("three S") unit, a name stemming from the belief that the unit was part of the Ministry of Home Affairs' Bureau of Special Investigation (BSI).[80] More likely, it was established by DDSI/OSS and answered directly to Khin Nyunt.[81] It operated with the support, but independently of, the Tatmadaw's regional military command structure. With a strength of around 200 personnel, the *Dam Byan Byaut Kya* was divided into four or five companies, each made up of sections of five to ten men. Their aim was to kill anyone suspected of association with the KNU or its military wing, the Karen National Liberation Army (KNLA), and to terrorize the local population into withdrawing their support for these organizations.[82] After Khin Nyunt's arrest in 2004, the unit was absorbed into the regular army, strengthening the belief that it was his creation.[83]

During this period, the military intelligence organization encompassed numerous support facilities. For example, there was a Defence Services Intelligence Centre (formerly the Military Intelligence Depot and before that the Military Intelligence Training Centre) at Mingaladon, north of Yangon. When the OSS was created in 1994, this facility was renamed the Defence Services Intelligence Collection Training School and its commanding officer upgraded to the level of colonel. The DDSI's Research and Information Unit at Mingaladon was upgraded in 1963 to become the Defence Services Intelligence Support Depot. It had four departments, covering administration, operations, interrogations and support. A second such facility was established in the late 1990s.[84] There were also depots in the main population centres that served as administrative offices, interrogation centres and detention facilities. One was the notorious Ye Kyi Aing detention centre at Mingaladon, where Prime Minister U Nu was held after the 1962 coup. According to former detainees, this facility had "been used continuously since then for the interrogation and confinement of political prisoners".[85]

In 2001, the OSS and DDSI merged to create the Defence Services Intelligence Bureau (DSIB). This represented another step in the progressive upgrading of Myanmar's military intelligence organization, and by extension the entire national intelligence apparatus. In terms of the Tatmadaw's formal structure, a "Bureau" is above an "Office", and ranks alongside major military formations such as the multiple Bureaux of Special Operations and Bureau of Air Defence.[86] All are commanded by Lieutenant Generals. At one stage, there seemed to be a possibility that intelligence might even become a fourth service arm of the Tatmadaw, alongside the army, navy and air force.[87] However, this appears to have been wishful thinking on the part of some members of DSIB, possibly including the ambitious Khin Nyunt. There was also speculation around the time that the DSIB would be separated from the armed forces and become a separate "civilian" organization, albeit still led and manned by military personnel.[88] Neither shift in status occurred, probably due to the opposition of other elements in the Tatmadaw leadership, but possibly also because of concerns over the command and control of military assets.

For reasons that are not clear, but may have had something to do with such rumours, the DSIB was more often referred to in public as the Office of the Chief of Military Intelligence (OCMI). This also served to highlight Khin Nyunt's elevated status.

After the 2001 merger, OCMI headquarters consisted of seven departments under Brigadier (one star) level officers. Sources differ, but five departments seem to have covered operational matters: Internal Affairs, Border Security, Counter Intelligence, International Relations, and IT. Also called the Science and Technology Department, the IT Department managed the "Cyber Warfare Centre". The other two departments at OCMI HQ handled Administration, and Security and Training.[89] When fully manned, each department had a staff strength of about 50–60 officers.[90] Once again, sources differ, but James McAndrew refers to 37 OCMI field units, divided into 31 army units (designated MI-1 to MI-31), three in the navy (NIU-1 to NIU-3) and three in the air force (AIU-1 to AIU-3).[91] The army units were organized into 12 "battalions" at the regional command level, each led by a lieutenant colonel.[92] Company size units, led by majors, were responsible for designated geographical areas.[93] As already noted, in large population centres like Yangon there were smaller offices and out-posted detachments.[94]

OCMI's size is very difficult to determine. Some Myanmar-watchers subscribe to a personnel strength of 10,000 or even 30,000, others to 3,000 or 4,000.[95] It is not always clear how these figures have been calculated, but James McAndrew and Miki Ebara represent the two main schools. Using his claim of 37 field units as a base, and assuming strengths of 200 to 250 men per unit, McAndrew calculates that there were between 7,400 and 9,250 field officers.[96] Add 350 to 400 men based at OCMI HQ and the total comes to about 10,000, not including the tens of thousands of paid and unpaid informers who were on OCMI's books. Ebara gives much lower estimates. She believes that there were only 29 army field units with about 100 men in each. Add three units in the navy and four units in the air force, plus HQ staff, and her total reaches about 4,000.[97] The latter more modest figures are more in line with the number of intelligence officers believed to have been purged from OCMI in 2004, but that figure too is subject to considerable debate. The large differences between these two estimates may be due to different accounting methods, or they may simply reflect differences in the kinds of personnel included. The actual number is unknown.

OCMI was an integral part of the Tatmadaw, and on organization charts was formally listed under the Myanmar Army's General Staff Office. However, in practice the military intelligence organization functioned almost as an autonomous body. At least until Ne Win was put under house arrest in 2002 and lost his power to influence high level decisions, Khin Nyunt seemed to have had the old dictator's ear and used this to great advantage.[98] For example, from 1992 military intelligence officers in the field were able once again to bypass the usual chain of command and report directly to their HQ in Yangon.[99] By exploiting their influence in Myanmar's economy and society, DDSI, OSS and later OCMI developed both legal and illegal business interests that provided a ready source of operating funds outside the official defence budget. Also, due to their control over key government processes and privileged access to sensitive information, including data collected on their fellow officers, military intelligence personnel could even challenge officers senior to them in rank. Indeed, they developed a reputation for corruption, arrogance and bullying.[100] All these factors contributed to friction between DDSI/OSS/OCMI and the rest of the Tatmadaw, including members of the senior officer corps.[101]

Lacking any combat power of its own (apart from the *Dam Byan Byaut Kya*), the DDSI/OSS/OCMI knew that its influence depended mainly on its privileged access to information. Accordingly, it jealously guarded the intelligence it collected.[102] Indeed, such was the extent of Khin Nyunt's control over the intelligence product and its distribution that Vice Senior General Maung Aye, Deputy Chairman of the SPDC and by most accounts Khin Nyunt's arch-rival, is reputed to have taken measures to secure access to independent sources of information. There were even reports that he created his own intelligence agency, and purchased "a powerful radio interceptor from a Western country".[103] A few observers have suggested that this "secret" shadow organization was specifically to keep an eye on Khin Nyunt and his colleagues in DDSI/OSS/OCMI.[104] Others have opined that the new unit was to protect Maung Aye and his family from assassination attempts, but without identifying his purported enemies.[105] If Maung Aye did create another intelligence agency, for whatever reason, it does not appear to have been granted any formal status. More likely, he organized an informal network of supporters in the armed forces and outside it, including in the business community, to keep informed of developments without having to rely on the established intelligence channels.

In August 2003, Khin Nyunt was appointed Prime Minister of Myanmar, and promoted to the rank of (four star) General.[106] This enhanced his position in the military hierarchy, but the SPDC, which had replaced the SLORC in 1997, emphasized collective leadership and sought to maintain a balance between competing personalities and factions.[107] Indeed, the Prime Minister's position had traditionally been largely ceremonial, leading some to view this appointment as a way of reducing the CI's influence. In typical fashion, however, Khin Nyunt threw himself into his new duties, determined to promote his change agenda, and doubtless his own career. Despite rumours that he had been asked to surrender his intelligence role, he also continued to act as CI. It appears that the management of day-to-day operations was left to OCMI's second-in-command, Major General Kyaw Win. Yet, Khin Nyunt's hand was still firmly on the tiller. He was described by insiders as a "consummate workaholic" who insisted on briefings with his senior advisors every day of the year, at 7:30 in the morning.[108] Despite the fact that he had other duties, both practical and ceremonial, his was still the strongest influence on the workings of the country's intelligence apparatus and it was he who made the critical decisions on most issues.

OTHER INTELLIGENCE AGENCIES

While always the dominant element in Myanmar's intelligence apparatus, the military intelligence organization did not operate alone. It worked with, and was supported by, a number of other agencies. Three were civilian bodies that fell into the portfolio of the Minister for Home Affairs.

In the MPF, there was a Special Intelligence Department (SID), referred to in some foreign sources as the Special Investigation Department, but more widely known as the Special Branch.[109] Its origins can be traced back to the colonial era, when an Intelligence Branch (IB) was formed in the Criminal Investigation Department (CID), soon after the latter's creation in 1887.[110] When Ne Win reorganized Myanmar's security forces in 1964, and transformed the old British-style Burma Police into the People's Police Force (PPF), the IB was absorbed into the newly organized SID. Given its antecedents, it was not long before the SID too became known as the Special Branch, or at times Special Branch 2 (SB2).[111] After the 1988 uprising, the SLORC allocated the SID a wide range of duties, including an important role in anti-narcotics operations. However, it was always primarily a "political police" charged with rooting out espionage, subversion and opposition to the government of the day. After another reorganization in 2000, it had a sanctioned strength of 1,213, under a Police Brigadier General.[112] At the working level, it was organized into eight branches, covering internal affairs, external affairs, prosecutions, investigations, operations, passports, security and administration. During Khin Nyunt's tenure as CI, SB became an important arm of the national intelligence apparatus and worked closely with DDSI/OSS/OCMI.

The MPF's Criminal Investigation Department also played a role in Khin Nyunt's intelligence empire. The CID was not an intelligence agency *per se* but, as occasion demanded, it too was directed by the National Intelligence Bureau (NIB) and MPF HQ to investigate, arrest and interrogate people suspected of opposition to the government.[113] A colonial-era police manual reprinted and reissued by the Inspector-General of Police in 1964 stated that "cases of a political nature" were part of the CID's responsibilities, and this seemed to remain the case even after the expansion of SB in the early 1990s.[114] Its size during that period is unknown but in 2000 the SPDC decreed a personnel strength of 803 men and women, under a Police Brigadier General.[115] There had always been CID offices in Yangon and Mandalay, but after a reorganization that year they were made responsible for newly-formed Lower Myanmar and Upper Myanmar branches of the department. There were also CID units in each state and division capital. Like the other intelligence agencies, the CID seemed to view the law as flexible in national security cases, but it tended not to take the kind of liberties that customarily marked SB and DDSI/OSS/OCMI operations. It was reputed to have a better surveillance record than SB, possibly because its members were better trained and tried to collect evidence that could be presented in an open court.[116]

Another component of Myanmar's national intelligence apparatus was the Bureau of Special Investigation, which was created by Prime Minister U Nu in 1951 to "eradicate termites" from the government bureaucracy.[117] It was based on the People's Property Protection Police, also known as P(4), and initially had a staff strength of about 315. Described by one scholar as "Burma's FBI", the BSI was given extensive powers.[118] Its role was primarily to investigate corruption and other financial crimes.[119] However, in the view of one contemporary observer, "an excess of zeal and suspicion and an insufficient regard for the privacy and motives of the individual, as well as disregard of due process of law, made the BSI more a menace than a help".[120] At first, the BSI answered directly to the Prime Minister but was later transferred to the Ministry of Home and Religious Affairs, where its original mission seems to have been given a lower priority than "running down suspected activity of a subversive or antigovernment nature".[121] Before 2004, the BSI was organized into six divisions, as part of the renamed Ministry of Home Affairs. It too had a reputation for "exercising violence with impunity".[122]

As already noted, the MFA did not enjoy a high status in Myanmar's civil bureaucracy, but it fulfilled an important intelligence function. It not only performed the usual diplomatic roles, including open source intelligence (OSINT) collection and analysis, but it also provided diplomatic cover and administrative support for military intelligence officers posted overseas.[123] Myanmar's defence attachés, for example, monitored military developments in their assigned countries and changes in the wider strategic environment. They also kept a watchful eye on expatriate groups and reported to DDSI/OSS/OCMI on their activities. Myanmar's ambassadors were often former military officers. Some had an intelligence background and a few had the option of reporting directly to Khin Nyunt.[124] Such officers were usually sent to the more important posts and to places, like Hong Kong and Chiang Mai, which did not have resident defence attachés. The MFA's cipher clerks were usually army non-commissioned officers (NCO) trained by the intelligence services.[125] The MFA also provided DDSI/OSS/OCMI, and the SLORC/SPDC, with strategic intelligence analyses. A senior MFA official was always attached to DDSI/OSS/OCMI headquarters to brief Khin Nyunt on international developments, for example before the visit of a foreign dignitary or delegation.[126]

In addition to these core agencies, there were a number of small investigative units in Myanmar, such as the Intelligence and Research Section of the Customs Department in the Ministry of National Planning and Economic Development, and the

Intelligence Squads operated by the Immigration Department of the Ministry of Immigration and Population. Occasionally, the MPF's Detectives Department has been included on this list.[127] The Ministry of Posts and Telecommunications (MPT), which until 2013 enjoyed a monopoly over the country's electronic communications, worked closely with DDSI/OCMI and helped extend its surveillance capabilities through telephone intercepts and other activities.[128] These organizations are rarely included in published descriptions of Myanmar's intelligence apparatus, however, probably because of their modest sizes or the fact that they are customarily engaged in specialized areas not usually associated with national security. Under the rule of the generals, however, any arm of the government could be ordered to contribute to the broader intelligence effort.

Together, all these agencies, units and ministries made up a large, diverse and multi-layered network that covered all five stages of the intelligence cycle, namely identifying requirements, collection, processing and exploitation, analysis and production, and dissemination.[129] As the country's intelligence apparatus grew, however, and assumed a wider range of responsibilities, questions of guidance, coordination and distribution became even more important.

After the 1962 military coup, Ne Win's Revolutionary Council took a number of steps to rationalize the country's security apparatus and exert greater control over its operations. In 1964, it created the National Intelligence Bureau (or Board). This was a small policy-making body responsible for coordinating the activities of the various intelligence and security agencies at the highest level.[130] When an ostensibly civilian parliament was created under a new constitution in 1974, the National Intelligence Bureau Law was passed to give the NIB formal status. It guided the activities of the DDSI, SB, CID, BSI and, where relevant, ministries such as the MFA and MPT. At that time, the NIB was attached to the Office of the Prime Minister, who chaired a NIB Control Board, but the Bureau was effectively controlled by the Director of the DDSI, acting as Chief of Intelligence. As Tin Maung Maung Than has noted, by holding such a position, the CI "had sweeping discretionary powers enjoying a form of autonomy that could lead to problems of accountability and abuse of power".[131] The DDSI also provided the NIB's staff, many of whom concurrently occupied positions in both organizations.

The NIB was revamped in 1983, and the NIB Law was amended, as part of a comprehensive review of Myanmar's intelligence apparatus.[132] Given continuing concerns over the CI's personal power, which had prompted a major purge of intelligence personnel earlier that year, it was decided to fill the NIB's most senior position by different agency heads on rotation.[133] However, in practice the Bureau was still dominated by the head of the military intelligence organization, the DDSI. After the 1988 uprising, this became the formal, as well as the actual, position. The Director of the NIB (referred to in some Western sources as the NIB's "Chairman") reported to the SLORC and, after the ruling council's reinvention in 1997, to the SPDC. While always relatively small, and lacking any organic operational capabilities, in formal terms the NIB was considered the highest intelligence organ in Myanmar, responsible for deciding broad policy, setting priorities and coordinating major operations. It soon became an important vehicle through which Khin Nyunt could manage his expanding intelligence empire, become involved in the business of other agencies and exercise his power as CI.

RELATED ORGANIZATIONS AND LAWS

As Human Rights Watch has observed, in Myanmar "The formal security agencies are only the first level of control. Even more invasive and prevalent are the different levels of the SPDC, operating from the national level right down to the township and ward level."[134] Well before the creation of the SPDC, the military government relied on other ways to monitor the population and root out disaffection. They augmented the efforts of the intelligence agencies and contributed to the regime's tight grip on Myanmar society.

For example, in 1988 the SLORC introduced an extensive network of subsidiary bodies to monitor the population and ensure that the regime's orders were carried out. Law and Order Restoration Councils (LORCs), consisting of army, police and civil service representatives were formed at the provincial, township, and ward/village level.[135] After the reinvention of the regime in 1997, they were renamed Peace and Development Councils (PDCs). These organs constituted "a steel frame reminiscent of the security and administrative councils created by the Tatmadaw in 1962".[136] As Monique Skidmore has written, through such structures the regime was able to reach down deep into Myanmar society and "exercise an astonishing degree of surveillance and control over individual, family and community life".[137] In addition, the General Administration Department (GAD), which formed the backbone of Myanmar's civil bureaucracy at both the national and provincial levels, had "a mandate to support government security efforts".[138] As the Asia Foundation has noted, "no other government organisation has such a wide presence in the country".[139] It too filled gaps in the intelligence agencies' collection efforts, routinely reporting to DDSI/OSS/OCMI as well as to its bureaucratic masters.[140]

After its formation in 1993, members of the mass Union Solidarity Development Association (USDA), dubbed the "White Shirts" by activist groups, were encouraged to report signs of "social deviance" and "disloyalty".[141] This practice echoed a pattern established after 1974 by the Burma Socialist Programme Party (BSPP), with its *Htein Chan Hmu* community-based intelligence gathering system, itself a development of the People's Reporter system introduced by Ne Win's "caretaker" government in 1958.[142] Selected USDA members were trained in information gathering techniques, at times acting in that capacity in concert with the official intelligence agencies.[143] As the association claimed 23 million members by 2010, when it was transformed into the Union Solidarity Development Party (USDP) to contest the national elections, its coverage of the population was potentially enormous.[144] The USDA was supported by ad hoc militia groups and vigilante gangs such as the *Swann Ar Shin*, or "Masters of Force". Other groups gave themselves names like the "Anti-Foreign Invasion Force", "State Defence Force" and "People's Vigorous Association".[145] The reliability of some USDA groups must be considered suspect, however, as many members were coerced into joining the association and were reluctant to act as informers or, in certain cases, enforcers.

Mention should also be made of the Border Area Immigration Control Command, known by its Burmese language initials as the *NaSaKa*. Established in 1992, it included representatives of DDSI/OCMI, the MPF, Customs, Immigration and, after 1993, the Ministry of Finance and Revenue.[146] The *NaSaKa* went through several iterations before it was disbanded in 2013, but all had key features in common. It was created to provide a coordinated bureaucratic and military response to the challenges of managing Myanmar's long and porous borders.

However, it only ever had about 1,200 or so members, which meant that it could only post units to the main commercial crossing points and sensitive areas like northern Rakhine State. Under the leadership of military intelligence officers, the *NaSaKa* and Border Supervisory Battalions known as *NaSaYa* exercised wide powers. In some areas, they went well beyond border control to the enforcement of restrictive laws, such as those aimed specifically at the Rohingyas in Rakhine State.[147] The *NaSaKa* soon acquired a reputation for brutality and corruption, but employed a large stable of agents and informers, and performed some useful intelligence functions.[148]

There were also several laws on the books in Myanmar which assisted the SLORC and SPDC to keep a close watch over the local population and foreign visitors. Some dated back to the colonial era, when the British gave sweeping legal cover to their intelligence collection efforts and suppression of all forms of dissent. For example, the Village Act (1907) and the Towns Act (1907) required citizens to report the identity of overnight guests to local government offices and administrative councils (at the ward/village level known in Burmese as *YaYaKa* or, after 1997, *YaWaTa*), which could refuse permission for various reasons. The population was also subject to periodic "guest checks". As Aung San Suu Kyi has written, "These checks can be a mere formality conducted with courtesy or they can be a form of harassment."[149] Regarding the latter, a report by the international NGO Fortify Rights has stated that "Successive military regimes in Myanmar employed these laws as a pretext for entering homes late at night in order to gather intelligence, monitor the movements of individuals of interest, and make arrests."[150] Civil officials conducting these inspections were often accompanied by armed military intelligence officers or members of SB.

Myanmar's intelligence officers were said to be highly regarded for their "spying skills".[151] However, it is difficult to judge how well the information and data collected by all these disparate agencies and ministries was collated, analysed and used. As a general rule, the government in Myanmar has never been very efficient. This was why, during the 1990s, the OSS stood out as exceptional. There were jurisdictional disputes and cumbersome bureaucratic procedures, some stemming from the British colonial days. Decisions of any consequence could only be taken by relatively senior officers, usually with a military or police background. Reflecting Myanmar's British bureaucratic heritage, reports and records were stored in mountains of paper files tied up with string or tape. These problems combined to make the sharing of data between agencies difficult, further complicating the production of timely and accurate assessments. There were also questions over the dissemination of intelligence products. As already noted, the military intelligence organization was selective in its circulation of reports, and the regime's secretive mindset added to the constraints surrounding their distribution.[152] All these factors militated against the efficient functioning of the country's intelligence apparatus.

To quote Martin Smith, by 2003 the SPDC had become, above all, "a 'military intelligence' government" that demanded to know everything that went on.[153] It was convinced that the country's fractured history and centrifugal political, ethnic and social forces threatened to break it apart, like Yugoslavia after the death of President Tito in 1980.[154] It believed that good intelligence and pre-emptive action helped them to prevent this from happening. The US Embassy in Yangon was harsher in its judgement, characterizing OCMI as "the Gestapo-fashioned military intelligence apparatus that keeps all of Burma's government, military, and society in check".[155] To a senior US diplomat who served in Myanmar around the same time, OCMI bore "a strong resemblance to the former Soviet Union's KGB".[156] Another Western observer compared it to the German Democratic Republic's (GDR) notorious secret police, known as the *Stasi*.[157] In the opinion of an experienced Myanmar-watcher, the country's vast intelligence apparatus was for one purpose only, and that was "to make sure that the military remains in power and that it would never again have to face the kind of massive, popular outburst of anti-government sentiment it did in 1988".[158]

If that judgement is accepted, then it is ironic that key elements of this apparatus were brought crashing down not by internal unrest or external challenges, but by rivalries in the military junta and schisms within the country's own armed forces.

Notes

1. INSCOM, "Directorate of Defence Services Intelligence (DDSI) Influence in Burma".
2. There is considerable confusion over the names of this organization. It appears that, from 1948 to the mid-1950s, the fledgling Tatmadaw had a number of Military Intelligence Sections, operating around the country and coordinated by a department (designated GS-3) in the General Staff Office of the Tatmadaw headquarters in Yangon (then known as the War Office). In 1956, the Ministry of Defence was formed, and these units were placed under a new Directorate of Defence Services Intelligence (DDSI), commanded by a lieutenant colonel. Even in official circles, however, the Tatmadaw's intelligence arm was known (in English) as the Military Intelligence Service (MIS) until the early 1970s, when "DDSI" became the more common formal title. See Maung Aung

Myoe, *Building the Tatmadaw: Myanmar Armed Forces Since 1948* (Singapore: Institute of Southeast Asian Studies, 2009), pp. 81–82; and James McAndrew, "From Combat to Karaoke: Burmese Military Intelligence, 1948–2006" (Unclassified thesis submitted to the faculty of the National Defence College in partial fulfilment of the requirements for the degree of Master of Science of Strategic Intelligence, Washington D.C., March 2007), p. 45.

3. See, for example, Bertil Lintner, "The Army Digs In", *Far Eastern Economic Review*, 2 September 1999, p. 23.
4. According to James McAndrew, "There are no reports of women MI members, but when a female operative is required, wives of MI members are reportedly utilised to provide a measure of accountability." McAndrew, "From Combat to Karaoke", p. 70.
5. As far as can be determined, there were about a dozen MI field units before 1988, 17 in 1989, 23 in 1992 and 27 in 1998. See Selth, "Burma's Intelligence Apparatus" (1998), p. 52; Bertil Lintner, "Unrest Swells the Burmese Ranks", *Jane's Defence Weekly*, 13 June 1992, p. 1020; and Ekkarat Banleng, "Burma – 007 Spies on Thai Soil". There are now fourteen Regional Military Commands.
6. RCCs (sometimes translated as Regional Operations Commands) are at the fifth tier of command (under the Commander-in-Chief, Chief of Army, Bureau of Special Operations and Regional Military Command). Their main duty is administration, not operations. OCCs (also known as Military Operation Commands) are similar to Light Infantry Divisions. Both RCCs and OCCs are commanded by Brigadier Generals.
7. This paragraph draws on *Staff Duty* (Yangon: Directorate of Training, Ministry of Defence, 1989); *The Infantry Battalion* (Yangon: Directorate of Training, Ministry of Defence, 2000); *Military Terms* (Yangon: Directorate of Training, Ministry of Defence, 2007) (all in Burmese); and interviews, Canberra, August 2018.
8. Miki Ebara, "The Fall of Military Intelligence Under Khin Nyunt: An Analysis of Power Dynamics in Myanmar" (Thesis submitted in partial fulfilment of the requirements for the Degree of Master

of Arts Program in Southeast Asian Studies (Inter-Department), Graduate School, Chulalongkorn University, Bangkok, 2005), p. 34. See also McAndrew, "From Combat to Karaoke", p. 76.
9. Aung San Suu Kyi was awarded the Nobel Peace Prize in 1991. In addition to those agents watching the party from a distance, the NLD assumed (probably correctly) that it had been infiltrated by "thousands of informers". Richard Cockett, *Blood, Dreams and Gold: The Changing Face of Burma* (New Haven: Yale University Press, 2015), p. 106.
10. Christina Fink, *Living Silence in Burma: Surviving under Military Rule*, 2nd ed. (London: Zed Books, 2009), p. 138.
11. "Country of Spies", *The Economist*, 13 April 1991, p. 38. In this context, the term "spy" seems to include various levels of informers.
12. See, for example, Martin Smith, *State of Fear: Censorship in Burma (Myanmar)*, An Article 19 Country Report (London: Article 19, December 1991), pp. 71–80; and Stephen Vines, "How Burma's Resistance Cheated the Secret Police", *Independent*, 1 September 1998, https://www.independent.co.uk/news/how-burmas-resistance-cheated-the-secret-police-1195287.html.
13. Fink, *Living Silence in Burma*, p. 138.
14. Morten B. Pedersen, *Promoting Human Rights in Burma: A Critique of Western Sanctions Policy* (Lanham: Rowman and Littlefield, 2008), p. 152.
15. Jonathan Falla, *True Love and Bartholomew: Rebels on the Burmese Border* (Cambridge: Cambridge University Press, 1991), p. 365. The threat from assassination squads was taken seriously by the Karen. See "Are Burma's Monks Planning Another Saffron Revolution?", *New Matilda*, 7 October 2009, https://newmatilda.com/2009/10/07/are-burmas-monks-planning-another-saffron-revolution/.
16. "Vicky Bowman, the Diplomat Who Caught the Burma Bug", *BNI Multimedia Group*, 5 April 2017, https://www.bnionline.net/en/opinion/interview/item/2912-vicky-bowman-the-diplomat-who-caught-the-burma-bug.html.

17. Almost all diplomatic missions were in Yangon, but for a time the United States maintained a Consulate-General in Mandalay. India still does. India and Bangladesh have also long had Consulates or Vice Consulates in Sittwe (formerly Akyab). In 2008, the United States opened the Jefferson Centre in Mandalay as an "outreach hub" of the embassy in Yangon.
18. See, for example, "Rangoon Incidents/Anomalies", Cable from the US Embassy, Rangoon, 25 November 2013, *Public Library of US Diplomacy*, https://wikileaks.org/plusd/cables/03RANGOON1519_a.html.
19. See, for example, Fergal Keane, "'Welcome to Myanmar, Mr BBC'", *XIndex*, 12 August 2012, https://www.indexoncensorship.org/2012/08/fergal-keane-reporting-burma/.
20. See, for example, Hannah Beech, "Aung San Suu Kyi: Burma's First Lady of Freedom", *Time*, 29 December 2010, http://content.time.com/time/magazine/article/0,9171,2040197,00.html.
21. See, for example, "A Land the World Forgot: A Photojournalist Sneaks into Myanmar to Report on the Freedom Movement", *Pulitzer Centre*, 18 June 2009, https://pulitzercenter.org/reporting/land-world-forgot-photojournalist-sneaks-myanmar-report-kachin-freedom-movement. See also Janelle Saffin, "Burma Emerges from a Shadowy Past, but Real Progress Lies Ahead", *The Conversation*, 3 July 2014, https://theconversation.com/burma-emerges-from-a-shadowy-past-but-real-progress-lies-ahead-27216.
22. See, for example, Sheridan Prasso, "Meeting Aung San Suu Kyi Was Worth Getting Blacklisted For", *Bloomberg*, 13 November 2015, https://www.bloomberg.com/news/articles/2015-11-13/meeting-aung-san-suu-kyi-was-worth-getting-blacklisted-for.
23. See, for example, *The Conspiracy of Treasonous Minions Within the Myanmar Naing-Ngan and Traitorous Cohorts Abroad* (Rangoon: Ministry of Information, October 1989); and *Burma Communist Party's Conspiracy to take over State Power* (Rangoon: News and Periodicals Enterprise, 1989).

24. "How Some Western Powers Have Been Aiding and Abetting Terrorism Committed by Certain Organisations Operating Under the Guise of Democracy and Human Rights by Giving Them Assistance in Both Cash and Kind", Special news briefing by the Secretary-1 of the State Law and Order Restoration Council, Lt-Gen Khin Nyunt, in the Defence Services Assembly Hall, Rangoon, 27 June 1997 (English language transcript in the author's possession). See also "Rangoon's Un-intelligence Show", *The Irrawaddy*, June 1997, http://www2.irrawaddy.com/article.php?art_id=717.
25. This report was clearly designed to demonstrate to the United States that Myanmar shared its concerns about international terrorism, and to cast the Rohingyas in a poor light, but it also indicated the extent of DDSI surveillance operations and the level of its analysis. "Arakan Rohingya National Organisation Contacts with Al Qaeda and with Burmese Insurgent Groups on the Thai Border", Cable from the US Embassy, Rangoon, 10 October 2002, *Public Library of US Diplomacy*, https://wikileaks.org/plusd/cables/02RANGOON1310_a.html.
26. Tin Kyi, "UN Envoy Finds Hidden Microphone in Myanmar Prison Interview: Sources", *AFP*, 23 March 2003, http://www.burmalibrary.org/TinKyi/archives/2003-03/msg00022.html.
27. "Burma Suspected of Bugging Indonesian Embassy", *ABC News*, 13 July 2004, http://www.abc.net.au/news/2004-07-13/burma-suspected-of-bugging-indonesian-embassy/2008910.
28. Rudyard Kipling, *Kim* (London: Penguin, 1989), p. 217. This novel was first published in 1901.
29. Gustaaf Houtman, *Mental Culture in Burmese Crisis Politics: Aung San Suu Kyi and the National League for Democracy*, Monograph Series No. 33 (Tokyo: Institute for the Study of Languages and Cultures of Asia and Africa, 1999), p. 29, note 9.
30. Houtman, *Mental Culture in Burmese Crisis Politics*, p. 29. See also Andrew Selth, "Burma and the Politics of Names", *The Interpreter*, 12 July 2010, https://archive.lowyinstitute.org/the-interpreter/burma-and-politics-names.

31. At least five of the names on the list were pseudonyms, a fact of which the intelligence officers compiling it seemed to be unaware. Supalak Ganjanakhundee, "An Intelligence-Made Enemy", *The Irrawaddy*, July 2002, http://www2.irrawaddy.com/article.php?art_id=2673.
32. *Myanmar: The Administration of Justice – Grave and Abiding Concerns*, AI Index ASA 16/001/2004 (London: Amnesty International, 2004), p. 11.
33. *Myanmar: Justice on Trial*, AI Index ASA 16/019/2003 (London: Amnesty International, 2003).
34. Kyaw Zwa Moe, "Bye Bye, Big Brother", *The Irrawaddy*, 24 October 2008, http://www2.irrawaddy.com/opinion_story.php?art_id=14493.
35. See, for example, *Tortured Voices: Personal Accounts of Burma's Interrogation Centres* (Bangkok: All Burma Students' Democratic Front, 1998); and Nang Zing La, *Life in Burma Military Prisons: Memoir of Pro-Democracy Advocate Nang Zing La* (Pittsburgh: RoseDog Books, 2005).
36. A distinction needs to be made between selective assassinations arranged by the intelligence apparatus and the extra-judicial killings and "disappearances" that have been hallmarks of military rule in Myanmar for decades. For an insight into the latter, see for example, *Crimes in Burma: A Report by the International Human Rights Clinic at the Harvard Law School* (Cambridge: Harvard Law School, 2009).
37. Dan Oakes and Mike Hedge, "Burma 'Hit Squad' in Australia", *Sydney Morning Herald*, 20 July 2011, https://www.smh.com.au/national/burma-hit-squad-in-australia-20110719-1hn8k.html. See also Lee Khoon Choy, *Golden Dragon and Purple Phoenix: The Chinese and Their Multi-Ethnic Descendants in Southeast Asia* (Singapore: World Scientific Publishing, 2013), p. 234.
38. See, for example, "Burmese Spies are Everywhere", *Bangkok Post*, 10 June 2001, http://www.burmalibrary.org/reg.burma/archives/200106/msg00053.html; and Thomas Bell, "Burma's Dissidents in Fear of Regime's Assassins", *The Daily Telegraph*, 18 October 2007, https://www.telegraph.co.uk/news/worldnews/1566599/Burmas-dissidents-fear-regimes-assassins.html.

39. In 1993, two members of the NLD elected in the 1990 general elections (which were ignored by the ruling military council) were found dead in unexplained circumstances, one in Kunming and the other near Bangkok. Both were "ministers" in the exiled National Coalition Government of the Union of Burma (NCGUB). See US Department of State, "Burma: Human Rights Practices 1993" (Washington D.C.: Department of State, 31 January 1994), http://www.ibiblio.org/obl/docs/USDOS-CR1993.htm.
40. Benedict Rogers, *Burma: A Nation at the Crossroads* (London: Ebury Publishing, 2015), p. xviii; and Nelson Rand, *Conflict: Journeys Through War and Terror in Southeast Asia* (Dunboyne: Maverick House, 2009), pp. 134–35.
41. Some of the Tatmadaw's Burmese language publications refer to the OSS as the Office of Strategic Defence Studies.
42. Khin Nyunt was promoted to Brigadier (one star rank, in the US system) in 1988 and to Major General (two stars) in 1990. The US Embassy in Yangon speculated that Khin Nyunt's promotion to Lieutenant General in 1993 may have come with a new title, such as "Director of Strategic Intelligence", but this does not appear to have been the case. See "Burma's Generals Promote Themselves", Cable from the US Embassy, Rangoon, 30 March 1993, *Public Library of US Diplomacy*, https://wikileaks.org/plusd/cables/93RANGOON1836_a.html.
43. Interview, Yangon, December 1996.
44. In 1994, Myanmar attended an ASEAN meeting in Bangkok and declared that it would sign the Treaty of Amity and Cooperation. It joined the ASEAN Regional Forum (ARF) in 1996 and became a full member of ASEAN in 1997. See Stephen McCarthy, "Burma and ASEAN: Estranged Bedfellows", *Asian Survey* 48, no. 6 (November/December 2008): 911–35. See also Larry Jagan, "Myanmar Looks to ASEAN First for Its Future", in *Myanmar: Reintegrating into the International Community*, edited by Li Chenyang, Chaw Chaw Sein and Zhu Xianghui (Singapore: World Scientific Publishing, 2016), p. 45.

45. *Myanmar: The Military Regime's View of the World*, Asia Report No. 28 (Yangon/Brussels: International Crisis Group, 7 December 2001), p. 8, https://www.files.ethz.ch/isn/28340/028_myanmar_military_regime_views_world.pdf.
46. Lintner, "Velvet Glove", p. 18.
47. *The Nation* website, Bangkok, in English, 27 August 2003.
48. Houtman, *Mental Culture in Burmese Crisis Politics*, p. 57. See also Selth, "Burma's Intelligence Apparatus" (1998), pp. 50–51.
49. "Leadership Change in Myanmar", *IISS Strategic Comments* 10, no. 9 (November 2004): 1–2.
50. "One Year after the Purge", *The Irrawaddy*, 18 October 2005, http://www2.irrawaddy.com/opinion_story.php?art_id=5097&page=1.
51. Interview, Canberra, July 1998. See also Trevor Wilson, *Eyewitness to Early Reform in Myanmar* (Canberra: Australian National University Press, 2016), pp. 38–40.
52. Callahan, "Junta Dreams or Nightmares?", p. 57. The reference to "fossils" harks back to Khin Nyunt's use of the OSS in 1997 to promote archaeological excavations at Pondaung, northwest of Myaing, in the expectation that the world's oldest known remains of higher primates would be found in Myanmar and "greatly enhance the stature of the country in the world". Gustaaf Houtman, "Remaking Myanmar and Human Origins", *Anthropology Today* 15, no. 4 (August 1999): 15.
53. Christina Fink, *Living Silence: Burma Under Military Rule*, 1st ed. (London: Zed Books, 2001), p. 157.
54. Pedersen, *Promoting Human Rights in Burma*, p. 113.
55. To some of its critics, the publicity-conscious OSS came to be known (in English) as the "Office of Stylish Shows". Bruce Matthews, "Burma/Myanmar: Government *A La Mode* – From SLORC to SPDC: A Change of Public Dress-Up and Manner?", *The Round Table* 349 (January 1999): 81.
56. Mary P. Callahan, *Making Enemies: War and State Building in Burma* (Ithaca: Cornell University Press, 2003), p. 212.
57. *Burma/Myanmar: How Strong is the Military Regime?*, pp. 11–12.

58. Lintner, "Velvet Glove", p. 18.
59. The most comprehensive study of these activities is Desmond Ball, *Burma's Military Secrets: Signals Intelligence (SIGINT) from 1941 to Cyber Warfare* (Bangkok: White Lotus, 1998). See also "Sigint Strengths form a Vital Part of Burma's Military Muscle", *Jane's Intelligence Review*, 1 March 1998, pp. 35–41. However, see Ebara, "The Fall of Military Intelligence Under Khin Nyunt", p. 28.
60. *Skyful of Lies: BBC, VOA: Their Broadcasts and Rebuttals to Disinformation* (Rangoon: News and Periodicals Enterprise, Ministry of Information, August 1988).
61. William Ashton [Andrew Selth], "Myanmar Boosts Cyberwar Capabilities", *Asia-Pacific Defence Reporter*, October 2001, pp. 20–21. See also A Resident of Kayin State, *Whither KNU?* (Rangoon: News and Periodicals Enterprise, 1995). This book graphically revealed the extent of the DDSI's intercept capabilities.
62. A Defence Services Computer Directorate was created in Tatmadaw HQ in the early 1990s, but this was not the same as the facility operated by the DDSI. See Robert Karniol, "Myanmar Spy Centre can listen in to Sat-Phones", *Jane's Defence Weekly*, 17 September 1997, p. 18; and Ball, *Burma's Military Secrets*, p. 84.
63. It has been claimed that the MPF operates a Russian-trained "cyber-crime unit" to detect undercover and citizen journalists trying to send copy out of Myanmar via the Internet. If so, it is unlikely that the MPF would duplicate a similar facility found within the DDSI. Sian Powell, "Underground Press in Burma Challenges Generals", *The Australian*, 13 September 2010, https://www.theaustralian.com.au/business/media/underground-press-in-burma-challenges-generals/news-story/54df081857a8ed2f16ac978c8e50d3b7?nk=a2b07ccc3754a6e925ab105d63672675-1538809947.
64. State Law and Order Restoration Council, The Computer Science Development Law No. 10/96, The Eighth Waxing of Tawthalin, 1358 M.E. (20 September 1996). See also Paul Todd and Jonathan Bloch, *Global Intelligence: The World's Secret Services Today* (Bangkok: White Lotus, 2003), pp. 185–89. In 1996, a close associate of

Aung San Suu Kyi was sentenced to three years in prison for having an unauthorized fax machine. Brooke-Wavell, "Obituary".

65. Ebara, "The Fall of Military Intelligence Under Khin Nyunt", pp. 61–68. See also Duncan McCargo and Ukrist Pathmanand, *The Thaksinization of Thailand* (Copenhagen: NIAS Press, 2005), pp. 53–55.
66. *Burma/Myanmar: How Strong is the Military Regime?*, p. 13.
67. "Burma: 2004 Annual Terrorism Report", Cable from the US Embassy, Rangoon, 23 December 2004, *Public Library of US Diplomacy*, https://wikileaks.org/plusd/cables/04RANGOON1627_a.html.
68. "Burma (Myanmar)", *OpenNet Initiative*, 6 August 2012, https://opennet.net/research/profiles/myanmar-burma.
69. "Intelligence Stations at Embassies", *Bangkok Post*, 30 July 1998, http://www.hartford-hwp.com/archives/54/144.html.
70. Douglas Bakshian, "China-Burma-India Intelligence", *Federation of American Scientists*, Background Report, 21 May 1998, https://fas.org/irp/news/1998/05/980521-prc3.htm. See also Andrew Selth, *Burma's Coco Islands: Rumours and Realities in the Indian Ocean*, Working Paper No. 101 (Hong Kong: Southeast Asia Research Centre, City University of Hong Kong, November 2008), http://www.cityu.edu.hk/searc/Resources/Paper/WP101_08_ASelth.pdf.
71. Andrew Selth, "Burma, China and the Myth of Military Bases", *Asian Security* 3, no. 3 (2007): 279–307.
72. "Opposition Radio says Myanmar Times backs Burma's Spies", *Democratic Voice of Burma*, 5 February 2001. Controlling this newspaper was a mixed blessing for the OSS, as any articles critical of the regime that were allowed through, to give the paper greater credibility, could be cited by the OSS's critics in the Tatmadaw as evidence of its disloyalty. Personal communication from Yangon, 2 December 2018.
73. For example, in July 2003 a six-part series of stories appeared in the *Global New Light of Myanmar* under the title "Daw Suu Kyi, the NLD Party and Our Ray of Hope". The author, who called

himself Maung Yin Hmaing, claimed to be a senior member of the NLD and close to Aung San Suu Kyi. In fact, the articles were supplied to the newspaper by OCMI. Despite being denounced by the NLD as regime disinformation, these articles were later published in a booklet for wider distribution. See *Daw Suu Kyi, the NLD Party and Our Ray of Hope and Selected Articles* (Yangon: News and Periodicals Enterprise, 2003). See also "Ghostwritten Article Series of the Burmese Junta: Goebbels – Clean Bowled", *Asian Tribune*, 12 July 2003, http://www.burmalibrary.org/TinKyi/archives/2003-07/msg00014.html.

74. See, for example, *Symposium on Socio-Economic Factors Contributing to National Consolidation: Papers and Discussions Presented at the Symposium Held at the International Business Centre, $6^1/_2$ Miles, Yangon, from 9th to 11th October 1996* (Yangon: Office of Strategic Studies, Ministry of Defence, 1996); and *Human Resource Development and Nation Building in Myanmar: Papers Presented at the International Business Centre, from 18th to 20th November 1997* (Yangon: Office of Strategic Studies, Ministry of Defence, 1998).

75. Hla Min, *Political Situation of Myanmar and its Role in the Region* (Yangon: Office of Strategic Studies, Ministry of Defence, 1997).

76. See, for example, "A Review of the Annual Report for the Year 2000 of the Reporters Sans Frontiers", *The Truth* 7 (16 May 2000), copy in the author's possession.

77. This did not prevent her hotel room from being "bugged" with clandestine listening devices. Barbara Victor, *The Lady: Aung San Suu Kyi, Nobel Laureate and Burma's Prisoner* (Chiang Mai: Silkworm Books, 1998), p. 8. See also Judith Shapiro, "Burma Road", *The New York Times*, 7 June 1998, http://movies2.nytimes.com/books/98/06/07/reviews/980607.07shapirt.html.

78. The Phoenix Program was designed to destroy the political infrastructure of the Viet Cong in South Vietnam. Its responsibilities were wide-ranging, but included the assassination of suspected Viet Cong operatives by so-called Provincial Reconnaissance Units.

See, for example, Douglas Valentine, *The Phoenix Program* (New York: Morrow, 1990). Desmond Ball has compared the *Dam Byan Byaut Kya* units to the *Einsatzgruppen* death squads used by the Nazis during the Second World War to destroy entire communities in the Ukraine and Baltic States. See Phil Thornton, *Restless Souls: Rebels, Refugees, Medics and Misfits on the Thai-Burma Border* (Bangkok: Asia Books, 2006), p. 35.

79. Members of this unit were also known as *Baw Bi Doh*, or "short pants" (in Karen), due to the eccentric mix of military and civilian clothes they usually wore, including camouflage pattern short pants.

80. The "three S" name came from *SaSaSa*, the Burmese abbreviation of *A'Htoo Son Zan Seh Seh Yay Oo Zi Ka Na*, or Bureau of Special Investigation.

81. Claudio O. Delang, ed., *Suffering in Silence: The Human Rights Nightmare of the Karen People of Burma* (Parkland: Universal Publishers and Karen Human Rights Group, 2000), pp. 42–74. See also "Extra-judicial Killing, Summary or Arbitrary Execution", *Human Rights Yearbook 2004* (Washington D.C.: National Coalition Government of the Union of Burma, 2005), http://www.ibiblio.org/obl/docs3/Burma%20Yearbook%202004/HTML%20Peages/Extra-judicial%20Killing.htm.

82. Guy Horton, *Dying Alive: A Legal Assessment of Human Rights Violations in Burma* (Chiang Mai: Images Asia and the Netherlands Ministry for Development Cooperation, April 2005), pp. 260ff. See also "Nyaunglebin District: Internally Displaced People and SPDC Death Squads", Karen Human Rights Group Information Update, 15 February 1999, http://khrg.org/1999/02/khrg99u1/internally-displaced-people-and-spdc-death-squads.

83. "Toungoo (Taw Oo) District", *Karen Human Rights Group*, http://khrg.org/reports/location/40.

84. Maung Aung Myoe, *Building the Tatmadaw*, pp. 82–83.

85. Selth, "Burma's Intelligence Apparatus" (1998), p. 53. See also *Myanmar: "In the National Interest": Prisoners of Conscience, Torture,*

Summary Trials under Martial Law, AI Index ASA 16/101/1990 (London: Amnesty International, 1990), p. 29; and Tinsa Maw-Naing and Y.M.V. Han, *A Burmese Heart* (US: Y.M.V. Han, 2015), pp. 219ff.
86. In 2001, there were only two Bureaux of Special Operations. There are now six.
87. Maung Aung Myoe, *Building the Tatmadaw*, p. 83.
88. John B. Haseman, "Myanmar Leaders Reorganise Military, Intelligence Structures", *Jane's Intelligence Review*, March 2002, pp. 40–41.
89. Another source has listed the seven departments as Politics and Counter-Intelligence, Border Security and Intelligence, Ethnic Nationalities and Ceasefire Groups, Narcotics Suppression, Naval and Air Intelligence, Science and Technology, and International Relations. See Maung Aung Myoe, *Building the Tatmadaw*, p. 83; and Ebara, "The Fall of Military Intelligence Under Khin Nyunt", pp. 32–34. McAndrew labels the Internal Affairs Department "Nationalities, Ceasefires, Narcotics, Naval and Air Intelligence". McAndrew, "From Combat to Karaoke", p. 76. The formal administrative structure was doubtless adjusted from time to time, in response to changing demands and priorities.
90. Ebara, "The Fall of Military Intelligence Under Khin Nyunt", p. 32.
91. One of McAndrew's sources for this figure is *The Darkness We See: Torture in Burma's Interrogation Centres and Prisons* (Mae Sot: Assistance Association for Political Prisoners (Burma), 2005), pp. 105–6.
92. At the time, there were twelve regional military commands, based at Yangon, Myitkyina, Lashio, Kentung, Taunggyi, Moulmein, Mergui, Bassein, Ahn, Monywa, Mandalay and Toungoo. See, for example, "Burma Reshuffles Military Intelligence", *Democratic Voice of Burma*, 15 December 2001; and Win Htein, "Behind the Military Shakeup", *The Irrawaddy*, 11 January 2002, http://www2.irrawaddy.com/article.php?art_id=2229.
93. There has been some confusion regarding the nomenclature of Tatmadaw units, with names like "division", "battalion", "regiment"

and "company" sometimes used in ways that defy direct comparison with their Western equivalents. See, for example, Andrew Selth, *Burma's Armed Forces: Power Without Glory* (Norwalk: EastBridge, 2002).

94. For example, in 2003 there were twenty-six township-level military intelligence offices in Yangon, plus three support units, all under army majors. There were also two special units under lieutenant colonels, each with three majors as deputies. The special units appear to have been formed to assist in the implementation of the seven-point road map to a "discipline-flourishing democracy" announced by Prime Minister Khin Nyunt on 30 August 2003. "Burma: New Secret Police Special Units", Cable from the US Embassy, Rangoon, 8 November 2001, *Public Library of US Diplomacy*, https://wikileaks.org/plusd/cables/03RANGOON1326_a.html.
95. By way of comparison, in 2018 the UK's Security Service (MI5) had about 3,000 full-time employees. Christopher Andrew, *The Secret World: A History of Intelligence* (London: Allen Lane, 2018), p. 142, note.
96. McAndrew, "From Combat to Karaoke", pp. 74–76; see also "Burma Dismantles Military Intelligence Unit", *Voice of America*, 19 December 2004, https://burmese.voanews.com/a/a-27-a-2004-12-20-1-1-93480834/1227853.html.
97. Ebara, "The Fall of Military Intelligence Under Khin Nyunt", p. 34.
98. See, for example, Hans-Bernd Zollner and Rodion Ebbighausen, *The Daughter: A Political Biography of Aung San Suu Kyi* (Chiang Mai: Silkworm, 2018), p. 168.
99. This had also been the practice before the 1983 purge, when some control of the intelligence apparatus was wrested back by the regional military commanders.
100. It was widely believed that DDSI/OCMI compiled dossiers on individual military officers, civil servants and business figures. See, for example, Aung Zaw, "A Burmese Spy Comes in from the

Cold", *The Irrawaddy*, June 2006, http://www2.irrawaddy.com/article.php?art_id=5828.

101. See, for example, Kyaw Yin Hlaing, "Myanmar in 2004: Why Military Rule Continues", in *Southeast Asian Affairs 2005*, edited by Daljit Singh and Liak Teng Kiat (Singapore: Institute of Southeast Asian Studies, 2005), pp. 231–56.

102. After the collapse of OCMI in 2004, one of its key critics complained that "Before, some news did not pass through us, they just censored themselves and submitted as they wish (sic)." See "Complete Explanation on the Developments in the Country given by General Thura Shwe Mann, member of the State Peace and Development Council and Lt. General Soe Win, Prime Minister, at Zeya Thiri Hall on October 24, 2004 and Explanation by Secretary-1, Lt. General Thein Sein, Chairman of the National Convention Convening Commission on October 22, 2004", supplement to the *Global New Light of Myanmar*, 7 November 2004.

103. Aung Zaw, "Et Tu, General?", pp. 45–46. See also Win Min, "Looking Inside the Burmese Military", *Asian Survey* 48, no. 6 (November/December 2008): 1028; Matthews, "Burma/Myanmar: Government *A La Mode*", p. 81; and "Power Play", *Far Eastern Economic Review*, 12 June 1997, p. 12.

104. Nehginpao Kipgen, *Democratisation of Myanmar* (New Delhi: Routledge, 2016), p. 85.

105. "Rangoon's Un-intelligence Show".

106. The Commanders-in-Chief of the Navy and Air Force are four star generals. The C-in-C of the Army, who is concurrently the Deputy Commander-in-Chief of the Defence Services, is a Vice Senior General, a relatively new rank usually accorded the equivalent of four and a half stars in the US system.

107. Some authors have suggested that Khin Nyunt was the most powerful member of the regime, if not its paramount leader. This was never the case. See, for example, Victor, *The Lady*, p. 139; and Floyd L. Paseman, *A Spy's Journey* (St. Paul: Zenith Press, 2004), pp. 174–75.

108. "Burma: Views From Military Intelligence", Cable from the US Embassy, Rangoon, 30 April 2004, *Public Library of US Diplomacy*, https://wikileaks.org/plusd/cables/04RANGOON545_a.html. See also "A Spy Never in the Cold", *The Irrawaddy*, November 2005, http://www2.irrawaddy.com/article.php?art_id=5153.
109. CID manuals used by the PPF in the 1960s referred to both the Intelligence Bureau and the Special Branch. However, these were reprints of colonial-era manuals, which were rarely updated to take account of changes in the force's structure and nomenclature. See, for example, "Directions for the Working of the Special Branch", *Criminal Investigation Department Manual*, Part 3 (Rangoon: Superintendent of Government Printing?, 1922?).
110. As Emma Larkin has pointed out, "Surveillance was the backbone of British police work in Burma." Emma Larkin, *Finding George Orwell in Burma* (London: Granta, 2011), pp. 58–59.
111. Selth, "Burma's Intelligence Apparatus" (1998), p. 44. See also Keith Dahlberg, *Bridge Ahead: A Medical Memoir* (New York: iUniverse, 2008), p. 112. Confusingly, the current Special Branch has a section known as SB2, which deals with foreign affairs, including the surveillance of foreign diplomats, visiting delegations and other foreigners in Myanmar. See, for example, M.S. Anwar, "Myanmar Government Deceive OIC Delegation in Maungdaw", *Rohingya Vision*, 15 November 2013, http://www.rvisiontv.com/myanmar-govt-deceive-oic-team-in-maung-daw/.
112. Ei Ei Zaw, "A Study on the Changing Role of Myanmar Police Force" (Unpublished thesis submitted to Yangon University for the degree of MRes in History, History Department, Yangon, 31 May 2002), p. 79.
113. AI, *Myanmar: "In the National Interest"*, p. 28.
114. *Criminal Investigation Department Manual*, Part 1 (Rangoon: Central Press, 1964), p. 7.
115. Ei Ei Zaw, "A Study on the Changing Role of Myanmar Police Force", p. 78.

116. Personal communication from Yangon, 1 March 2017.
117. Cited in Richard Butwell, *U Nu of Burma* (Stanford: Stanford University Press, 1963), p. 120.
118. Hugh Tinker, *The Union of Burma: A Study of the First Years of Independence* (London: Oxford University Press, 1957), pp. 83 and 87. See also Mya Maung, *Totalitarianism in Burma: Prospects for Economic Development* (New York: Paragon House, 1992), p. 36.
119. Five laws initially listed for BSI attention were the Essential Services and Supply Act (1947), the Public Properties Protection Act (1947), the Foreign Exchange Regulation Act (1948), the Anti-Corruption Act (1948), and the Export and Import Supervision (Temporary) Act (1948). However, this list has since been extended to include at least thirteen other laws. See San Win, "Administrative and Criminal Justice Measures for Preventing Corruption in Myanmar", presentation to the Fifth Regional Seminar on Good Governance for Southeast Asian Countries, Tokyo, Japan, 7–9 December 2011 (English language copy in the author's possession).
120. Louis J. Walinsky, "The Rise and Fall of U Nu", *Pacific Affairs* 38, no. 3/4 (Autumn 1965–Winter 1965–66): 278.
121. T.D. Roberts et al., *Area Handbook for Burma* (Washington D.C.: US Government Printing Office, June 1968), p. 324.
122. Nicholas Cheesman, *Opposing the Rule of Law: How Myanmar's Courts Make Law and Order* (Cambridge: Cambridge University Press, 2015), p. 164.
123. See, for example, "Myanmar Attache in US Absconds with Family", *The Himalayan*, 3 April 2005, https://thehimalayantimes.com/world/myanmar-attache-in-us-absconds-with-family/.
124. Personal communication from Washington D.C., 3 November 2018.
125. Interview, Canberra, July 1998. These officers appear to have been managed by a "Special Branch" in the MFA responsible for, among other things, the physical security of official premises and the proper handling of classified documents.

126. Personal communication from Yangon, 1999, and interview, Canberra, October 2013.
127. Selth, "Burma's Intelligence Apparatus" (1998), p. 51.
128. Priscilla A. Clapp, "Burma: Poster Child for Entrenched Repression", in *Worst of the Worst: Dealing with Repressive and Rogue Nations*, edited by Robert I. Rotberg (Cambridge and Washington D.C.: World Peace Foundation and Brookings Institution, 2007), p. 142.
129. Some authorities add two other steps, consumption and feedback. See, for example, Mark M. Lowenthal, *Intelligence: From Secrets to Policy* (Los Angeles: Sage, 2012), p. 57.
130. In some sources, the NIB at this time was called (in English) the National Intelligence Board, possibly reflecting its small size and oversight functions. Selth, "Burma's Intelligence Apparatus" (1998), p. 41.
131. Tin Maung Maung Than, "Burma in 1983: From Recovery to Growth?", in *Southeast Asian Affairs 1984*, edited by Pushpa Thambipillai (Singapore: Institute of Southeast Asian Studies, 1984), p. 118.
132. National Intelligence Bureau Law (Pyitthu Hluttaw Law No. 10 of 1983).
133. Min Thu, "Burmese Intelligence Revamped", *Bangkok Post*, 13 November 1983.
134. *Vote to Nowhere: The May 2008 Constitutional Referendum in Burma* (New York: Human Rights Watch, 30 April 2008), https://www.hrw.org/report/2008/04/30/vote-nowhere/may-2008-constitutional-referendum-burma.
135. These organs were known by their Burmese language initials as the *NaWaTa* (SLORC), *PaWaTa* (provincial LORC), *MaWaTa* (township LORC) and *YaWaTa* (ward/village LORC). After 1997, the names of the latter two were changed to *MaYaKa* (township PDC) and *YaYaKa* (ward/village PDC). A ward is a subdivision of a city or town, equivalent to a rural village tract.
136. James T. Guyot and John Badgley, "Myanmar in 1989: Tatmadaw V", *Asian Survey* 30, no. 2 (February 1990): 188.

137. Monique Skidmore, *Karaoke Fascism: Burma and the Politics of Fear* (Philadelphia: University of Pennsylvania Press, 2004), p. 66.
138. Kyi Pyar Chit Saw and Matthew Arnold, "Administering the State in Myanmar: An Overview of the General Administration Department", Discussion Paper No. 6 (Yangon: Asia Foundation, October 2014), p. 12.
139. Kyi Pyar Chit Saw and Arnold, "Administering the State in Myanmar", p. 1.
140. Clapp, "Burma: Poster Child for Entrenched Repression", p. 142.
141. Todd and Bloch, *Global Intelligence*, p. 186. The nickname "White Shirts" seems to be an attempt by opponents of the military regime to equate the USDA with the Nazi *Braunhemden* or "Brown Shirts", and Benito Mussolini's Fascist "Black Shirts" or *Camicie Nere*.
142. Also written as *Htane Chan Mhu*. It refers to the "criminal concealment" of the truth. See Ebara, "The Fall of Military Intelligence Under Khin Nyunt", p. 29. For the People's Reporter system, see *Is Trust Vindicated? A Chronicle of the Various Accomplishments of the Government headed by General Ne Win during the Period of Tenure from November, 1958 to February 6, 1960* (Rangoon: Director of Information, Government of the Union of Burma, 1960), pp. 33–34.
143. *The White Shirts: How the USDA Will Become the New Face of Burma's Dictatorship* (Mae Sot: Network for Democracy and Development, May 2006), pp. 54–55. See also "NLD in Central Burma: Treading Water", Cable from the US Embassy, Rangoon, 6 July 2006, *Public Library of US Diplomacy*, https://wikileaks.org/plusd/cables/06RANGOON946_a.html.
144. By 2006, there were 17 USDA branches at the state and region level, 65 at district level, 320 at township level and 15,308 at ward/village level. Kyi Win Nyunt, "Cherish the Union, Perpetually Serve National and People's Interest", *Global New Light of Myanmar*, 7 November 2006, http://www.ibiblio.org/obl/docs2/NLM2006-11-07.pdf.

145. *The White Shirts*, p. 53.
146. In 1972, the Ministry of Planning and Finance was formed by combining the Ministry of Finance and Revenue, and the Ministry of National Planning, both of which had been created in 1948. In 1993, the ministry was divided into the Ministry of Finance and Revenue and the Ministry of National Planning and Economic Development.
147. The structure of the *NaSaKa* is not clear, but it would appear that the *NaSaYa* (also known as Work Inspection Battalions) were units at border crossings commanded by majors, or possibly even a military intelligence officer of lieutenant colonel rank. A few observers have suggested that the *NaSaYa* was an expanded and upgraded version of the *NaSaKa*. This appears to be incorrect. See "More on NaSaKa", *Shan Herald Agency for News*, 1 January 2000, http://www.burmalibrary.org/reg.burma/archives/200101/msg00004.html.
148. *Myanmar's "Nasaka": Disbanding an Abusive Agency* (Yangon/Brussels: International Crisis Group, 16 July 2013), http://blog.crisisgroup.org/asia/2013/07/16/myanmars-nasaka-disbanding-an-abusive-agency/.
149. Aung San Suu Kyi, "Visiting Rites", in *Letters from Burma* (London: Penguin, 1996), pp. 51–53.
150. *Midnight Intrusions: Ending Guest Registration and Household Inspections in Myanmar* (Bangkok: Fortify Rights, March 2015), p. 12, https://www.fortifyrights.org/downloads/FR_Midnight_Intrusions_March_2015.pdf.
151. Supalak Ganjanakhundee, "An Intelligence-Made Enemy".
152. Open source information readily available to the public outside Myanmar was often restricted inside the country. Even some international news reports attracted high security classifications if they dealt with sensitive subjects. Interviews, Yangon, December 1999.
153. Martin Smith, "Army Politics as a Historical Legacy: The Experience of Burma", in *Political Armies: The Military and*

National Building in the Age of Democracy, edited by Kees Koonings and Dirk Kruijt (London: Zed, 2002), p. 290.

154. See, for example, Maureen Aung-Thwin, "Burma: Plus ça Change", in *Asian Security Handbook: Terrorism and the New Security Environment*, edited by William M. Carpenter and David G. Wiencek (London: M.E. Sharpe, 2005), p. 72.
155. The Gestapo (*Geheime Staatspolizei*) was the secret state police of Nazi Germany and German-occupied Europe during the Second World War. It had carte blanche to operate widely without judicial review. "Burmese General Khin Nyunt as Prime Minister: Promotion or Demotion?", Cable from the US Embassy, Rangoon, 26 August 2003, *Public Library of US Diplomacy*, https://wikileaks.org/plusd/cables/03RANGOON1029_a.html.
156. Clapp, "Burma: Poster Child for Entrenched Repression", p. 142. Khin Nyunt once claimed that OCMI was similar to well-known intelligence organizations like the CIA, KGB and Mossad, and should be accepted by international observers as equally legitimate. See "From Feared Myanmar Spymaster to Art Gallery Owner", *Dawn*, 2 January 2014, https://www.dawn.com/news/1077899.
157. Hannah Beech, "Fallen Idol", *The New Yorker*, 2 October 2017, p. 28, https://www.newyorker.com/magazine/2017/10/02/what-happened-to-myanmars-human-rights-icon.
158. Bertil Lintner, "The Army Digs In", *Far Eastern Economic Review*, 2 September 1999, p. 24.

Chapter 3

THE FALL OF GENERAL KHIN NYUNT

> Military intelligence organisations go in for torture and oppression and a whole lot of nastiness, so as somebody who represents such an organisation I suppose you can call Khin Nyunt all sorts of things, but expressions like 'prince of darkness' are rather too dramatic.
>
> Aung San Suu Kyi
Asiaweek, 17 December 1999[1]

On 19 October 2004, Myanmar's national television station MRTV announced that Prime Minister Khin Nyunt had been "permitted to retire for health reasons".[2] On 24 October, a briefing was given on MRTV by the newly-appointed Prime Minister, Lieutenant General Soe Win, and General Shwe Mann, the Defence Services Chief of Staff and Coordinator of Special Operations. Both were leading members of the SPDC. They stated that the government had discovered evidence of large scale and systematic corruption involving military intelligence officers on the Myanmar-China border. General Khin Nyunt had ignored instructions to halt these activities and, on being told that he was being relieved of his intelligence duties, had ordered OCMI to gather information on other senior members of the Tatmadaw. According to the two generals, this not only jeopardized the unity of the armed forces but also "posed a serious threat to the nation".[3] Accordingly, Khin Nyunt had been dismissed from all his official positions and placed under arrest.

Any suggestion that Khin Nyunt's health was ever a factor in his dismissal was soon forgotten, as the former Chief of Intelligence was publicly labelled "culpable", "corrupt" and "insubordinate". It was a remarkable exposure of the tensions that had been festering within the Tatmadaw for years. Even more startling was the tacit admission that one senior officer had the potential to bring down the military government, even to threaten the stability of the country.[4] On 7 November, the full text of the eighteen-page briefing by Soe Win and Shwe Mann was issued as a supplement to the English-language *Global New Light of Myanmar*.[5] Burmese-language newspapers issued similar annexes. Even before then, however, state-run news outlets had repeatedly proclaimed that "no-one is above the law", and that the SPDC would move decisively against anyone who "adversely affects the national policies".[6] Referring to Khin Nyunt's historic speech of 30 August 2003, in which he had outlined the country's proposed transition to a "discipline-flourishing democracy", the paper made it clear that the "Seven-Point Road Map is not Policy of Individual but State Policy" (sic).[7]

The 24 October 2004 briefing identified four specific offences committed by Khin Nyunt. First, he had disobeyed orders from a senior officer, something which, if allowed to go unpunished, could lead to the "disintegration of the military".[8] Second, OCMI had become involved in illegal economic activities. Third, Khin Nyunt and his family were guilty of bribery and corruption. Fourth, OCMI had exceeded its powers and become involved in activities outside its formal sphere of responsibility.[9] To anyone familiar with Myanmar, and the conduct of its government and security forces, the accusations of illegal behaviour, including bribery and corruption, were risible, as most officials and servicemen with any power used their positions to enrich themselves or to promote their own and their family's interests. Indeed, the charge of corruption was a device commonly used by the regime to remove military officers and other officials who had fallen out of favour, for one reason or another. In the kleptocracy that was modern Myanmar there was never any difficulty in finding the necessary evidence to justify measures of this kind. The other charges, however, were more serious.

Lacking any popular mandate, the cohesion and loyalty of the Tatmadaw was essential for the generals to remain in power. It was the main reason that military personnel were watched so closely, and any signs of deviance pounced upon. There had always been personal and professional rivalries, and resentment at the privileges claimed by the military intelligence community, but any suggestion of a serious split in the ranks of the senior officer corps demanded decisive action. Also, if Khin Nyunt had indeed ordered OCMI staff to investigate regional military commanders and those in charge of major combat formations, apparently with a view to exposing their own corrupt practices, then that too would have caused concern.[10] It had long been accepted that Khin Nyunt (and other intelligence chiefs before him) compiled files on fellow officers, but any suggestion that he planned to use the information collected to protect himself and his organization would have raised red flags. Such a course of action threatened the entire military leadership, potentially weakened the cohesion of the armed forces, and thus its grip on power.

In the months following Khin Nyunt's dismissal, there was a spate of reports both inside and outside Myanmar speculating on its precise causes and likely consequences. Thanks largely to his four star rank and control of the state's massive intelligence apparatus, Khin Nyunt was arguably the third-most powerful member of the SPDC, after Senior General Than Shwe and Vice Senior General Maung Aye.[11] Several pundits have suggested that even before 2004 he was being marginalized, as demonstrated by his transfer in 2003 from the key position of SPDC Secretary-1 to the largely ceremonial post of Prime Minister. Others have traced his apparent decline in influence to Ne Win's arrest and subsequent death in 2002, which deprived Khin Nyunt of the "Old Man"'s personal protection.[12] Most accounts of the CI's dismissal, however, began with a description of events on the Myanmar-China border in September 2004, which seemed to have sparked the move by the SPDC to crush Khin Nyunt and dismantle his power base. Not all these reports were factually accurate and the accompanying discussion of the regime's possible motives often contained inconsistencies. Different observers gave different weight to different factors, but most accounts tended to follow the same broad pattern.

It is still not clear exactly what transpired in September 2004. The official line is that a "dutiful citizen" complained about corruption at the Pang Hpak Man checkpoint south of Muse, near the Myanmar-China border.[13] The accused was a notorious *NaSaKa* unit. The story goes that this complaint was dutifully passed on to Khin Nyunt who refused to take any action, prompting Major General Myint Hlaing, the commander of Northeastern Command, to send a detachment of soldiers to detain those responsible. According to unconfirmed reports, they met resistance (some commentators have even described an exchange of gunfire), before up to 200 *NaSaKa* and military intelligence officers were arrested.[14] Other reports state that a seventy-member *NaSaKa* unit was merely "roughed up" before its leaders, drawn from the OCMI, Myanmar Police Force, Customs and Immigration, were arrested.[15] According to the SPDC, they had 3 billion kyat in cash (US$3.25 million at the then market rate), 42 tons of jade, 1,300 pearls and a number of unlicensed cars in their possession.[16] In late 2004, 186 members of the Tatmadaw and three civil service departments were convicted for their involvement in the Muse corruption case, suggesting that the first account is more accurate.[17]

This incident has been portrayed by most observers as a power play directed personally at Khin Nyunt, who was in Singapore on an official visit at the time. Certainly, the move against the *NaSaKa* unit by army combat forces was unprecedented and could not have been made without high level clearance from Yangon. This was probably given by SPDC Vice Chairman Maung Aye, or possibly even SPDC Chairman Than Shwe.[18] A few commentators have pointed out that Major General Myint Hlaing was formerly one of Maung Aye's personal staff officers, fuelling speculation that the initial complaint, if it existed at all, was merely an excuse for his infantry units to move against the *NaSaKa*, thus indirectly challenging Khin Nyunt, under whose broad control the latter operated.[19] Conspiracy theorists have gone further and claimed that the initial complaint was made by a "secret intelligence group" controlled by Maung Aye.[20] Others believe that the incident was sparked by the *NaSaKa*'s refusal to share the spoils of their corrupt activities with Myint Hlaing and his fellow officers, a complaint about the *NaSaKa* also heard from other regional military commanders who controlled key sections of the international border.[21]

Even now, fifteen years after the event, the actual trigger for the raid on the Muse *NaSaKa* unit is shrouded in mystery. At the time, a story circulated that the *NaSaKa* had knowingly intercepted a convoy of smuggled goods intended for high ranking officials in Yangon, prompting a sharp reaction. Another rumour was that the *NaSaKa* had killed a young smuggler who was related to a senior member of a Kachin ceasefire group.[22] One of the more plausible explanations was passed on to the State Department in Washington without comment by the US Embassy in Yangon. According to an embassy cable sent in January 2007, *NaSaKa* officials at the Muse checkpoint confiscated some communications equipment bought by a Myanmar Army colonel based in Lashio, the HQ of Northeastern Command. The regional military commander reported this to Maung Aye, who gave his permission for the "regular army" to raid the *NaSaKa* compound in Muse and recover the equipment. When it did so, the soldiers involved encountered resistance, which they were able to deal with easily, before finding a large amount of contraband.[23] This gave Khin Nyunt's enemies in the military hierarchy sufficient grounds to move against him, and the public justification for doing so.

In a volume of his memoirs published in 2017, Khin Nyunt gives few details of the incident. However, he sheets home responsibility for the whole affair to corrupt *NaSaKa* officers and, somewhat surprisingly and without further explanation, to "unscrupulous Chinese officials".[24]

FIVE THEORIES

Whatever the precise circumstances of the raid on the Muse *NaSaKa* unit, it is clear that Khin Nyunt's fall from grace was due to a combination of factors, some short term and some long term. No single issue was responsible. For heuristic purposes, however, it is possible to divide explanations for Khin Nyunt's fall into five broad camps, and to label them the policy, power, personal, pillage and preservation theories.²⁵

Those subscribing to the "policy" theory suggest that Khin Nyunt fell foul of the regime's top leadership because he was a relative "moderate", more prepared to envisage a future political role for Aung San Suu Kyi, more open to deals with the EAGs, and more receptive to the concerns expressed by foreign countries than the supposed "hardliners" surrounding Than Shwe and Maung Aye.²⁶ Accordingly, these observers saw Khin Nyunt's arrest as a major setback for the processes of democratization and national reconciliation. It has also been suggested that Khin Nyunt was brought down because he was more favourably disposed towards China (and by extension its allies, such as Pakistan) than most other SPDC members, whose fervent nationalism prompted a more isolationist stance.²⁷ There was some basis for all these claims, but the policy differences reported in the higher echelons of the armed forces were often overstated. The senior generals argued among themselves from time to time, but there was little serious disagreement on fundamental issues like the country's future direction, the Tatmadaw's continuing control of national affairs and the need for Myanmar to be wary of getting too close to any particular foreign power.²⁸

As regards the "power" theory, the US Embassy in Yangon reported in 2004 that "a more probable explanation for the SPDC's anti-Khin Nyunt campaign is a long-standing hatred, and fear, associated with an MI apparatus that knew no limits and focused attention not only on overt threats to the status quo, but also on the regime itself".²⁹ It functioned "like a state within a state".³⁰ Because of OCMI's control of information flows and its files on senior officials, even regional military commanders were reluctant to take action against intelligence officers, no matter what the rank difference and the offence. The 2010 memoir of former Lieutenant General Tun Kyi, for example, describes a remarkable example of insubordination by a military intelligence Major towards a regional commander, who was a Major General.[31] Such behaviour ran counter to accepted military discipline and the normal chains of command, but appeared to be tolerated at the highest levels, where Khin Nyunt controlled the intelligence apparatus and Maung Aye the regional commands.[32] It was a source of great friction, however, and in 2004 there were many in the Tatmadaw who were happy to see the combat arm reassert its authority and bring the intelligence apparatus to heel.[33]

The "personal" theory contrasted the backgrounds of Maung Aye and Khin Nyunt. Maung Aye was a graduate of the prestigious Defence Services Academy (DSA) at Pyin Oo Lwin (formerly Maymyo) while Khin Nyunt was a product of the Defence Services (Army) Officer Training School (OTS) at Bahtoo.[34] Maung Aye was a career soldier and combat veteran. Khin Nyunt, on the other hand, had never served as a divisional or regional commander, nor had any direct combat experience.[35] After 1983, he operated through the intelligence apparatus, from an office in Yangon. The two generals were believed to disagree on the best path for the military government to follow, for example with regard to Aung San Suu Kyi's future role and the management of the EAGs. Maung Aye was also reputed to be jealous of the high profile enjoyed by Khin Nyunt in the international press, where the latter was lauded as a pragmatic visionary with whom foreigners could do business.[36] In 1994, for example, US Congressman Bill Richardson was reported to have said: "I think that the future of Burma will be decided by two people—Khin Nyunt and Aung San Suu Kyi."[37] Singaporean leader Lee Kuan Yew once described Myanmar's generals as "dense", "stupid" and "obtuse", but publicly said that Khin Nyunt was "the most intelligent of the lot".[38] Khin Nyunt's downfall thus represented a personal victory for Maung Aye over his long-time rival.[39]

The "pillage" theory sees the events of late 2004 more in terms of the competition between DDSI/OSS/OCMI and other parts of the Tatmadaw for the perks and economic benefits of military rule. As seen from Yangon, the business interests of the regional military commanders and leaders of major combat formations were based on "graft and muscle". Under pressure to be self-supporting, they engaged in black market deals, imposed road tolls, leant on local businesses and offered protection services.[40] One popular scam was to purchase petrol through the Tatmadaw's central logistics system, then sell it on the black market through intermediaries at a marked-up price. In contrast, the vast DDSI/OSS/OCMI apparatus was "a far more sophisticated 'mafia-like' operation".[41] It too relied on corruption and protection rackets, but controlled a large economic empire, with numerous business fronts, especially hotels and restaurants. It managed essential junctures of the economy, such as the informal "hundi" financial remittance system and border trade smuggling.[42] It was also deeply involved in the entertainment industry, including gambling, karaoke, nightclubs and prostitution. The enormous profits generated by all these interests provided a steady income stream for the intelligence apparatus (and for individual officers) that others in the Tatmadaw could only envy.

There is another way of looking at the events of late 2004, and that is through Khin Nyunt's wish to preserve his power through the intelligence apparatus. Kyaw Yin Hlaing, for example, has written that even before the Muse incident, Than

Shwe had asked Khin Nyunt to give up his position as CI and focus on his role as Prime Minister. It appears that, although Khin Nyunt was not happy about the idea, he agreed to do so by the end of 2004. After the Muse incident, he apparently refused Than Shwe's order to discipline the intelligence officers involved, probably in the hope that, after he had relinquished his position as CI, officers loyal to him would continue to dominate the powerful intelligence apparatus.[43] In an attempt to preserve OCMI's authority, and thus his own, Khin Nyunt ordered his men to compile dossiers on other senior officers. This was not part of an attempt to take over government, as some have suggested, but was essentially a move to convince Than Shwe that intelligence officers were not the only corrupt ones, and should therefore be spared retribution.[44] This response reportedly infuriated Than Shwe, who saw Khin Nyunt's actions as insubordinate and a threat to the unity of the Tatmadaw.[45]

All five theories probably contain elements of the truth about the dramatic events of 2004, but to what extent, and in what combination, remain difficult to tell.

PERSONALIZED POWER

As the eminent Myanmar-watcher David Steinberg has pointed out, there is no tradition in Myanmar of sharing power. Its distribution has usually been seen as a zero-sum game, with only winners and losers. As he has written, "Traditional concepts conceive of power as finite and personalised."[46] Throughout the country's history, this has led to factionalism and the formation of entourages owing loyalty to an individual rather than to an institution. Despite its formal organization, hierarchical structure and strict codes of conduct, this pattern of behaviour can also be seen within the armed forces. Such a system can have practical benefits, in terms of cooperation between disparate elements and flexibility in dealing with institutional obstacles. However, it can also pose problems, particularly if an entourage comes to be seen as a potential threat to Tatmadaw unity and discipline. Thus, when a powerful figure like Khin Nyunt falls, his proteges and supporters usually fall with him.[47] This can be at great cost to the efficiency of the wider organization, but is deemed preferable to having disgruntled and possibly mutinous elements in the ranks.

Starting with a raid on OCMI headquarters on 18 October, when Khin Nyunt was in Mandalay, and his arrest the following day, Myanmar's intelligence apparatus was subject to an extraordinary purge, far exceeding that of the 1983 crackdown in its scope and severity.[48] The details are not clear but it seems that, within the space of only a week, all OCMI offices around the country were raided by members of the "regular army". The major intelligence units were disbanded and the smaller offices either closed or reduced to skeleton staffs.[49] Few members of the army's intelligence corps were spared, regardless of their rank. Some 300 senior officers appear to have been arrested. Many had their assets seized. Junior officers and enlisted men with more than two years' service in the intelligence corps were "allowed to retire". Those who had served less than two years were reassigned to infantry units and barred from promotion. The latter measures appear to have affected about 2,700 men.[50] The total numbers involved in the purge vary wildly between sources, ranging from "scores" to 30,000. There is no authoritative figure. However, it is thought that about 3,000 military officers and other ranks were directly affected.[51]

Although sometimes portrayed as a periodic reshuffle of official appointments, the purge extended to other government agencies, including the public service and even civil society. The Commander of Special Branch and the Director-General of BSI were replaced. Two ministers and four deputy ministers close to Khin Nyunt were removed, as were several high level officials from the judicial system.[52] Dozens of officers from civil departments handling immigration, customs and revenue, who either had military intelligence backgrounds or were perceived to be closely associated with OCMI, were dismissed.[53] Only those officers able to secure a ministerial guarantee were retained. All of Myanmar's thirty-seven ambassadors were recalled for "familiarisation" and "reorientation" courses, as were some defence attachés.[54] According to exiled activists, about twenty diplomats and embassy staff members with links to OCMI were later dismissed, including the ambassadors to Singapore and Indonesia, both senior positions.[55] A number of diplomats had their postings cut short. None, however, were imprisoned. As Michael Charney has noted, "The purge continued into 2005, as individual trials and confessions yielded more information on the extent of corruption and Khin Nyunt's connexions."[56]

Anyone who was believed to be close to Khin Nyunt, had worked with OCMI, or benefited from its operations, was suspect, regardless of their rank or occupation. Khin Nyunt's two sons (one a businessman and the other an army officer) and his son-in-law were arrested, charged and sentenced to long prison terms.[57] The Myanmar Maternal and Child Welfare Association and the Myanmar Women's Affairs Federation, both of which were managed by Khin Nyunt's wife, were investigated.[58] According to Larry Jagan, "even students admitted to college and university who had been recommended by Khin Nyunt's people were all expelled".[59] One rumour current at the time claimed that Than Shwe had even ordered the detention of Khin Nyunt's favourite astrologer, Bodaw Than Hla.[60] Portraits of General Khin Nyunt in the Defence Services museum in Yangon and plaques detailing his donations to religious institutions disappeared almost overnight. As a local informant told the US Embassy at the time, the purge extended "not just to the roots, but to the soil attached to the roots". This was an allusion to the Burmese phrase *thoke thin ye*, which means "to wipe clean, or eliminate".[61] As Emma Larkin explained, it refers to "a vanishing so complete that it is almost as if nothing had ever existed".[62]

In June 2005, Khin Nyunt was tried by a special tribunal convened in Yangon's Insein Gaol. He faced eight charges including insubordination, "attempt to disintegrate the armed forces", bribery, corruption, diverting public property and the violation of import-export regulations (including the illegal import from China and Thailand of 30,000 luxury vehicles).[63] The first two charges were clearly the most serious. Khin Nyunt was widely considered to be one of the least corrupt members of the senior officer corps, but he had strayed over the strict bounds of the law often enough to provide the regime with the public justification to charge him with various economic crimes. In July, after a short trial, Khin Nyunt was sentenced to forty-four years in prison, but this was later commuted to house arrest. Inevitably, given Myanmar's "tea culture" and penchant for conspiracy theories, his arrest and trial gave rise to countless rumours, some of them highly implausible.[64] For example, it was suggested that when he was in gaol Khin Nyunt was injected with "brain-scrambling chemicals, ensuring he could never attempt a come-back".[65] Another story was that he was allowed to serve his prison sentence at home after his interrogators found passages favourable to Than Shwe in his personal diary, which had been seized at the time of his arrest.

About fifty people linked to Khin Nyunt, including thirty-eight of OCMI's most senior members, were also put on trial.[66] All but four high-ranking officers, and all commanding officers of intelligence units and *NaSaKa* units, were convicted and sentenced, mainly for "economic crimes" but also, in a few cases, for treason.[67] They were given sentences ranging from 20 to nearly 200 years. The latter were the longest in Myanmar's history, and were clearly aimed at dissuading any others who were contemplating a challenge to the status quo.[68] There were rumours that several military intelligence officers died under torture, while being interrogated, but this remains unconfirmed.[69] Deputy OCMI chief Major General Kyaw Win was allowed to retire, and escaped any punishment, apparently because he was close to Than Shwe. Indeed, it was widely believed that Kyaw Win had been "planted" inside OCMI by the Senior General as part of a "checks and balances" system and "to keep a close eye on Khin Nyunt".[70] One activist news outlet even suggested that Kyaw Win "was complicit in the coup that unseated PM Gen Khin Nyunt".[71]

According to the Australian ambassador in Yangon, the SPDC remained "obsessed" by the Khin Nyunt case, months after the CI's arrest.[72] This was partly due to the collapse of Myanmar's military intelligence organization, and the problems this caused, but also because some of the 5,000 or so military intelligence officers and Khin Nyunt associates reportedly named on the SPDC's arrest warrants had gone underground or escaped to neighbouring countries, where they constituted a potential threat.[73] Also, it was claimed that during the crackdown on OCMI in October 2004 a large number of intelligence files had gone missing.[74] Many appear to have been destroyed, although by who and why is not clear. Peter Popham states, without any explanation, that "Truckloads of documents were seized and incinerated."⁷⁵ If this is true, then it is likely that some files were destroyed simply to remove the evidence of sins committed by particular officers or military units. However, more sinister motives cannot be ruled out. OCMI itself had reason to hide some of its past practices. The loss of data apparently required newly-appointed case officers to call in people who had been arrested in the past, and to seek their help in reconstructing their old files. The regime also lost track of which foreign academics and journalists had already visited Myanmar.⁷⁶

It has been suggested by a few commentators that the disappearance of sensitive OCMI files, and their possible future emergence in embarrassing circumstances, may help account for the commutation of Khin Nyunt's long prison sentence to the more comfortable option of house arrest in Yangon.⁷⁷ For example, among the files reputed to have gone missing were those covering the so-called Depayin (or Depiyin) massacre in May 2003, when then SLORC Secretary-2 Lieutenant General Soe Win, apparently on Than Shwe's orders, arranged for a large gang of USDA militia members to attack Aung San Suu Kyi's motorcade.⁷⁸ Activist groups and others have claimed that this was a "concerted and well-planned attempt to kill" the popular opposition leader.⁷⁹ The SPDC stated that only five people died in the incident, but the NLD has always maintained that around seventy people were murdered and many others injured.⁸⁰ Khin Nyunt, who was apparently not consulted before the attack, was later reported to have said that, by belatedly ordering OCMI to intervene and protect Aung San Suu Kyi, he saved her life.⁸¹ Khin Nyunt has denied ever saying this, but it is widely believed to be the case. Even so, the possibility that he used his inside knowledge of sensitive issues like this to win concessions from the SPDC is pure speculation. He was smart enough to know that he and his family were completely at the mercy of the SPDC, and that any indiscretions would have severe consequences.

Writing in August 2005, the departing Charge d'Affaires of the US Embassy in Yangon, Carmen Martinez, offered her reflections on the events of the past year.[82] In a valedictory cable to the State Department in Washington, she wrote that Myanmar's generals were "retreating into their collective shell, recalling former dictator Ne Win's experiment with self-imposed isolation". She continued:

> Many observers point to the October 2004 ouster of former military intelligence czar (and original member of the 1988 junta), Khin Nyunt, as the source of the current retreat. The hypothesis being that the disgraced Prime Minister was a moderate or a reformer who lost out to the hard-liners in a power struggle. We disagree. General Khin Nyunt was a hard-liner, albeit a more polished and approachable one. He was a pragmatist who cultivated foreign countries and a purported dialogue with the opposition simply as a means to mollify the international community and perpetuate the regime's absolute control. His ouster was a consolidation, not simply of hard-liners, but of the top generals who time and again demonstrate a remarkable ability to eat their own in order to preserve a carefully constructed system of patronage and power sharing. Khin Nyunt made himself a tempting morsel — fattening on his patronage network and the power of his intelligence apparatus — and the SPDC maw swallowed him up just as it has others before him.[83]

Many observers agreed with this assessment. A few used similar, or even more colourful, language to make their views known. Writing in the *Bangkok Post* earlier that year, for example, Larry Jagan described the purge of the intelligence apparatus as "tantamount to the Burmese armed forces turning on themselves: it was a form of 'cannibalism' according to many senior military officers, the 'Army eating its own flesh'".[84]

It is with these thoughts in mind that the military regime's efforts after 2004 to rebuild Myanmar's national intelligence apparatus should be considered.

Notes

1. "We Restored Order", *Asiaweek*, 17 December 1999, http://edition.cnn.com/ASIANOW/asiaweek/interview/khin.nyunt/. Khin Nyunt's nicknames (in English) included "Prince of Darkness" and "Prince of Evil". See, for example, Hannah Beech, "Burma's Feared Ex-Spy Chief Finds a New Life as a Gallery Owner", *Time*, 30 May 2013, http://world.time.com/2013/05/30/burmas-feared-ex-spy-chief-finds-a-new-life-as-a-gallery-owner/. Khin Nyunt was also dubbed "TV Actor" by the Myanmar public for his frequent appearances on Myanmar's state television.
2. Kate McGeown, "Khin Nyunt's Fall from Grace", *BBC News*, 19 October 2004, http://news.bbc.co.uk/2/hi/asia-pacific/3756052.stm.
3. Bo Hla Tint, "Political Reforms Needed", *The Irrawaddy*, 2004, http://www2.irrawaddy.com/article.php?art_id=4208&page=1.
4. "The Burmese Regime Airs its Dirty Laundry: Former PM 'Corrupt and Insubordinate'", Cable from the US Embassy, Rangoon, 12 November 2004, *Public Library of US Diplomacy*, https://wikileaks.org/plusd/cables/04RANGOON1462_a.html.
5. "Complete Explanation on the Developments in the Country".
6. "Khin Nyunt's Ouster: One Week Later", Cable from the US Embassy, Rangoon, 26 October 2004, *Public Library of US Diplomacy*, https://wikileaks.org/plusd/cables/04RANGOON1401_a.html.
7. "Seven-point Road Map is Not Policy of Individual but State Policy", *Global New Light of Myanmar*, 7 November 2004, http://www.ibiblio.org/obl/docs/NLM2004-11-07.pdf.

8. "Complete Explanation on the Developments in the Country".
9. Ibid. See also Ebara, "The Fall of Military Intelligence Under Khin Nyunt", p. 2.
10. Some sources claim that Khin Nyunt ordered his staff to gather harmful information about Senior General Than Shwe and Vice Senior General Maung Aye, not just regional and division commanders. Files on these officers probably existed, but whether Khin Nyunt would have dared to use them at this time is debateable. See, for example, Aung Zaw, "The Spring before Khin Nyunt's Fall", *The Irrawaddy*, 2 October 2008, http://www2.irrawaddy.com/opinion_story.php?art_id=14354&page=1.
11. A Correspondent, "Major Shakeup in Myanmar's Intelligence Apparatus", *Asia-Pacific Defence Reporter*, February 2005, p. 8.
12. Personal communication from Singapore, 10 January 2019. Ne Win was placed under house arrest in March 2002, after several members of his family were accused of trying to overthrow the military government. He died on 5 December 2002, aged 91. See, for example, David Lamb, "Burmese Leader Ne Win", *Washington Post*, 6 December 2002, https://www.washingtonpost.com/archive/local/2002/12/06/burmese-leader-ne-win/e7be1659-d203-44cc-bf54-d05a18048ccc/.
13. The checkpoint was also known as 105 Mile, on the Mandalay-Lashio-Muse Road at Nant Phetkar. "Complete Explanation on the Developments in the Country", p. 6.
14. Terence Lee, *Defect or Defend: Military Responses to Popular Protests in Authoritarian Asia* (Baltimore: Johns Hopkins University Press, 2015), p. 183; and "Myanmar's Prime Minister Khin Nyunt Removed from Office", Priority Alert, *AsiaInt.com*, 19 October 2004.
15. The US Embassy favoured the lower figure. "Burma's Grunts vs MI: Round One?", Cable from the US Embassy, Rangoon, 14 October 2004, *Public Library of US Diplomacy*, https://wikileaks.org/plusd/cables/04RANGOON1345_a.html.
16. "Complete Explanation on the Developments in the Country".

17. "More Background on the Coup", *The Irrawaddy*, November 2004, http://www2.irrawaddy.com/article.php?art_id=4200&page=1.
18. "Burma's Grunts vs MI: Round One?".
19. Win Min, "Looking Inside the Burmese Military", p. 1028.
20. Some sources claimed that this "counter-intelligence group" was formed to keep a watchful eye on the military intelligence officers under Khin Nyunt. If it existed at all, it may have been the same as the private "intelligence agency" reputed to have been formed by Maung Aye. See Bo Kyaw Nyein, "Understanding the Burma's SPDC Generals", *Mizzima News*, 26 January 2006, https://web.archive.org/web/20061022043204/http://www.mizzima.com/Solidarity/2006/January/26-Jan-06-02.htm.
21. Win Min, "Looking Inside the Burmese Military", p. 1029.
22. "Burma's Grunts vs MI: Round One?"
23. "No Big Power Struggle Behind Customs Arrests", Cable from the US Embassy, Rangoon, 16 January 2007, *Public Library of US Diplomacy*, https://wikileaks.org/plusd/cables/07RANGOON52_a.html.
24. Khin Nyunt, *I, the Military Intelligence, SLORC and SPDC*.
25. Some analysts have proposed only three theories. See, for example, R. Hariharan, "Burma (Myanmar): Why the Prime Minister was Sacked?", *South Asia Analysis Group*, Paper No. 1150, 25 October 2004.
26. "Leadership Change in Myanmar", pp. 1–2. See also "An Ugly Regime Becomes Even Uglier", *The Economist*, 19 October 2004, p. 1, https://www.economist.com/unknown/2004/10/21/an-ugly-regime-becomes-even-uglier.
27. See, for example, Larry Jagan, "Ousting Likely to Disappoint Beijing", *South China Morning Post*, 20 October 2004, https://www.scmp.com/article/474774/ousting-likely-disappoint-beijing. See also Wayne Bert, "Burma, China and the USA", *Pacific Affairs* 77, no. 2 (Summer 2004): 268. On Khin Nyunt's reputed Pakistan sympathies, see Prakash Nanda, *Rediscovering Asia: Evolution of India's Look-East Policy* (New Delhi: Lancer Publications, 2003), pp. 304–5.

28. "Economic Tensions in the Burmese Military", Cable from the US Embassy, Rangoon, 30 July 2004, *Public Library of US Diplomacy*, https://wikileaks.org/plusd/cables/04RANGOON967_a.html.
29. "The Burmese Regime Airs its Dirty Laundry".
30. Bertil Lintner, "In the Dark", *Far Eastern Economic Review*, 4 November 2004, p. 22.
31. See Bo Tun Kyi (Monywa), *My Experiences Over Fifty Years* (Yangon: Moe Ywae, 2010) (in Burmese). Also, personal communication from Singapore, January 2019.
32. In the second volume of his memoirs, Khin Nyunt apologized for the arrogance and disrespect shown by some of his men towards "high ranking army officers" and members of the public. See *The Experiences of My Life*, volume 2 (Yangon: Daw Maw Maw, 2016) (in Burmese), unofficial translation in the author's possession.
33. See, for example, Kyaw Yin Hlaing, "Myanmar in 2004", pp. 231–56; and Selth, "SLORC's 'Intel-Net'", pp. 4–18.
34. Maung Aye was a member of the DSA's first graduating class (DSA-1) in 1959. Khin Nyunt was from the 25th batch of OTS graduates (OTS-25) in 1960.
35. Win Min, "Looking Inside the Burmese Military", p. 1028. Khin Nyunt did, however, command the 20th Light Infantry Regiment in 1978, when it participated in Operation *Naga Min*, which led to the expulsion of almost a quarter of a million Muslim Rohingyas from Myanmar. Khin Nyunt, *Secretary One* (Yangon: Daw Maw Maw, 2018) (in Burmese), unofficial translation in the author's possession.
36. See, for example, Aung Zaw, "Khin Nyunt, the Man to Watch", *The Irrawaddy*, 24 August 2004, http://www2.irrawaddy.com/opinion_story.php?art_id=3837; and Christopher Len and Johan Alvin, *Burma/Myanmar's Ailments: Searching for the Right Remedy*, Silk Road Paper (Washington D.C.: Central Asia — Caucasus Institute and Silk Road Studies Program, March 2007), pp. 32–34, https://www.files.ethz.ch/isn/31357/200704-BurmaMyanmar.pdf.

37. Philip Shenon, "Mutual Need Ties Dictator and Dissident in Myanmar", *The New York Times*, 20 February 1994, https://www.nytimes.com/1994/02/20/weekinreview/the-world-mutual-need-ties-dictator-and-dissident-in-myanmar.html.
38. "Lee Kuan Yew on Burma's 'Stupid' Generals and the 'Gambler' Chen Shui-Bian", Cable from the US Embassy, Singapore, 19 October 2007, *Public Library of US Diplomacy*, https://wikileaks.org/plusd/cables/07SINGAPORE1932_a.html. See also "Tom Plate and Jeffrey Cole interview Lee Kuan Yew", *This Little Red Dot*, 9 October 2007, http://thislittlereddot.blogspot.com/2007/10/tom-plate-and-jeffrey-cole-interview.html. Andrew Marshall was less complimentary, describing Khin Nyunt as "Burma's Poo Bah, Big Brother and (it was rumoured) most prominent closet homosexual". Andrew Marshall, *The Trouser People: A Story of Burma — In the Shadow of Empire* (Washington D.C.: Counterpoint, 2002), p. 193.
39. Aung Zaw, "One Down, Two to Go", *The Irrawaddy*, October 2004, http://www2.irrawaddy.com/article.php?art_id=4132&page=1. See also Hariharan, "Burma (Myanmar): Why the Prime Minister was Sacked?".
40. In Myanmar, all military units were under pressure to be self-sufficient as much as possible but in 1997, facing severe resource constraints, Tatmadaw HQ issued orders for all regional military commands to meet their basic logistical needs locally, rather than rely on the central supply system. Selth, *Burma's Armed Forces*, p. 136.
41. "Economic Tensions in the Burmese Military".
42. On the hundi system, see for example Rhys Thompson, "'Underground Banking' and Myanmar's Changing Hundi System", *Journal of Money Laundering Control* 22, no. 2 (2019), https://doi.org/10.1108/JMLC-04-2018-0030. Also useful is Sean Turnell, "Banking and Financial Regulation and Reform in Myanmar", *Journal of Southeast Asian Economies* 31, no. 2 (August 2014): 225–40.
43. Kyaw Yin Hlaing, "Myanmar in 2004", p. 236.

44. Maung Aung Myoe, *Building the Tatmadaw*, p. 103.
45. Kyaw Yin Hlaing, "Myanmar in 2004", p. 236. See also ibid., p. 67.
46. David I. Steinberg, *Burma: The State of Myanmar* (Washington D.C.: Georgetown University Press, 2001), p. 19.
47. This phenomenon is examined in David I. Steinberg, *Turmoil in Burma: Contested Legitimacies in Myanmar* (Norwalk: EastBridge, 2006).
48. Ye Htut, "A Background to the Security Crisis in Northern Rakhine", *ISEAS Perspective*, no. 2017/79, 23 October 2017, p. 7, https://www.iseas.edu.sg/images/pdf/ISEAS_Perspective_2017_79.pdf.
49. A Correspondent, "Major Shakeup in Myanmar's Intelligence Apparatus", p. 9. See also "Leadership Change in Myanmar", p. 1.
50. Here too, different sources give different figures. Some claim that in total about 2,700 were retired or reassigned. Others say that 2,500 were allowed to retire while another 2,500 were reassigned. See Ebara, "The Fall of Military Intelligence Under Khin Nyunt", p. 22; and *Burma: Human Rights Yearbook 2008* (Washington D.C.: Human Rights Documentation Unit, National Coalition Government of the Union of Burma, 2009), p. 19, http://www.burmalibrary.org/docs08/HRYB2008.pdf.
51. Larry Jagan states that 30,000 uniformed personnel were purged. Helen James gives a figure of 8,000. See Larry Jagan, "Deposed PM's Allies Face Sentencing", *South China Morning Post*, 21 February 2005, https://www.scmp.com/article/489760/deposed-pms-allies-face-sentencing; and Helen James, "Myanmar in 2005: In a Holding Pattern", *Asian Survey* 46, no. 1 (January/February 2006): 163. For other estimates, see Bertil Lintner, "Myanmar Payback Time", *Jane's Defence Weekly*, 20 April 2005, p. 23. "Myanmar Junta Dismantling Intelligence Unit Headed by Former PM", *Agence France Presse*, 19 December 2004, http://www.burmanet.org/news/2004/12/20/agence-france-presse-myanmar-junta-dismantling-intelligence-unit-headed-by-former-pm/; McGeown, "Khin Nyunt's Fall from Grace"; and "Burma Dismantles Military Intelligence Unit", *Voice of America*, 29 October 2009, http://www.

voanews.com/content/a-13-2004-12-19-voa18-67335807/272118.html.
52. Apparently, several jurists were removed from office after declining to give legal advice pertaining to crimes committed by Khin Nyunt and his men. See "Impunity and the Un-rule of Law in Myanmar", Asian Legal Resource Centre, *Reliefweb*, 17 February 2005, https://reliefweb.int/report/myanmar/impunity-and-un-rule-law-myanmar.
53. "Criminal Charges Reportedly Filed Against Military Intelligence Officers", *The Irrawaddy*, 17 January 2005, http://www2.irrawaddy.com/article.php?art_id=4296.
54. "Burmese Regime Recalls Foreign Envoys for 'Reorientation'", Cable from the US Embassy, Rangoon, 1 December 2004, *Public Library of US Diplomacy*, https://wikileaks.org/plusd/cables/04RANGOON1524_a.html.
55. "Burma Fires Diplomats Linked to Former Military Intelligence Chief", *Democratic Voice of Burma*, 9 June 2005.
56. Michael W. Charney, *A History of Modern Burma* (Cambridge: Cambridge University Press, 2009), p. 182.
57. Khin Nyunt's sons were charged with economic crimes and received gaol sentences of 68 and 51 years. "Ex-Prime Minister's Sons are Put on Trial", *Los Angeles Times*, 15 May 2005, http://articles.latimes.com/2005/may/15/world/fg-briefs15.2.
58. "Burma Probing Bodies Formerly Led by Ex-Premier's Wife", *Democratic Voice of Burma*, 2 November 2004.
59. Larry Jagan, "Khin Nyunt in the Dock at Insein", *Bangkok Post*, 12 July 2005.
60. David Wallechinsky, *Tyrants: The World's 20 Worst Living Dictators* (New York: Regan, 2006), p. 69. There was a precedent for this. When Ne Win's family was arrested in 2002 their astrologer was also put in prison.
61. "Burma: US Bilateral Initiatives Victim of Post-Khin Nyunt Purge", Cable from the US Embassy, Rangoon, 14 January 2005, *Public Library of US Diplomacy*, https://wikileaks.org/plusd/cables/05RANGOON104_a.html.

62. Emma Larkin, *Everything is Broken: A Tale of Catastrophe in Burma* (New York: Penguin, 2010), pp. 162–63.
63. Charney, *A History of Modern Burma*, p. 181.
64. Andrew Selth, "Burma: Conspiracies and Other Theories", *The Interpreter*, 5 June 2013, https://www.lowyinstitute.org/the-interpreter/burma-conspiracies-and-other-theories.
65. Justin Wintle, "A Victim of Burma's Boneheaded Rulers", *Far Eastern Economic Review*, May 2007, pp. 43–46.
66. Jagan, "Khin Nyunt in the Dock at Insein". See also "Over 300 in Defunct Spy Unit on Trial in Myanmar", *The Star*, 25 January 2005, https://www.thestar.com.my/news/regional/2005/01/25/over-300-in-defunct-spy-unit-on-trial--in-myanmar/.
67. Ye Htut, "A Background to the Security Crisis in Northern Rakhine", p. 7.
68. A life sentence in Myanmar is usually twenty years.
69. See, for example, "Senior Intelligence Officers Killed in the Junta's Torture Chamber", NCGUB Information Committee, Press Release, 14 January 2005. This is not to rule out the deaths of some imprisoned OCMI officers and Khin Nyunt associates for other reasons.
70. Aung Zaw, "Et Tu, General?", p. 46.
71. Bruce Hawke, "Maj-Gen Kyaw Win – Renaissance Spy", *The Irrawaddy*, October 2004, http://www2.irrawaddy.com/article.php?art_id=4131.
72. "Australia Sees Grim Burma Getting Grimmer", Cable from the US Embassy, Rangoon, 14 September 2005, *Public Library of US Diplomacy*, https://wikileaks.org/plusd/cables/05RANGOON1054_a.html.
73. It is not known how the Australian ambassador arrived at the figure of 5,000 people, which seems rather high. "Australia Sees Grim Burma Getting Grimmer". See also "Gag the Messenger", *Asia.view*, 26 September 2007, https://www.economist.com/asia/2007/09/26/gag-the-messenger.
74. "Australia Sees Grim Burma Getting Grimmer".

75. Peter Popham, *Perfect Hostage: A Life of Aung San Suu Kyi* (London: Hutchinson, 2007), p. 421.
76. According to one frequent visitor to Myanmar, the regime's embassy in the United States "lost" all its data on him in 2004, and had to ask for his help in recovering details of his earlier visits. Personal communication from Washington D.C., 3 November 2018. See also "Gag the Messenger".
77. "Australia Sees Grim Burma Getting Grimmer".
78. See, for example, Helen James, *Security and Sustainable Development in Myanmar* (London: Routledge, 2006), p. 48.
79. Peter Popham, *The Lady and the Peacock: The Life of Aung San Suu Kyi* (London: Rider, 2011), p. 362.
80. Zarni Mann, "A Decade Later, Victims Still Seeking Depayin Massacre Justice", *The Irrawaddy*, 31 May 2013, https://www.irrawaddy.com/news/burma/a-decade-later-victims-still-seeking-depayin-massacre-justice.html. See also *Preliminary Report of the Ad hoc Commission on Depayin Massacre (Burma), July 4, 2003* (Bangkok: National Council of the Union of Burma and the Burma Lawyers' Council, 2004), http://www.ibiblio.org/obl/docs/Depayin_Massacre.pdf.
81. Saw Yan Naing, "I Saved Suu Kyi at Depayin Massacre: Ex-Spy Chief", *The Irrawaddy*, 10 April 2012, https://www.irrawaddy.com/news/burma/i-saved-suu-kyi-at-depayin-massacre-ex-spy-chief.html.
82. When US ambassador Burton Levin left Yangon at the end of his assignment in September 1990, he was not replaced, as the Bush administration wished to register a protest against the new military regime. The position was not filled again until Derek Mitchell's appointment as ambassador in July 2012. In the intervening period, the United States was represented in Yangon by a succession of Charges d'Affaires.
83. "Parting Thoughts on Burma", Cable from the US Embassy, Rangoon, 4 August 2005, *Public Library of US Diplomacy*, https://wikileaks.org/plusd/cables/05RANGOON901_a.html. Carmen Martinez was US Charge d'Affaires ad interim in Yangon from August 2002 to August 2005.

84. Larry Jagan, "Power Struggle Intensifies Uncertainty", *Bangkok Post*, 31 January 2005. Jagan used a similar quotation, from a retired Tatmadaw officer, in "Deposed PM's Allies Face Sentencing", *South China Morning Post*, 21 February 2005, https://www.scmp.com/article/489760/deposed-pms-allies-face-sentencing. See also Renaud Egreteau and Larry Jagan, *Soldiers and Diplomacy in Burma: Understanding the Foreign Relations of the Praetorian State* (Singapore: NUS Press/IRASEC, 2013), p. 199.

Chapter 4

POWER SHIFTS AND STRUCTURAL CHANGES

> The Government reinforced its rule with a pervasive security apparatus. Until its dismantling in October, the Office of the Chief of Military Intelligence (OCMI) exercised control through surveillance, harassment of political activists, intimidation, arrest, detention, physical abuse, and restrictions on citizens' contacts with foreigners. After October, the Government's new Military Affairs Security (MAS) assumed a similar role, though apparently with less sweeping powers. The Government justified its security measures as necessary to maintain order and national unity.
>
> "Burma", 2004 Country Report on Human Rights Practices US Department of State, 28 February 2005[1]

In his comments on MRTV on 24 October 2004, General Shwe Mann stated that "we have placed Military Intelligence Service in its bounds and have prevented not to get involved in other matters" (sic).[2] However, the SPDC was clearly determined to go further and destroy Khin Nyunt's intelligence empire, removing him forever as a potential threat to the SPDC's senior leadership, notably Than Shwe and Maung Aye. It was for this reason that the entire OCMI organization was dismantled. There was no question, however, that the regime would continue to rely heavily on intelligence for its command and control of both the security forces and Myanmar's diverse population.

For all its shortcomings in the eyes of many in the Tatmadaw, over the years OCMI, its predecessors and other intelligence agencies had proven their value to the regime. They had helped it to stay informed about developments, to anticipate threats and to remain secure in its pursuit of the three "national causes" of unity, stability and sovereignty, as it perceived them. For the sake of its own survival, and in its eyes the country's survival, the SPDC was bound to establish some kind of organization to fill the vacuum that it had unexpectedly created.

OUT WITH THE OLD

The details are not clear, but it appears that, as a first step, the SPDC disbanded the Myanmar Army's Intelligence Corps as a separate entity and gave the country's then twelve regional commanders effective control over all military intelligence field units.[3] As a consequence, these units no longer functioned as extensions of a discrete bureau based in the Tatmadaw's HQ. Kyaw Yin Hlaing has suggested that "the dismissal of the entire intelligence corps brought an end to a long-standing factional struggle between the army and intelligence units".[4] It also meant, however, that military intelligence in Myanmar was suddenly deprived of any central coordination and guidance. Also, it would be surprising if the country's strategic intelligence effort did not suffer at the expense of the operational and tactical intelligence that was more in demand at the level of the regional military commanders. These problems were exacerbated by the abolition of the NIB.

Immediately following Khin Nyunt's arrest, the SPDC moved to prevent a reoccurrence of the problem it felt it had just solved, namely the rise of an all-too-powerful Chief of Intelligence. On 22 October 2004, the regime abolished the NIB and repealed the 1983 NIB Law. Shwe Mann attempted to explain these steps, as follows:

> Although the National Intelligence Bureau Act and the National Intelligence Bureau were necessary in the past, but today they are not necessary anymore. Heads of department and some deputy heads of department at the Office of the Chief of Military Intelligence Headquarters, while serving in the National Intelligence Bureau, for various reasons, committed other improper and unlawful acts. As they were committed either unknowingly or knowingly, the Bureau and the law if allowed to still exist, the bribery and corruption that had occurred in the past will still remain. It will be a hindrance in reaching the State's goal of a modern developed and disciplined country (sic).[5]

Shwe Mann later stated that the NIB Law and the NIB had been removed "to deter bribery, corruption and influence by improper ways, and intimidation by the State service personnel (sic)".[6] The NIB and its law "did not serve the interests of the public".[7] They were "no longer suitable for the welfare of the public to be in conformity with the changing situations and with a view to ensuring security and peace" (sic).[8]

It was obvious to most observers, however, that the real reason for the repeal of the NIB Law and the dissolution of the NIB was to deprive anyone, especially the heads of Myanmar's security agencies, of a platform from which they could dominate the country's entire intelligence apparatus and build an independent power base. As had occurred at least twice before, in 1965 and 1983, the CI had become too powerful and had to be removed before he threatened the status quo, or made a bid for the national leadership.⁹ This posed a dilemma for the regime. There was clearly a need for Myanmar's vast intelligence apparatus to be centrally managed and for its operations to be coordinated at a senior level. However, the power this gave the CI under the old arrangements not only challenged the military chain of command, but also threatened the leadership's ability to dictate policy and balance the competing interests found among the higher levels of the Tatmadaw. As Khin Nyunt's case demonstrated, these concerns were heightened by the CI's ability to collect sensitive information on his fellow officers, which could possibly be used against them in any internal power struggle.¹⁰

After October 2004, these concerns were underlined by the appointment of Than Shwe and Maung Aye loyalists to positions formerly held by Khin Nyunt, his proteges and supporters. Khin Nyunt's successor as Prime Minister, for example, was Lieutenant General Soe Win, a former head of the USDA and the so-called "Butcher of Depayin". The SPDC also struck at a wide range of economic interests that were formerly controlled by the military intelligence organization. These efforts seemed designed not only to assume control of lucrative businesses formerly managed by OCMI but also to gather evidence of corruption that could be levelled against it.¹¹

For example, after the SPDC stopped issuing import licences for motor vehicles in 1996, it was very difficult for anyone in Myanmar to import a car.¹² The resale of import licences was prohibitively expensive and import tariffs were very high. The import of cars from Thailand and China, a highly lucrative trade, soon fell under the control of the DDSI/OSS. It was also a profitable source of income for the EAGs on the country's periphery with which Khin Nyunt had negotiated ceasefires and in some cases forged special relationships. Two obvious examples were the United Wa State Army (UWSA) in the north and the Democratic Karen Buddhist Army (DKBA) in the east. From the late 1990s, smugglers, in collaboration with DDSI/OSS/OCMI and their affiliate the *NaSaKa*, brought tens of thousands of new and second-hand cars, trucks and motorcycles across Myanmar's porous borders, particularly that with Thailand. DDSI/OSS/OCMI used local ceasefire groups like the UWSA and DKBA to deliver these vehicles to purchasers inside the country.[13] After October 2004, the SPDC clamped down on this trade, restricting imports, while still taking the lion's share of the profits.

Also, following Khin Nyunt's fall, thirty-two journals and magazines that had been operating under licence from OCMI were temporarily closed down. They included the high profile *Myanmar Times*, run by an Australian businessman and "Sonny" Myat Swe, the son of Brigadier General Thein Swe, who for some years was head of OCMI's International Relations Department.[14] The *Myanmar Times* was the only publication that received censorship clearance directly from the OSS, rather than from the Press Scrutiny Board. Other publications targeted included several news-oriented magazines and weeklies with a wide readership, including *Living Colour, New Gazette, 7-Days, First Eleven, Myanmar Interview, Idea, International News Journal* and *Kumudra* ("The Lotus").[15] Media outlets not affiliated with military intelligence were not affected by the crackdown.[16] Also, a large OCMI front trading company was closed and operating licences were withdrawn from two banks believed to have close ties with OCMI.[17] Bagan Cybertech, which had been run by one of Khin Nyunt's sons, and had reportedly benefited from a large payment made from official OCMI funds, was taken over by the Myanmar Army's Signal Corps before being sold on to regime cronies.[18] Lacking OCMI's expertise and authority, however, it soon ran into difficulties, despite being Myanmar's main Internet service provider.

In November and December 2004, 14,318 convicts were released from Myanmar's forty-five known gaols.[19] The regime justified this unusual move by citing "improper deeds" on the part of the old NIB.[20] Reflecting the NIB's wide remit, the prisoners released included members of ethnic minorities, including some former members of EAGs, people who had violated immigration laws, and a large number of white collar criminals. Also released were seventy-six political prisoners, most of whom were political party members and activists.[21] Several were prominent 1988 generation student leaders, who the SPDC claimed had been treated "incorrectly" and detained for excessive periods by DDSI/OSS/OCMI.[22] While at one level these releases were welcomed both in Myanmar and abroad, they were dismissed by the opposition NLD, which saw the decision not as a gesture of goodwill but rather as "a malicious action directed at military intelligence".[23] The US Embassy in Yangon agreed, reporting in a cable to Washington that the prisoner release was "another frontal assault on Khin Nyunt and the next step in an ongoing campaign to blame the country's ills on the former PM and his expansive empire, which included his once-powerful military intelligence network as well as broad commercial interests".[24]

Following Khin Nyunt's arrest, there was a spate of rumours in Yangon that the inter-agency organization known as the *NaSaKa* was also to be disbanded, and replaced on Myanmar's frontiers by separate units of MPF, Immigration and Customs officials.[25] This did not occur, although OCMI officers attached to the *NaSaKa* were replaced, usually by less experienced men.[26]

The *NaSaKa* continued to operate, albeit under tighter controls, until July 2013, when it was disbanded without explanation by President Thein Sein.[27] However, from 2005 the *NaSaKa* no longer enjoyed a monopoly over border controls. In January that year, a Border Area Trade Directorate, known by its Burmese initials as *NaKaTha*, was formed.[28] It was composed of personnel seconded from the MPF, Customs, Immigration, the Myanmar Economic Bank and Internal Revenue. A notable omission was anyone from military intelligence. The new organization was led by more junior officers than had commanded the *NaSaKa*. It was formally managed by the Ministry of Commerce, but was widely believed to answer to Maung Aye through the Trade Policy Council. *NaKaTha* units were reportedly posted to 11 border towns; 5 on the Chinese border, 3 on the Thai border, 2 on the Indian border and 1 on the Bangladesh border.[29] Without the coordinating role formerly exercised by OCMI, the overlapping responsibilities of *NaKaTha* members led to considerable confusion. Also, it was not long before it too was accused of corruption.

Despite all these measures, the US Embassy in Yangon could report at the end of 2004 that "Big Brother's still on the job despite the recent evisceration of military intelligence".[30] The SPDC continued "to rely on [its] broad intelligence network to counter any perceived threats to the junta's staying power". However, things were not the same. In January 2005, the embassy told the State Department that:

> The October ouster of former Prime Minister and MI chief Khin Nyunt, and the purge of his intelligence and business empire, has created a significant void within the regime. ... this has led to considerable paralysis with regard to decision-making and interaction with the international community.

> Furthermore, and perhaps more significant, the demise of Khin Nyunt and MI, chief enforcers of SPDC control, has also severely hampered the regime's ability to maintain its vast network of spies and surveillance. The previously omnipotent military intelligence apparatus was not only the mechanism that stifled dissent and opposition, but was also the eyes and ears that allowed senior SPDC leaders to make many administrative decisions for the regime — and to keep tabs on each other.[31]

Many of those holding official positions in Myanmar at the time felt a sense of drift and, despite early confirmation of the seven-step roadmap to a "discipline-flourishing democracy" announced by Khin Nyunt in August 2003, the lack of a clear direction for the future. There were numerous anecdotal reports of SB and other intelligence officers being unsure of their new roles and seeking guidance on their responsibilities.[32] Also, it is believed that many informers stopped reporting developments of interest until their tasking and lines of communication were clarified. Some were doubtless happy to have a good reason to do so.

IN WITH THE NEW

The SPDC was well aware of all these problems. It was determined to pay back the country's intelligence apparatchiks for years of humiliation, but it also knew that it had to take steps to restore the country's intelligence capabilities.

In the immediate aftermath of Khin Nunt's arrest and the dismantling of OCMI, the MPF was given greatly increased responsibilities for internal security. They were to be exercised mainly through SB which, according to unconfirmed press reports, moved quickly to boost its strength and acquire new capabilities. In December 2004, for example, an instruction was issued to each State and Division police force to fill quotas of twenty officers and thirty sergeants. They were to be not older than forty-five years of age and to have high school diplomas.[33] According to news stories broadcast at the time, the extra 700 or so personnel were required urgently "since the Police Special Branch must take over the activities carried out by the now defunct Military Intelligence units".[34] It is likely that the CID was also ordered to play its part in filling the gap left by OCMI's demise, at least for a period. MPF officers familiar with this period have said that, for the first time, they felt that the force was accorded the respect it deserved by senior military officers, and was no longer treated as the "younger brother" of the armed forces.[35] Even so, it was clearly going to take some time for the MPF to develop the capabilities required to exercise the new role that had been so unexpectedly thrust upon it, adding to the urgency of finding a replacement for OCMI.

In late 2004 or early 2005, the SPDC created the Office of the Chief of Military Affairs Security (OCMAS), later known (in English) as the Office of the Chief of Military Security Affairs (OCMSA), or simply as MAS (or MSA).[36] Appointed as its chief was Lieutenant General Myint Swe, the Yangon Division commander and reportedly a loyal protégé of SPDC Chairman Than Shwe. (It was Myint Swe who had arrested Khin Nyunt in October 2004). OCMSA was made subordinate to the Tatmadaw's General Staff Office. At least in its early days, its structure seems to have remained much the same as OCMI, but with a number of adjustments. For example, the rank level of department heads was reduced to lieutenant colonel.[37]

This was justified on the grounds that OCMSA HQ now only performed administrative and analysis functions.[38] New military intelligence battalions were formed, but they were put under the control of the regional military commanders.[39] Intelligence companies were deployed to population centres, but they too answered to the relevant regional commanders.[40] Field units no longer reported directly to their HQ in Yangon or (after the capital's move in November 2005) to Naypyidaw. Intelligence reports were sent through RMC channels to the General Staff and thence to the Commander-in-Chief of the Army. Only courtesy copies went to the Chief of MSA.

Predictably, OCMSA endured a shaky start. As the US Embassy noted in early 2005, the "new intelligence chief has considerably less political stature and experience than ousted Prime Minister and Military Intelligence Czar Khin Nyunt and oversees a military intelligence apparatus with a reduced mandate and less authority".[41] OCMSA's influence was balanced against the increased power granted to the MPF, and in particular to the force's SB.[42] Also, the new military intelligence organization struggled to meet the relatively high standards that had been set by OCMI.[43] One major failing was the inexperience of its new officers who, despite an intensive ten-week training course in Yangon, struggled to fill the shoes of those they had replaced.[44] Also, OCMSA being so much smaller than OCMI, its personnel were spread very thinly around the country.[45] According to several accounts, information flows from the field were down to mere trickles.[46] Often, OCMSA officers had to persuade their MPF counterparts and various township officers to share information with them, simply to satisfy their superiors and maintain the credibility of the new military intelligence organization.[47] Activists and others used to being watched by OCMI and SB agents found themselves free from effective surveillance, some for the first time in years.[48]

Inevitably, mistakes were made. For example, in 2005 OCMSA and the MPF were at a loss to explain several bombings in Yangon that killed eleven and injured at least 162.[49] One of the bombs exploded at a Thai trade fair, causing the regime considerable diplomatic embarrassment. These attacks followed a similar anonymous bombing in Mandalay. After the Yangon attacks, the security authorities accused three different EAGs and the exiled National Coalition Government of the Union of Burma (NCGUB) of being responsible, but failed to discover the real culprits.[50] Fingers were also pointed at "a world famous organisation of a certain superpower nation", a clear allusion to the CIA, which was accused of having trained the bombers in "a neighbouring country", obviously Thailand.[51] It was also rumoured that the bomb attacks were carried out by disgruntled former military intelligence officers.[52] In another incident, this time in 2006, a Karen leader was named as a suspect in a bomb plot, despite having died three years earlier. In 2011, a female Karen doctor who founded a medical clinic in Mae Sot in 1989 and had received numerous international awards was mistakenly identified by OCMSA as the political leader of the KNU.[53] These errors did not enhance the credibility of Myanmar's revamped intelligence apparatus, either inside the country or outside it.[54]

As various problems became apparent, however, steps were taken by the regime to solve them. Some entailed a reassessment of the 2004 purge. For example, it was reported that in early 2005 a large number of former military intelligence officers ranked below the level of sergeant had been reinstated to their original positions, and ordered to resume their old duties.⁵⁵ This was apparently because the surveillance being conducted by OCMSA's new recruits was considered ineffective.⁵⁶ It has also been suggested that there were problems in processing all the paperwork generated by OCMSA's activities. In addition, according to the *Democratic Voice of Burma* (DVB), after the collapse of OCMI lower level military intelligence officers were posted frequently, rarely staying in one place for more than a few months. This appears to have been aimed at reducing the likelihood of agents engaging in corrupt practices and developing suspect relationships with local power brokers. However, the high tempo of postings significantly reduced their effectiveness, as it took time to get to know the working environment and nurture relationships with contacts and informers. In 2010, it was apparently decided that postings should return to the OCMI pattern, and be changed every two to five years.⁵⁷

According to a US Embassy Yangon report dated 7 December 2007, OCMSA was "one of the two intelligence agencies created following former intelligence chief Khin Nyunt's ouster in 2006".⁵⁸ It is not known to what other agency the embassy might have been referring in this cable, which contained a number of errors. It is most likely, however, to be the Myanmar Financial Intelligence Unit (MFIU), which was created in January 2004, following the passage of the 2002 Control of Money Laundering Law. To quote its website, the MFIU:

> serves as the central agency to receive, request and analyse the reports submitted by the reporting entities and other information relating to money laundering, financing of

terrorism and predicate offences and to disseminate the result of analysis, and related information to relevant persons or organisations or internal or external counterpart agencies upon request or spontaneously, if it suspects that it relates to money laundering, financing of terrorism, or any predicate offences (sic).[59]

Ideally, national financial intelligence units should operate autonomously and have timely access to all reports of suspicious transactions. However, as noted by Brian Moore, the MFIU operated as part of the Ministry of Home Affairs, under the supervision of the Chairman of the Central Control Board on Money Laundering, which was formed in 2002.[60] The MFIU also lacked its own budget and suffered from inadequate laws regarding terrorist financing, thus limiting its effectiveness.[61]

Other changes were made to fill the gaps left by OCMI's demise. For example, the USDA assumed a higher profile in the intelligence system. According to one study, "The SPDC has met with USDA CEC [Central Executive Committee] members and other loyal members to train them as Intelligence officers, forming teams in each Township."[62] Another report stated that the USDA had "local intelligence branches which monitor the general population in various neighbourhoods across the country".[63] Also, from time to time, the MPF recruited USDA members to provide it with information about the NLD and other suspect organizations. All the information collected was reported directly to the USDA's General HQ, before being passed on to OCMSA and SB. It was the opinion of some dissidents that the vast size and reach of the USDA made it a much more effective collector of information than the new military intelligence agency.[64] Given its influence, and the impunity which it seemed to enjoy, the organization appeared to many observers to have been "empowered to do the dirty work of the military regime".[65]

In May 2006, Lieutenant General Myint Swe was replaced as the chief of OCMSA by Lieutenant General Ye Myint, reportedly a protégé of Vice Senior General Maung Aye. As Ye Myint had been the commander of Central Command, based at Mandalay, this step was widely interpreted as another attempt by the SPDC to break down the institutional divide between the Tatmadaw's combat (particularly infantry) and intelligence arms.[66] Ye Myint remained head of OCMSA until August 2010, when he was replaced by Lieutenant General Kyaw Swe, the former commander of Southwest Regional Command.[67] Like his predecessor, he had no specific intelligence background. Before then, however, Ye Myint was called upon to respond to the regime's greatest domestic security problem since the 1988 uprising.

In what began as a small and largely spontaneous movement, public demonstrations in August 2007 over economic hardships blossomed into wider protests, mainly in Yangon, led by Buddhist monks (or *pongyis*). With the encouragement of NLD members and other activists, some based abroad, the demonstration took an overtly political turn and soon became a major challenge to the military regime.[68] The brutal suppression of these protests involved all elements of Myanmar's coercive apparatus, notably the Tatmadaw and OCMSA. According to Human Rights Watch:

> The MSA played a central role in monitoring the protests, collecting photos and other intelligence during the protests, and using the information collected to help coordinate the widespread arrests that followed the crackdown on the

protesters. The Military Security Affairs also took a leading role in the interrogation of detainees who were believed to have connections to exiled dissident organisations and armed groups fighting the Burmese government.[69]

The BSI, SB, CID and other parts of the MPF (particularly its paramilitary security battalions) were also involved. All these organizations were later identified as having been active in suppressing the civil unrest, identifying suspects or interrogating detainees.[70] A large network of informers, including USDA officials and militia members, also helped track down demonstrators and protest organizers.[71]

After the protests were quelled, the SPDC produced an eighteen-page report outlining a "longstanding plot involving 'bogus monks', a little known group, the Forum for Democracy in Burma, and billionaire financier George Soros' Open Society organisation to bring down the regime".[72] The report included the names of alleged plotters and their supposed backers. Also, at a press conference held in Naypyidaw that December, senior officials described the "threat" to Myanmar from all these elements. Their comments were supported by displays of weapons, mobile phones and other items allegedly seized from the demonstrators.[73] Both public relations exercises reflected the considerable efforts made by the national intelligence apparatus to identify the perpetrators and supporters of the 2007 unrest, based on surveillance records, interrogations of those detained and other sources. They also confirmed that OCMSA, SB and other agencies, including members of the USDA, had rounded up and questioned anyone who had played even a minor role in the protests, often relying on still photographs and film footage taken during the disturbances to identify their targets. Benedict Rogers has claimed that, within a few weeks of the protests, the regime had arrested at least 6,000 people, including 1,400 Buddhist monks.[74] About 1,000 people were eventually imprisoned—some for terms of sixty-five years—for "speech crimes" and a range of other offences.[75]

Given the nature of the military regime in Myanmar, it is difficult to know the extent to which the SPDC's report and press briefing actually reflected its thinking or were part of an elaborate propaganda campaign. The findings put forward were in many cases highly tendentious and, if meant to be taken seriously, did not always reflect well on the intelligence community's ability objectively to analyse and assess the massive amounts of data that it collected, let alone grasp the root causes of popular unrest in Myanmar. As Kyaw Yin Hlaing has written, "Although many exile activists tried to take credit for the monk-led protests, all available evidence showed that they played very little role. Monks and lay protesters engaged in the protests out of their frustration with the economic and political situation of the country."[76] However, the regime believed that it faced an existential threat from a coalition of official and private actors, domestic and foreign.[77] According to the Chief of Police:

> The recent incidents in last August and September were the results of timely conspiracies of a western power and anti-government groups inside and outside the country as well as at the border (sic).[78]

The generals were convinced that the United States (the "western power" in question) had facilitated the protests as part of a concerted and multi-faceted programme to precipitate regime change in Myanmar. This belief strengthened the

SPDC's determination to maintain a large and powerful intelligence apparatus that was capable of detecting such threats before they became a serious threat to the military regime and, as they perceived them, to Myanmar's unity, stability and sovereignty.

Indeed, the 2007 "Saffron Revolution" (as it was dubbed by the foreign press, although in Myanmar the *pongyis'* robes tend to be a darker shade) underlined the fact that, although the military government managed to suppress the protests, the purge in 2004 had severely reduced its intelligence capabilities. To quote Kyaw Yin Hlaing once again, "Before former intelligence chief Khin Nyunt was dismissed and his intelligence agency disbanded, the junta could almost always uncover opposition groups that were planning to organise protests ... the absence of an effective intelligence agency allowed activists to mobilise and sustain the protests quite freely."[79] Other observers suggested that, had Khin Nyunt still been CI and his more experienced intelligence agents been around, the protests would have been managed in a more sophisticated manner, and not been allowed to reach the dangerous proportions they did.[80] As another commentator observed, "the so-called 'Saffron Revolution' illustrated how far the intelligence apparatus had deteriorated: the dissent caught the government completely by surprise, and it resorted to extensive arrests and torture to find the ringleaders".[81]

Senior General Than Shwe seemed to share this view. Even though he more than anyone else was responsible for many of its weaknesses, he was reportedly highly critical of the country's intelligence apparatus in the wake of the 2007 unrest.[82] Rather than objectively examine its root causes, however, and take measures to address popular grievances, the regime's response was once again to strengthen the country's coercive apparatus so that similar protests would not reoccur, or at least could be foreseen and prevented before they became a serious problem. This included a revitalization of the military intelligence organization. Priscilla Clapp had foreseen just such a development. Not long before the Saffron Revolution, she wrote:

> It would be a surprising aberration in the long history of military rule in Burma ... if the leadership did not eventually recreate a means of ensuring strong military control over an intelligence function that is so critical to its political power.[83]

By December 2007, diplomatic observers in Yangon were reporting that Lieutenant General Ye Myint had "significantly strengthened MAS's authority and resources".[84] A special effort was put into increasing the level of surveillance of students, political activists and other potential sources of civil unrest. Both OCMSA and SB numbers were significantly increased and more informers recruited.[85]

As time passed, there were a growing number of anecdotal reports suggesting that Myanmar's intelligence apparatus had in part at least recovered from the 2004 purge and returned to business as usual. A broad division of responsibilities seemed to have been agreed. In 2008, for example, a Canadian government report noted that OCMSA appeared to handle the most serious and sensitive political issues, such as the incarceration of Aung San Suu Kyi, who was once again under house arrest, and problems related to the ethnic armed groups, including those that had agreed to ceasefires with the SPDC.[86] The MPF's SB handled cases involving the leading dissident organizations, including the NLD and the 88 Generation Students Group. The latter, founded in 2005, was made up mainly of students who had participated in, and subsequently been imprisoned for their role in, the 1988 pro-democracy uprising.[87] Most had been released, subject to certain conditions, by 2012. For their part, the BSI continued to address financial crimes, including fraud and corruption, while the CID mainly handled serious criminal matters such as rape and murder.[88]

At the same time, steps were taken to prevent the leak of confidential information from military and government offices, including the intelligence agencies.[89] The regime had always been sensitive to public discussions about its inner workings and national security issues. However, these concerns increased when a series of dramatic stories appeared in the international news media. In 2009, for example, a confidential report on the visit to North Korea by a high level Tatmadaw delegation in 2008 was leaked.[90] The revelation in 2009 that North Korea was helping to construct underground facilities in Myanmar was another embarrassment, as were accusations in 2010 that the regime had launched a nuclear weapons programme.[91] Many of the stories that appeared on these subjects were either factually inaccurate or misguided in their conclusions, but they all hit a raw nerve in Naypyidaw. Together with a few other projects reported in the news media, such as the Tatmadaw's plans for a fibre-optic military communications network, these matters were all considered top secret.[92] Their public exposure prompted renewed pressure on OCMSA to monitor and control the electronic media in Myanmar. Also, committees were organized at every military command level to prevent further damaging leaks, and new measures were introduced to protect computer-based data.[93]

The intelligence services were also pursuing a number of new initiatives. According to former OCMI agents, a "data thief" project to steal computer-based information had been launched.[94] Emails were being hacked and mobile phone calls intercepted, reportedly with the help of computer systems set up under Khin Nyunt by North Korean, Singaporean and Russian experts.[95] Websites considered hostile to the regime found themselves under cyber attack.[96] Activists, journalists and foreign academics once again reported being followed by OCMSA and SB officers.[97] Some believed, with good reason, that their hotel phones were tapped.[98] One astute Myanmar-watcher, who travelled widely throughout the country, described the regime's "surveillance machine" in 2010 as "frighteningly thorough and efficient".[99] "Active cells" of intelligence officers were reportedly still operating in Bangladesh, India and Thailand.[100] All these activities suggested that the new intelligence apparatus was settling down, gathering strength, and returning to familiar patterns of behaviour.

Despite all the changes made to individual agencies, however, and improvements in the overall performance of the national intelligence apparatus, there were still complaints in military circles that it was not up to par, compared with its predecessor.[101] For example, between 2005 and 2007 there were nearly twenty anonymous bomb attacks, most of them in population centres, that were never solved.[102] Despite all the accusations thrown around, few culprits were identified and even fewer were arrested. Another failing that repeatedly came up in discussions after 2004 was the lack of a central oversight mechanism like the old NIB that could decide broad intelligence policies, coordinate operations and eliminate any duplication of effort. So obvious was the need for a new NIB that, even after its abolition, many observers were confident that it would be recreated, albeit under the control of the "regular" armed forces.[103] There was also gossip about a new "Inland Security Ministry" under someone loyal to Than Shwe, to manage such issues. Rumours periodically surfaced that such a body was under consideration but it did not eventuate, possibly out of fear that it would give too much power to one person.[104] For obvious reasons, that was something the regime wished to avoid.

After 2011, all these issues were seen from a different perspective as Myanmar made the carefully orchestrated transition from a military dictatorship to a "discipline-flourishing democracy". While the basic rationale behind the national intelligence apparatus remained, and had been given greater urgency by the Saffron Revolution, there was increasing pressure for it to change the way it operated and was perceived, both by the local population and the wider world.

Notes

1. US Department of State, "Burma", 2004 Country Reports on Human Rights Practices, Bureau of Democracy, Human Rights and Labour (Washington D.C.: Department of State, 28 February 2005), https://www.state.gov/j/drl/rls/hrrpt/2004/41637.htm.
2. "Complete Explanation on the Developments in the Country", p. 15.
3. It is not known how, or even if, the intelligence elements in the Myanmar Navy and Myanmar Air Force were affected, but it is assumed that they were included in the purge as they were integral parts of OCMI.
4. Kyaw Yin Hlaing, "Myanmar in 2004", p. 238.
5. "Complete Explanation on the Developments in the Country", p. 12.

6. Ibid., p. 15.
7. Connie Levett, "Burma Shuts Down Military Intelligence Office", *Sunday Age*, 24 October 2004.
8. Burma Lawyers Council, "Promulgation of Law Repealing National Intelligence Bureau Law and Dissolution of the National Intelligence Bureau", 22 October 2004, http://web.archive.org web/20110902222829/http://www.blc-burma.org/html/Myanmar%20Law/lr_e_ml04_07.htm.
9. In 1965, Colonel Maung Lwin was removed, and in 1983 it was Brigadier General Tin Oo's turn. The latter was CI from 1972 to 1978, but later became Military Assistant to the President, Director of the National Intelligence Bureau and Joint General Secretary of the BSPP, thus retaining considerable influence in intelligence circles.
10. According to anecdotal evidence, the intelligence agencies were interested not only in evidence of corruption and the misuse of power, but also personal traits such as a weakness for mistresses, the patronage of prostitutes, a taste for pornography, a gambling habit or excessive drinking. See, for example, Aung Zaw, "A Burmese Spy Comes in from the Cold".
11. "Burma: Tatmadaw Takes Away M.I.'s Keys", Cable from the US Embassy, Rangoon, 24 November 2004, *Public Library of US Diplomacy*, https://wikileaks.org/plusd/cables/04RANGOON1503_a.html.
12. Exceptions were made for senior Buddhist monks and selected organizations.
13. "Burma: Tatmadaw Takes Away M.I.'s Keys".
14. Sonny Swe was later forced to transfer his stake in the *Myanmar Times* to the Ministry of Information.
15. The popular monthly *Living Colour* was licensed to one of Khin Nyunt's sons, but operated under independent management. Jennifer Leehey, "Writing in a Crazy Way: Literary Life in Contemporary Urban Burma", in *Burma at the Turn of the 21st Century*, edited by Monique Skidmore (Honolulu: University of Hawaii Press, 2005), p. 202.

16. "Military Intelligence-Affiliated Media Shut Down", Cable from the US Embassy, Rangoon, 20 October 2004, *Public Library of US Diplomacy*, https://wikileaks.org/plusd/cables/04RANGOON1366_a.html.
17. Lintner, "Myanmar Payback Time", p. 23.
18. "Burma: Khin Nyunt's Cronies Feeling the Squeeze", Cable from the US Embassy, Rangoon, 30 November 2004, *Public Library of US Diplomacy*, https://wikileaks.org/plusd/cables/04RANGOON1518_a.html.
19. This figure does not include up to fifty labour camps and numerous interrogation centres scattered around the country. See *Burma's Prisons and Labour Camps: Silent Killing Fields* (Mae Sot: Assistance Association for Political Prisoners (Burma), 2009?), http://www.burmalibrary.org/docs07/Burma%27s_prisons_and_labour_camps-silent_killing_fields.pdf; and "Torture, Abuse Common in Burma's Prisons", *Asia Sentinel*, 1 October 2007, https://www.asiasentinel.com/politics/torture-abuse-common-in-burmas-prisons/.
20. "Burma", 2004 Country Reports on Human Rights Practices.
21. In April 2004, Amnesty International estimated that there were 1,350 political prisoners in Myanmar. See Burmese Women's Union and Assistance Association for Political Prisoners (Burma), *Women Political Prisoners in Burma*, September 2004, p. 4, http://aappb.org/wp-content/uploads/2014/03/Women-Political-Prisoners-in-Burma.pdf.
22. Win Min, "Internal Dynamics of the Burmese Military: Before, During and After the 2007 Demonstrations", in *Dictatorship, Disorder and Decline in Myanmar*, edited by Monique Skidmore and Trevor Wilson (Canberra: ANU E Press, 2008), p. 32.
23. "Burmese Regime Begins Release of 4,000 Prisoners", Cable from the US Embassy, Rangoon, 19 November 2004, *Public Library of US Diplomacy*, https://wikileaks.org/plusd/cables/04RANGOON1488_a.html.

24. Ibid.
25. "Burma: 2004 Annual Terrorism Report".
26. "Burma's Least Wanted: The Rohingyas", Cable from the US Embassy, Rangoon, 22 February 2007, *Public Library of US Diplomacy*, https://wikileaks.org/plusd/cables/07RANGOON181_a.html.
27. Jared Ferrie, "Myanmar President Disbands Controversial Border Force", *Reuters*, 15 July 2013, https://www.reuters.com/article/us-myanmar-security/myanmar-president-disbands-controversial-border-force-idUSBRE96E0B420130715.
28. It has also been called "Border Commerce". See, for example, *A Choice for China: Ending the Destruction of Burma's Northern Frontier Forests*, A Briefing Document by Global Witness, October 2005, p. 57.
29. "Rangoon Shares Border Tax with Ceasefire Groups", *Shan Herald Agency for News*, 3 February 2005, https://bugashihtawn.wordpress.com/2011/02/15/rangoon-shares-border-tax-with-ceasefire-groups/.
30. "Burma: Khin Nyunt's Gone, But Big Brother's Still Watching", Cable from the US Embassy, Rangoon, 1 December 2004, *Public Library of US Diplomacy*, https://wikileaks.org/plusd/cables/04RANGOON1522_a.html.
31. "Is the Burmese Regime Coming Unglued?".
32. Evan Osnos, "The Burmese Spring", *The New Yorker*, 6 August 2012, https://www.newyorker.com/magazine/2012/08/06/the-burmese-spring.
33. At the time, there were fourteen provinces in Myanmar, including seven states named after the main ethnic minority groups and seven divisions. These became the fourteen states and regions listed in the 2008 constitution.
34. "Burma Plans Expansion of Police Special Branch to Monitor Political Activities", *Democratic Voice of Burma*, 25 December 2004.
35. Personal communication from Yangon, March 2017.

36. It is widely assumed that the different names were the result of different translations of the original title in Burmese. See, for example, *Country of Origin Information Report: Burma (Union of Myanmar)* (London: UK Border Agency, Home Office, 23 July 2010), http://www.refworld.org/pdfid/4c529d1a2.pdf. However, a former Information Minister of Myanmar has written that the name (in English, at least) changed from OCMAS to OCMSA at some stage. See Ye Htut, "A Background to the Security Crisis in Northern Rakhine", p. 7, note 34.
37. McAndrew, "From Combat to Karaoke", p. 131.
38. *Country of Origin Information Report: Burma (Union of Myanmar)*.
39. See, for example, A Correspondent, "Major Shakeup in Myanmar's Intelligence Apparatus", pp. 8–9; and McAndrew, "From Combat to Karaoke".
40. "New Spy Machine Starting from Scratch", *Shan Herald Agency for News*, 17 February 2005, http://www.ibiblio.org/obl/docs3/BNI2005-02-19.htm.
41. "Burma: US Bilateral Initiatives Victim of Post-Khin Nyunt Purge".
42. Win Min, "Internal Dynamics of the Burmese Military", p. 34.
43. Aung Zaw, "Burmese Spy Reveals MI's Dirty Deeds", *The Irrawaddy*, 24 April 2006, http://www2.irrawaddy.com/article.php?art_id=5681&Submit=Submit.
44. "Intelligence Officers to be Replaced by Military Officers in Burma", *Democratic Voice of Burma*, 14 December 2004. Khin Nyunt has written that an intelligence officer needed ten years' experience before he could consider himself fully qualified. See Khin Nyunt, *Secretary One*.
45. "Burma Reportedly Reorganises Military Intelligence Structure", *Democratic Voice of Burma*, 29 June 2005.
46. Min Lwin, "Intelligence Unit to Return to Khin Nyunt Days", *Democratic Voice of Burma*, 18 October 2010, http://www.dvb.no/news/intelligence-unit-to-return-to-khin-nyunt-days/12265.

47. Moe Zay Nyein, "What is *SaYaHpa*", in *What's Swann Ar Shin and Other Articles* (Yangon: Ma Hla Hla Win, 2014) (in Burmese), unofficial translation in the author's possession.
48. Osnos, "The Burmese Spring".
49. "11 Killed in Burma Bomb Blast", *ABC News*, 8 May 2005, https://www.abc.net.au/news/2005-05-08/11-killed-in-burma-bomb-blast/1565752.
50. "Bomb Blasts Rock Capital", *BBC News*, 7 May 2005, http://news.bbc.co.uk/2/hi/asia-pacific/4524815.stm.
51. Richard Ehrlich, "Triple Bombing in Burma Leads to CIA Intrigue", *Scoop*, 18 May 2005, http://www.scoop.co.nz/stories/HL0505/S00219/triple-bombing-in-burma-leads-to-cia-intrigue.htm.
52. See Donald M. Seekins, *Historical Dictionary of Burma (Myanmar)* (Lanham: Scarecrow Press, 2006), p. 294; and "Bomb Explosions Occur in Yangon Due to Inhumane Acts Committed by Terrorists", *Global New Light of Myanmar*, 8 May 2005, http://www.ibiblio.org/obl/docs2/NLM2005-05-08.pdf.
53. The Thai intelligence authorities apparently shared this belief, which Anne Decobert has described as "laughable". Anne Decobert, *The Politics of Aid to Burma: A Humanitarian Struggle on the Thai-Burmese Border* (Oxford: Routledge, 2016), p. 220.
54. Shah Paung, "Dead KNU Man Spooks Burmese Sleuths", *The Irrawaddy*, 9 May 2006, http://www2.irrawaddy.com/article.php?art_id=5718.
55. "Intelligence Agents Reappointed by Burma Junta", *Democratic Voice of Burma*, 18 January 2005.
56. Fink, *Living Silence in Burma*, p. 138.
57. "Exile Radio Reports 'Shake-up' in Burma's Military Intelligence", *Democratic Voice of Burma*, 16 October 2010.
58. Khin Nyunt was arrested in 2004, not 2006. "Burma: Who's Who in the Regime", Cable from the US Embassy, Rangoon, 7 December 2007, *Public Library of US Diplomacy*, https://wikileaks.org/plusd/cables/07RANGOON1170_a.html.

59. Myanmar Financial Intelligence Unit, https://mfiu.gov.mm/en.
60. The Anti-Money Laundering Central Board, https://mfiu.gov.mm/anti-money-laundering-central-board.
61. Brian Moore, "How Myanmar Can Curb Illicit Financial Flows", *Asia Times*, 10 January 2017, http://www.atimes.com/myanmar-can-curb-illicit-financial-flows/.
62. *The White Shirts*, p. 55.
63. "Myanmar (Burma): Whether the Military Intelligence Force in Myanmar has been Fully or Partially Disbanded and Who is Carrying out their Duties (2004–February 2008)" (Ottawa: Research Directorate, Immigration and Refugee Board, 25 February 2008), https://www.justice.gov/sites/default/files/eoir/legacy/2014/01/31/MMR102757.E.pdf.
64. *The White Shirts*, p. 56. See also "Burma's New Intelligence Agents and the NLD", *Democratic Voice of Burma*, 8 November 2004.
65. Kyaw Zwa Moe, "Lawlessness and Disorder in Burma", *The Irrawaddy*, 23 March 2007, http://www2.irrawaddy.com/opinion_story.php?art_id=6941.
66. Maung Aung Myoe, *Building the Tatmadaw*, p. 83.
67. "More Detail on Military Reshuffle Emerges", *The Irrawaddy*, 30 August 2010, http://www2.irrawaddy.com/article.php?art_id=19337&page=1.
68. Andrew Selth, "Burma's 'Saffron Revolution' and the Limits of International Influence", *Australian Journal of International Affairs* 62, no. 3 (September 2008): 281–97.
69. *Crackdown: Repression of the 2007 Protests in Burma* (New York: Human Rights Watch, 22 September 2009), https://www.hrw.org/report/2007/12/06/crackdown/repression-2007-popular-protests-burma. See also Bertil Lintner, *The Resistance of the Monks: Buddhism and Activism in Burma* (New York: Human Rights Watch, 22 September 2009), https://www.hrw.org/report/2009/09/22/resistance-monks/buddhism-and-activism-burma.
70. *Crackdown*. See also Lintner, *The Resistance of the Monks*; and *Bullets in the Alms Bowl: An Analysis of the Brutal SPDC Suppression of the September 2007 Saffron Revolution* (Washington D.C.?:

NCGUB, March 2008), http://www.ibiblio.org/obl/docs4/BulletsInTheAlmsBowl.pdf.
71. "Chapter 4.4, Surveillance: Lawful Interception & Other Surveillance Methods", *ICT Sector-Wide Impact Assessment* (Yangon: Myanmar Centre for Responsible Business, 24 September 2015), http://www.myanmar-responsiblebusiness.org/pdf/SWIA/ICT/Chapter-04.04-Surveillance.pdf, p. 171. See also "Burma Intelligence Officer Says 'Thousands' Killed", *Krungthep Thurakit*, 3 October 2007 (in Thai).
72. Chris McGreal, "Spies, Suspicion and Empty Monasteries – Burma Today", *The Guardian*, 15 December 2007, https://www.theguardian.com/world/2007/dec/15/burma.chrismcgreal.
73. "Information Committee of State Peace and Development Council Holds Press Conference 2/2007 on Protests in August and September in Myanmar", *Global New Light of Myanmar*, 4 December 2007, http://www.ibiblio.org/obl/docs4/NLM2007-12-04.pdf. There were also separate articles in the same edition of the paper reporting "clarifications" made by other officials, including a lengthy statement by MPF Director-General Police Brigadier General Khin Yi.
74. Benedict Rogers, *Than Shwe: Unmasking Burma's Tyrant* (Chiang Mai: Silkworm Books, 2010), p. 179.
75. "Scenesetter for Codel Webb to Burma", Cable from the US Embassy, Rangoon, 5 August 2009, *Public Library of US Diplomacy*, https://wikileaks.org/plusd/cables/09RANGOON494_a.html.
76. Kyaw Yin Hlaing, "The State of the Pro-Democracy Movement in Authoritarian Myanmar/Burma", in *Myanmar/Burma: Challenges and Perspectives*, edited by Xiaolin Guo (Stockholm: Institute for Security and Development Policy, 2008), p. 71.
77. There is a useful summary of foreign assistance to exile news media organizations in "An Overview of Northern Thailand-based Burmese Media Organisations", Cable from the US Consulate General, Chiang Mai, 14 February 2007, *Public Library of US Diplomacy*, https://wikileaks.org/plusd/cables/07CHIANGMAI33_a.html.

78. "Minister for Information Brig-Gen Kyaw San speaks at Press Conference 2/2007", *Global New Light of Myanmar*, 4 December 2007, http://www.ibiblio.org/obl/docs4/NLM2007-12-04.pdf.
79. See, for example, Kyaw Yin Hlaing, "Challenging the Authoritarian State: Buddhist Monks and Peaceful Protests in Burma", *The Fletcher Forum of World Affairs* 38, no. 1 (Winter 2008): 137–38.
80. Kyaw Yin Hlaing, "Challenging the Authoritarian State", p. 138.
81. Neil A. Englehart, "Two Cheers for Burma's Rigged Election", *Political Science Faculty Publications* 1 (2012): 675, https://scholarworks.bgsu.edu/cgi/viewcontent.cgi?article=1001&context=poli_sci_pub.
82. "New Intelligence Chief Undertakes Major Overhaul", *The Irrawaddy*, 16 October 2010, http://www2.irrawaddy.com/article.php?art_id=19748.
83. Clapp, "Burma: Poster Child for Entrenched Repression", p. 142.
84. "Burma: Who's Who in the Regime".
85. Moe Zay Nyein, "What is *SaYaHpa*".
86. Aung San Suu Kyi was incarcerated six times between 20 July 1989 and 13 November 2010, for periods totalling almost fifteen years. She spent most of that time under virtual house arrest in her University Avenue home.
87. Bertil Lintner, "Myanmar's 88 Generation Comes of Age", *Asia Times*, 25 January 2007, http://www.atimes.com/atimes/Southeast_Asia/IA25Ae04.html.
88. "Myanmar (Burma): Whether the Military Intelligence Force in Myanmar has been Fully or Partially Disbanded and Who is Carrying out their Duties (2004–February 2008)".
89. "New Intelligence Chief Tries to Plug Leaks", *The Irrawaddy*, 1 October 2010, http://www2.irrawaddy.com/article.php?art_id=19603. See also *Country of Origin Information (COI) Report: Burma (Myanmar)* (London: UK Border Agency, Home Office, 2 February 2012), https://www.refworld.org/pdfid/538876b34.pdf.
90. See, for example, Kyaw Min Tun, "Burma, North Korea Said to Expand Military Ties", *Radio Free Asia*, 2 July 2009, https://www.

rfa.org/english/news/myanmar/nkorea-07012009231914.html. See also "Death Sentences in Burma over Document Leak", *RTE*, 8 January 2010, https://www.rte.ie/news/2010/0108/126112-burma/.

91. For a sensible overview of the nuclear issue, see Jeffrey Lewis, "Does Burma Still Have Nuclear Dreams?", *Foreign Policy*, 16 November 2012, https://foreignpolicy.com/2012/11/16/does-burma-still-have-nuclear-dreams/. On the tunnels, see Bertil Lintner, "Tunnels, Guns and Kimchi: North Korea's Quest for Dollars, Part 1", *Yale Global Online*, 9 June 2009, https://yaleglobal.yale.edu/content/tunnels-guns-and-kimchi-north-koreas-quest-dollars-part-i; and Bertil Lintner, "Tunnels, Guns and Kimchi: North Korea's Quest for Dollars, Part 2", *Yale Global Online*, 11 June 2009, https://yaleglobal.yale.edu/content/tunnels-guns-and-kimchi-north-koreas-quest-dollars-part-ii.
92. The fibre optic network was not just for routine communications. It also supported an upgraded air defence capability, considered essential for Myanmar's security in times of conflict.
93. Moe Zay Nyein, "What is *SaYaHpa*".
94. Aung Zaw, "A Burmese Spy Comes in from the Cold".
95. Aung Zaw, "Burmese Spy Reveals MI's Dirty Deeds".
96. Brian McCartan, "Myanmar on the Cyber-Offensive", *Asia Times*, 1 October 2008, http://www.atimes.com/atimes/Southeast_Asia/JJ01Ae01.html.
97. It is usually assumed that these agents are military intelligence officers, but these days they are more than likely to be from SB.
98. Personal communication from Washington D.C., 3 November 2018.
99. Larkin, *Finding George Orwell in Burma*, p. 57.
100. Aung Zaw, "Burmese Spy Reveals MI's Dirty Deeds". See also "Burmese Spy Arrested by Bangladesh Army", *Defence Update Bangladesh*, 18 September 2017, https://medium.com/@DefenseUpdateBangladesh/breaking-burmese-spy-arrested-by-bangladesh-army-12fac9845ea5.

101. "Exile Radio Reports 'Shake up' in Burma's Military Intelligence".
102. There had been at least 70 bomb attacks since 1989, killing about 80 people and injuring more than 250. Aung Naing Oo, "Burma Bombings Raise Questions—Who and Why?", *The Irrawaddy*, 18 January 2007, http://www2.irrawaddy.com/opinion_story.php?art_id=6619.
103. "Khin Nyunt's Ouster: One Week Later".
104. Min Lwin, "Intelligence Unit to Return to Khin Nyunt Days".

Chapter 5

INTELLIGENCE DEVELOPMENTS SINCE 2011

> The level of oppression has eased markedly since President Thein Sein, a former army general, took office in 2011 after an opposition-boycotted election. But while many political prisoners have been released, newspapers are no longer censored and freedom of speech has largely become a reality, the government has not ceased spying on its own people.
>
> Todd Pitman
> "In Burma, Internal Spy Network Lives on" (2013)[1]

Little definite is known about developments in Myanmar's intelligence community after the SPDC formally handed over political power to President Thein Sein's quasi-civilian government in March 2011. Understandably, many observers remained sceptical that there was any real shift in its status. One journalist summed up the popular mood in 2015 when he wrote that "the Tatmadaw's current intelligence arm ... is a shadow of the old MI. Supposedly".[2] The same uncertainty surrounds the period since March 2016, when Aung San Suu Kyi's NLD administration took office. As always, observers are dependent largely on anecdotal evidence, unconfirmed news reports and rumours. There have been a few autobiographies and memoirs published in Burmese by former military officers, including Khin Nyunt himself, but like all such works they must be treated with caution. At one level, there are unmistakeable signs of change but, at the same time, a great deal appears to have remained the same. One way of examining this subject is by dividing it into possible organizational changes, and observable behavioural changes.

ORGANIZATIONAL CHANGES

As in the past, the lines of authority for the management of intelligence matters in Myanmar are blurred and the responsibilities of particular agencies seem to overlap. However, in the absence of any official announcements, or new laws passed by the Union parliament, it would appear that the basic structure and roles of the country's intelligence apparatus have remained broadly the same as they were before 2011. Perhaps the most notable development has been the progressive civilianization of security matters and the concomitant rise in importance of the MPF, which is now widely (if not entirely accurately) accepted as "the primary institution charged with internal security".[3] The police force's efforts in this regard appear to be directed mostly through Special Branch. However, OCMSA still plays an important and probably under-appreciated role. Outside of conflict areas (on which more below) it is believed to focus on the maintenance of law and order in the rural and border areas. If accurate, this division of duties may reflect some kind of formal demarcation with the MPF, but is more likely to be a function of the Tatmadaw's much larger size and wider geographical distribution.[4] It also performs a range of other functions that fall outside the MPF's usual responsibilities.

It is always risky to rely on a single source for descriptions of intelligence organizations, their structure, manpower and responsibilities, but sometimes analysts are left with little choice. One such example is a book published in Burmese in 2014 by "Moe Zay Nyein", titled *What's Swann Ar Shin and Other Articles*. It contained a chapter which asked the question "What is *SaYaHpa*" and provided a relatively detailed description of the military intelligence organization at that time.[5] Dubbed "the Myanmar Edward Snowden" by some journalists, Moe Zay Nyein seems to be the pseudonym of a former intelligence officer, probably around the colonel level.[6] Alternatively, it may be the collective pen-name of a group of well-informed dissidents keen to expose the inner workings of the new government's coercive apparatus. Either way, what is striking about Moe Zay Nyein's description of OCMSA (known in Burmese as the *SaYaKha*) around this time is the breadth of the agency's operational responsibilities, which in some respects harks back to the days of Khin Nyunt's OCMI.

Some aspects remain unclear but, thanks to Moe Zay Nyein's unique contribution to the public record, a reasonable picture of Myanmar's military intelligence organization around 2014 can be discerned.

According to Moe Zay Nyein, during the first decade after its creation OCMSA gradually expanded and, as circumstances demanded, it took on a range of new tasks.[7] It also acquired a new head, former army chief of staff Lieutenant General Mya Tun Oo.[8] When he took command in September 2014 the organization's HQ reportedly consisted of six departments. Two dealt with administration and training. According to an unofficial translation of Moe Zay Nyein's book, the four operational departments were labelled Internal, External, Counterintelligence and Technology. The departments were subdivided into branches, each responsible for discrete functions. The departments varied in size, but most seem to have had between forty-five and ninety senior staff, making a total strength of roughly 450 commissioned officers plus an unknown number of NCOs and other ranks. By that time, the rank level of department heads had been restored to Brigadier, with most deputy head positions held by colonels. The lowest ranked officers were captains. Leaving aside the training and administration departments, the functions of which can largely be assumed, it is worth looking a little more closely at the other four.

The "Internal" Department seems to have been the largest. Including its head and his deputy, there were a total of 89 officers, including 8 lieutenant colonels, 21 majors and 58 captains. They were spread between eight branches, responsible for operations, ethnic affairs, the navy, the air force, economic research, narcotics, security and administration. As suggested by this structure, the department performed a wide variety of roles. It analysed and distributed combat-related intelligence to other parts of the Tatmadaw. It compiled and assessed intelligence about the military training, capabilities and activities of Myanmar's neighbours and any other countries which might constitute a threat. It assisted navy and air force units responsible for the surveillance and policing of Myanmar's territorial waters and airspace. It gathered information about narcotics trafficking and collected economic intelligence. It liaised with ethnic groups and helped manage their affairs in accordance with various ceasefire agreements. The department provided security for senior officers when they were travelling, both in Myanmar and abroad, and arranged for the close personal protection of visiting military dignitaries. It also managed certain personnel matters, such as the granting of security clearances and the issue of passports to military officers going abroad.⁹

According to Moe Zay Nyein, the "Counterintelligence" Department consisted of 50 officers, including the department head and his deputy, 4 lieutenant colonels, 11 majors and 33 captains. They were divided into four branches, a political branch, an economic branch and two special duty branches. Their roles fell into three broad categories, namely "safeguarding measures, detective measures and deception activities".¹⁰ As such, they went beyond intelligence collection to include the infiltration of various organizations and groups with a view to forestalling or disrupting any activities considered inimical to national security. Those targeted included religious institutions, student groups, political parties, businesses, workers' unions and peasant organizations. As circumstances required, OCMSA agents fabricated rumours and stirred up racial animosities. According to Moe Zay Nyein, they even planted bombs in population centres to cause confusion and provoke fears that could be exploited by the government. Another task was to keep a close eye on foreign journalists and local news media outlets that might be seeking sensitive information. To achieve all these aims, the department recruited informers, *agents provocateurs*, double agents and "stool pigeons".¹¹

Another department described in detail by Moe Zay Nyein was the "Technology" Department. In 2014, it consisted of 46 officers, including the head and his deputy, 4 lieutenant colonels, 8 majors and 22 captains. They were divided between four branches, dealing with domestic affairs, foreign affairs, electronic counter-measures and electronic news media and information. Spurred on by the shrewd use of the Internet by activists during the 2007 Saffron Revolution, and the critical international coverage of the SPDC's woeful response to Cyclone Nargis in 2008, OCMSA had made a major effort to develop IT skills and to acquire a range of modern computer hardware and software. The department was charged with monitoring electronic coverage of Myanmar, including activist websites, and with promoting the image of the country and armed forces. It was also responsible for protecting Myanmar's military communications systems and for preventing hacking and interception by hostile individuals and agencies. This extended on occasion to the implementation of active measures, such as jamming or disabling "enemy" transmissions. The department also managed a research programme to investigate possible further improvements to the country's official IT systems.[12]

Unfortunately, in his book Moe Zay Nyein does not include any description of the "External" Department, save to say that it was focused on the collection of military intelligence. This implied that it was similar to the branches in DDSI and OCMI that had handled intelligence received from agents outside Myanmar, and about foreign countries. From other sources, however, it is highly likely that, like these earlier bureaucratic bodies, the functions of OCMSA's "External" Department went well beyond those tasks to include the management of active measures and liaison arrangements with foreign intelligence services. These are discussed in a separate chapter below.

Moe Zay Nyein's book paints a picture of an intelligence agency that seems to have recovered many of the capabilities, and probably some of the influence, that it had lost in the 2004 purge. The key difference, however, was that ten years after Khin Nyunt's ouster the military intelligence organization was firmly under the control of the army hierarchy and the SPDC. These changes were significant, but they were not the only developments in the national intelligence apparatus. Since 2011, there has been a constant stream of news reports about other structural changes. Some may have more than a grain of truth in them.

For example, soon after Thein Sein took office, there were unconfirmed reports that the Tatmadaw Commander-in-Chief (C-in-C), Senior General Min Aung Hlaing, had formed a new intelligence agency, under his own control, to investigate domestic political and security affairs. It was said to have a very wide remit:

> The new intelligence unit will reportedly investigate the movements of political parties, ethnic armed forces and ceasefire groups, violent domestic actions such as bomb explosions and any matter that affects the state's security and stability, including non-disintegration of the military, and take necessary measures.[13]

It was claimed that the new body was about 200 strong, and consisted of members of all three service arms, from colonel down to captain in rank. It also included representatives from the MPF, BSI and the Ministry of Border Affairs. Despite the story's rather dramatic headline in *The Irrawaddy* magazine, the unit was said to be "not a separate entity". However, it would oversee all intelligence agencies and report to both military and civilian authorities at the provincial and national levels.[14]

These press reports have yet to be confirmed, and the nature of the "new intelligence unit", if it exists, clarified. However, the story seems to be related to recurring claims that the government planned to reconstitute the National Intelligence Bureau, to provide a formal mechanism for the oversight and coordination of a "new security system" that included an expanded surveillance network, including increased electronic monitoring.[15]

From time to time over the past ten years, stories have appeared in Myanmar's news media claiming that the recreation of the NIB, or an organization like it, was being contemplated, or had even occurred. For example, in October 2010 it was reported by the exile radio station *Democratic Voice of Burma* that the newly appointed head of OCMSA, Lieutenant General Kyaw Swe, was unhappy about the fragmentation of the country's intelligence effort and the lack of operational coordination, and was planning to re-establish the NIB. According to the DVB's anonymous source, "Right now, every agency is going alone on its own; the Special Branch comes up with its own theory, the intelligence agency another theory, and the MAS is useless (sic)."[16] This view was shared by one experienced Old Myanmar Hand, who described the system in 2012 as being like "a creature that has lost its central nervous system. The legs are flailing, and it doesn't know which way to turn."[17] These problems were adding to pressures to reconstitute the NIB.

In June 2011, a meeting of the country's regional military commanders reportedly discussed the reform of Myanmar's intelligence apparatus, including the possible re-establishment of the NIB, which was said to have been the subject of government attention since the beginning of the year. According to *The Irrawaddy*, a "Burmese intelligence report" suggested that a "new collaboration" called the "National Defence and Security Force" would oversee the activities of OCMSA, SB and BSI, under the Minister for Home Affairs.[18] The story did not explain how a major military unit could be answerable to a civilian ministry, bearing in mind that, under the 2008 constitution, the Home Affairs Minister is always a senior Tatmadaw officer appointed by the C-in-C. In September 2011, there were more unconfirmed reports that the government planned to recreate the NIB and expand the country's surveillance network, prompted this time by Aung San Suu Kyi's stated plans to extend the NLD's geographical reach and to make extra efforts to mobilize her party's supporters before the 2015 general election.[19]

Nothing appears to have come from any of these stories, but the issue did not go away. In August 2013, for example, a Thai journalist opined:

> Khin Nyunt's security outfit might have been more efficient, given its top-down nature. In a way, what Myanmar has now is more like the Thai intelligence agencies — every unit seems to have its own spies and operatives and no single person or agency is overseeing the big picture.[20]

In November that year, there were calls by Yangon Division lawmakers to re-establish the NIB under the National Defence and Security Council (NDSC), a high level executive body that had been created under the 2008 constitution.[21] These calls followed another round of anonymous bomb attacks in the former capital. The Yangon MPs were also concerned about security for the Southeast Asian Games, which were due to be held in Myanmar that December, as well as Myanmar's chairmanship of ASEAN in 2014, which would see an influx of foreign dignitaries and thus a heightened risk profile. In December 2014, several local news media outlets, including *Eleven Media*, *Voice Daily* and *Tomorrow News*, reported that a body similar to the NIB was actively being considered. The following month, the President's Office denied that there were moves to re-establish the NIB, or an equivalent organization.[22] Only days later, however, the *Myanmar Times* newspaper reported that the MPF had been ordered to re-establish the NIB, under the aegis of the Minister for Home Affairs.[23]

It is always possible, of course, that the NIB or a similar body has been revived but not yet publicly acknowledged. For example, in 2014 a confidential report prepared by an international NGO in close collaboration with the Ministry of Home Affairs referred specifically to a "National Intelligence Bureau".[24] This body was said to coordinate the activities of SB with those of other agencies that made up the national intelligence apparatus. If and when this new NIB was formed, who makes up its membership, how it operates, how its director is chosen and to whom it reports, is not known. The size and role of the MPF has grown significantly since 2011, as Myanmar's internal security has increasingly become "civilianised" but, as noted above, the OCMSA has become more powerful since its creation and could not fail to be a core member of any organization created to consider high level intelligence matters. Even if this NGO report proves to be inaccurate, however, and there is no new NIB, the need for high level direction and coordination of Myanmar's national intelligence effort remains.

While the news media has been focused on the possible re-emergence of the NIB, other components of the intelligence apparatus have been steadily growing in size and stature.

In 2015, SB had a personnel strength of about 2,500, of which 300 were based at the HQ in Naypyidaw, under a Police Brigadier General.[25] Sources differ, but the HQ is reportedly divided into five departments, dealing with internal security, intelligence, international relations, company forces, and management and training.[26] Others describe separate departments for passports and prosecutions, although they may be referring to an earlier structure.[27] SB investigation and documentation centres have been established in Naypyidaw and Yangon. There are also 55 mobile platoons, covering 165 areas across the country. Each of the 14 states and regions has its own SB Command. Yangon and Mandalay Regions are commanded by Police Colonels, the other provinces are under Police Lieutenant Colonels. There are SB outposts in all townships. Sensitive areas like northern Rakhine State are allocated extra resources.[28] In addition to its role as Myanmar's "political police", SB provides security for diplomatic premises and personnel, as well as high level visitors and MPs. Selected officers have been trained in counter-terrorism and bomb disposal. SB is also responsible for providing basic security and intelligence training courses to other parts of the MPF.

It has been reported that, since February 2015, SB answers directly to the Deputy Minister for Home Affairs, who is concurrently the Chief of Police.[29] SB is still part of the MPF, but units are now believed to send reports up the line to the SB commander, then on to the Deputy Minister. For reasons that are not clear, it appears that intelligence is not shared with other parts of the force, although SB and CID still work closely together in shared areas of interest, like passport issues. These arrangements may be an attempt to increase efficiencies and limit the number of leaks, but some observers suspect deeper motives. Official spokesmen have described these and a number of other bureaucratic changes introduced around the same time as "simply intended to streamline the administrative apparatus by combining government departments".[30] However, they have prompted public concern, as the Minister for Home Affairs is a serving military officer appointed by the Tatmadaw C-in-C, and the move seemed designed to give SB greater independence and authority. It was also feared that its operations will become even less transparent and accountable.

Little is known about the CID during the turbulent period following Khin Nyunt's dismissal, but it was most likely enlisted to act in support of the expanded SB. As time has passed, however, and OCMSA has grown into its new role, the department seems to have returned to its traditional focus on the investigation of serious criminal offenses. It has also assumed a greater role in the fight against narcotics production and distribution. After Afghanistan, Myanmar is the world's second largest producer of illicit opiates. It is also a major producer of amphetamine-type stimulants. The CID also assists other departments with forensic investigations. In 2015, it had about 700 members.[31] It was headed by a Police Brigadier, based in Naypyidaw. There were regional branches in Naypyidaw, Yangon and Mandalay, headed by Police Lieutenant Colonels, as well as twenty local units spread between the state and regional capitals. In addition, there were eleven specialist sections based in Yangon, where there was also a forensics laboratory and a training school. The CID has long suffered from a shortage of modern equipment, and personnel with the necessary education and skills, but it still has the capacity to make a significant contribution to the national intelligence effort.

Once again, the details are not clear but it appears that following OCMI's collapse the jurisdiction of the BSI was expanded to include a range of political crimes. Like SB, it reported to the Minister for Home Affairs who, in the absence of a Chief of Intelligence, assumed a greater responsibility for providing the SPDC and key officials with security-related briefings. Since 2011, the BSI seems to have reverted largely to its formal investigative functions, relating to corruption, fraud and other financial crimes.[32] This role has been reinforced by the creation of an Action Committee Against Corruption in 2013, passage of an Anti-Corruption Act the same year, and the formation in 2014 of an Anti-Corruption Commission backed by President Thein Sein.[33] According to the Ministry of Home Affairs' website, however, one of the BSI's four main objectives is still "to collect intelligence for national security".[34] It thus remains a major player in the national intelligence apparatus. The BSI currently has six divisions in its Naypyidaw HQ, titled Administration, Law and Prosecution, Information Technology, Investigation and Financial, Crime, and Inspection. There are BSI offices in the capitals of the seven states and seven regions.[35] Its current size is unknown.

In 2015, there was a spate of stories in the Myanmar press that the SB and BSI were going to be taken out of the Ministry of Home Affairs and placed under the control of the President's Office, as part of a new intelligence organization called the Office of Security and Information. These reports were dismissed by the President's Office as "groundless".[36] As far as is known, no such organization has yet been created.

In 2014, the revised Anti-Money Laundering Law reaffirmed the MFIU as Myanmar's national agency responsible for detecting and taking action against illegal financial transactions, under the control of a Central Body on Anti-Money Laundering.[37] The actual sequence of events is not clear, but around the same time the MFIU was transferred to the Myanmar Police Force, where it formed the basis of the MPF's Financial Intelligence Division.[38] This amalgamation was publicly confirmed by the Central Body in 2016, the same year that the international Financial Action Task Force removed Myanmar from its watch list of countries that did not meet its standards regarding measures taken against money-laundering and terrorist financing.[39] Based in Naypyidaw, the Financial Intelligence Division initially had about thirty personnel, led by a Police Brigadier General, but there were plans to expand it to about 180 members. It consists of five branches, handling finance, investigation, administration, communications and logistics. There were also plans to upgrade its computer facilities and open an office in Yangon, where most major businesses in Myanmar were registered and had their headquarters.

From time to time, references to other agencies or units with intelligence connections have cropped up in discussions or the news media, but they are not always clear.

To take one example, the Yangon Region MPF commander appears to have created a unit of "preventative police" to help investigate and manage special cases.[40] Known as the *TaLaYa-Naing*, its duties seem to overlap with those of SB. For example, the unit was behind the arrest in 2013 of Ye Min Oo, the Secretary of the Federation of Students' Unions (Organizing Committee).[41] He was subsequently charged with inciting people to "commit an offence against the state or public tranquillity". According to the *Myanmar Times*, the charge was related to his alleged role in instigating protests by *pongyis* and others in 2012 against the opening of an office of the Organisation of the Islamic Conference (OIC) in northern Rakhine State.[42] At times, the *TaLaYa-Naing* even seems to operate in competition with SB, and may be an attempt by the local force to take back a measure of control over political cases.[43] Another report has suggested that this unit is part of OCMSA, but that is not the case. Indeed, the *TaLaYa-Naing* does not appear to share information about specific cases with any other intelligence body.[44] Some other provincial police forces may have similar units.

To take a couple of other examples, in 2005 an article in the Australia-based *Asia-Pacific Defence Reporter* mentioned the Home Affairs Ministry's "special police", but this was probably just a reference to SB.[45] In 2006, the international NGO Reporters Sans Frontieres (Reporters Without Borders, or RSF) referred to a "Military Security Force" which it said "replaced Military Intelligence (MI)".[46] The following year, the New York-based Committee to Protect Journalists referred to "the Military Security Force, a government intelligence agency". Both appear to be references to OCMSA, as suggested by the RSF's concurrent use of the Burmese abbreviation *SaYaHpa*.[47]

There was one development during this period, however, that can be confirmed. In 2012, the Thein Sein government repealed the two colonial-era laws that required households to report the details of overnight guests to the local authorities. The Ward or Village Tract Administration Law of 2012, which replaced the old laws, retained a requirement for visitors to be listed with the local authorities, hence its popular name as the "midnight inspections law". There was also a requirement to report foreigners and "suspected strangers" in the interests of "security, prevalence of law and order, community peace and tranquillity".⁴⁸ However, the requirement to report overnight guests was removed in an amendment narrowly passed by both houses of parliament in 2016. This step was opposed by the 25 per cent of MPs appointed by the C-in-C, on the grounds that such reports were necessary for the maintenance of national security. The military bloc in parliament claimed that, without such laws, strangers would be "free to roam" around Myanmar.⁴⁹ The latest version of the law still requires guests remaining in a ward or village for more than one month to inform local officials of their presence.⁵⁰

There have been a few other developments since 2011 that have affected the intelligence system. For example, under the 2013 Telecommunications Law, the government may direct carriers to help it regarding "information or telecommunications damaging to national security and the prevalence of law".⁵¹ A framework for making such requests has yet to be agreed with the country's three main international service providers.⁵² Up to March 2016, the authorities had sought permission to access private customers' information eighty-five times, but the two foreign carriers then operating in Myanmar reportedly agreed to provide the information in less than a quarter of cases. There does not appear to have been a test case yet, but it is difficult to see an operator refusing a request if the government applies strong pressure. In any case, local agencies may soon have their own means of accessing the desired data. The Telecommunications Law also permits the government to order the suspension of services "when an emergency situation arises".⁵³ This occurred during the 2007 "Saffron Revolution". As Human Rights Watch has pointed out, such expressions as "national security", "emergency" and "public interest" are not clearly defined in the law, leaving their interpretation to the government.[54]

Since the transition to a mixed civilian-military government in 2011, the role of the General Administration Department has expanded to include the provision of staff for state and region governments. More importantly, in December 2018 the department was transferred from the Ministry of Home Affairs to the Ministry of the Office of the Union Government.[55] A former deputy minister in the President's Office has been appointed as the Minister for the Union Government. These are potentially important changes, as they bring the department under nominal civilian control. Its new status will likely prompt some changes in the way that it operates. However, the GAD's "insidious tentacles" still give the intelligence agencies the ability to gather information in over 70,000 towns and villages.[56] Also, the department is "staffed overwhelmingly by military appointees and retired Tatmadaw personnel", which means that security services will doubtless continue to enjoy privileged access to its databases and periodic reports. Zoltan Barany wrote in January 2018 that "Although it has not played an obstructionist role, the GAD does give the army valuable on-the-ground information from every corner of the country that the NLD has no way of obtaining."[57] That is likely to remain the case for some time.

The USDP, which was formed from the mass USDA to win a large parliamentary majority in the 2011 elections, now seems to be a spent force. After a well-publicized leadership struggle in August 2015, it was soundly defeated by the NLD in the November 2015 elections, gaining only 41 parliamentary seats out of the 664 available.[58] It is not known to what extent the USDP still actively supports the country's intelligence apparatus but, if it has survived recent developments, this role appears to be significantly reduced. It has been speculated by a few observers that, to a limited extent, the USDP's role may have been picked up by the extremist Buddhist organization known as the *MaBaTha*, or the Association for the Protection of Race and Religion. That group has reportedly been penetrated by the country's intelligence agencies and informs on those who do not support its racist agenda.[59] Also, ad hoc groups used by the government to assist the state's coercive apparatus have fallen by the wayside. For example, after Thein Sein took power in 2011 local governments continued to recruit vigilante gangs to enforce unpopular administrative decisions and inform on their fellow citizens.[60] However, since the appointment of NLD chief ministers in most states and regions by the Aung San Suu Kyi government this practice seems to have been abandoned.

Organizational changes can only give part of the story. A better indicator of developments since 2011 is the observable behaviour of the intelligence agencies, but here too the evidence is unreliable and contradictory.

BEHAVIOURAL CHANGES

As decades-old restrictions on political activity, freedom of expression and freedom of association were relaxed under President Thein Sein, so the level of overt oppression in Myanmar declined. Even organizations like Amnesty International and Human Rights Watch acknowledged that under the new quasi-civilian government there was a marked decline in the number of reported arrests, arbitrary detentions, cases of torture and sham trials.[61] Most restrictions on the news media were either suspended or removed.[62] In 2012, about

650 political prisoners were released and visa restrictions were lifted on about 2,000 expatriate Myanmars and foreigners who had been blacklisted by the military government as security threats, or simply as "undesirables".[63] Exiled dissidents began to return to Myanmar, some to continue their political activities in relative freedom.[64] In 2014, 3,000 more prisoners were released, including some former military intelligence officers convicted in 2005.[65] In 2016, another 600 names were removed from the government's blacklist.[66] As Nick Davies noted in March that year, when Aung San Suu Kyi took office, "People can move without being tracked, speak without being arrested."[67] To many in Myanmar, it seemed like a new world.

Despite the freer atmosphere prevailing throughout most of the country, however, old habits seemed to die hard. There were still serious human rights abuses. In its 2015 human rights country report, for example, the US State Department noted that "Security forces continued to exert a pervasive influence on the lives of inhabitants through the fear of arbitrary arrest and detention and through threats to individual livelihoods. These forces enjoyed impunity."[68] The intelligence agencies were often implicated in such activities. For example, by law warrants were required to conduct searches and make arrests, but OCMSA and SB continued to carry out both at will. Violence was still a routine part of military and police interrogations.[69] The local representatives of foreign media organizations, and those who spoke to them, still seemed to be viewed as "spies" and were subject to harassment, if not arrest.[70] Some 2,000 people remained on the government's blacklist, for reasons that have never been spelt out.[71] This was in addition to the widespread human rights violations reported in conflict zones around Myanmar's borders, perpetrated against recognized ethnic minorities like the Chin, Kachin, Shan and Karen, and communities claiming ethnic minority status like the Muslim Rohingyas concentrated in Rakhine State.[72]

Also, as Karin Dean in particular has noted, "The decrease of authoritarianism does not necessarily lead to a decline in surveillance for political and social control, and Myanmar is an exemplary case."[73] After 2011, the level of overt surveillance may have declined, but a number of mechanisms were kept in place to permit the civilian and military authorities to keep a close watch on anyone suspected of challenging the state or its security forces. Some intelligence agencies actually expanded the range of their interests. The activities of the SB, for example, at times exceeded the scope of those it exercised under the military regime.[74] Also, from numerous reports, it is clear that surveillance of community leaders, political party members, diplomats and journalists continued.[75] Typical was one report in 2013, in which one activist described:

> Men on motorcycles tailing closely. The occasional phone call. The same, familiar faces at crowded street cafes.[76]

In 2015, the UN's Special Rapporteur on the situation of human rights in Myanmar, Yanghee Lee, reported that:

> Human rights defenders informed the Special Rapporteur of regular surveillance through phone calls, and monitoring of and enquiries about their movements and activities.[77]

She repeated this verdict in 2017, naming the MPF's SB as the agency most likely to be responsible.[78] She highlighted the pressing need for judicial and parliamentary oversight of the executive's use of surveillance powers.

It has been suggested by a few observers that after Thein Sein took office some of these activities may have been driven by junior officers, as a precautionary measure in the absence of any clear direction from their superiors.[79] Also, not entirely tongue in cheek, Emma Larkin has raised the possibility of "bored spies" doing something to justify their existence during a period of uncertainty and low operational tempo.[80] However, if either explanation was ever true, it is unlikely to have remained the case after an initial period of confusion over intelligence priorities and practices.

Since Aung San Suu Kyi's government took power, reports of intelligence activity in Myanmar have been mixed. In its country report for 2016, for example, the US State Department observed:

> Outside of conflict areas, security forces generally operated with respect for the rule of law, and various organisations noted the significant decrease under the new government of the pervasive and threatening influence security forces previously exerted on the lives of inhabitants.[81]

The same assessment was made in the country report for 2017, but included the caveat that "others noted an increase in police surveillance and monitoring during the year".[82] Indeed, Aung San Suu Kyi's critics have charged that, in some respects, Myanmar has changed little from the days of the military regime, when the authorities were quick to crack down on dissent.[83] They claim that the intelligence apparatus may be less in evidence, but many of the same restrictions on their speech and activities remain in force.[84]

Karin Dean shares this view. There may be fewer arrests and summary trials in Myanmar under the NLD government, but to her mind the overall level of surveillance "remains comparable to that in the past or is even wider, while its pattern has changed". Critically, there has been "a shift from high intensity force to low intensity coercion of lesser visibility, with shifting targets and modes of performance".[85] This pattern can be seen in the use since 2016 of Myanmar's restrictive laws and regulations, many of which date back to the colonial era and the military regime, to limit protests and silence critics of the government and security forces. As Amnesty International wrote in its 2017/2018 annual report:

> The authorities continued to use a range of vaguely worded laws that restricted the rights to freedom of expression, association and peaceful assembly to arrest and imprison people solely for peacefully exercising their rights.[86]

For example, there has been a marked increase in the use of Section 66(d) of the 2013 Telecommunications Act to punish "offensive" or "insulting" online comments about the authorities.[87] People have been imprisoned for calling the president an idiot on Facebook, or for mocking the Tatmadaw C-in-C.[88] One young woman was sentenced to six months in gaol for a Facebook post comparing a new light green army uniform to a woman's *longyi* (sarong).[89] Journalists and human rights campaigners have claimed that under Aung San Suu Kyi's government press and other freedoms are actually going backwards.[90]

More importantly, Myanmar's intelligence apparatus has been able to supplement its traditional collection activities, which have relied heavily on human intelligence (HUMINT), with technical sources.⁹¹ OCMSA and SB, in particular, have benefited not only from the rapid advances made in electronics and related fields, but also the commercialization and spread of formerly restricted technologies. The extraordinary growth in telecommunications in Myanmar in recent years, for example, has prompted much greater attention to communications intelligence (COMINT).⁹²

In 2001, there were 295,000 telephone subscribers, a national penetration of only 0.6 per cent.⁹³ There are now almost 57 million mobile phone subscribers, a penetration of 110.43 per cent (Myanmar's population is a little over 54 million).⁹⁴ In 2000, there were barely 1,000 Internet users in Myanmar. There are now over 18 million, or about 34 per cent of the population.⁹⁵ In December 2017, there were some 16 million Facebook subscribers, a penetration of almost 30 per cent, and by all accounts the number is growing rapidly.⁹⁶ These developments make Myanmar vulnerable to SIGINT collectors and information warfare specialists. In 2011, for example, a former army officer was arrested because his emails contained material critical of the armed forces.⁹⁷ From time to time, the Facebook pages of local news media organizations have been disabled by unknown hackers.⁹⁸ There have been unconfirmed reports that, for several years, a Russian-trained, 700-man unit based outside Naypyidaw has been engaged in an intelligence collection and disinformation campaign including, since 2016, the promotion of the Tatmadaw's extreme views on the Rohingya question.⁹⁹ It may have even hacked into the websites of foreign governments.¹⁰⁰ There have also been indications that Myanmar has invested in advanced electronic surveillance technologies that permit it to restrict access to the Internet and monitor its usage.¹⁰¹

Foreigners have not been exempt from this kind of attention. In 2013, for example, at least a dozen journalists and academics who follow developments in Myanmar, some from outside the country, were advised by Google that "state-sponsored attackers" had attempted to hack into their Gmail accounts.[102] Google would not reveal how they knew the hackers were "state-sponsored", and the Myanmar Government has denied accusations of any misconduct. Private operators or another country may have been responsible (China immediately springs to mind), as even some official Myanmar websites have been subject to outside interference.[103] However, the clear implication of the advice from Google was that OCMSA had tried to gain access to the private correspondence of reporters seen as potentially hostile to the Myanmar Government and armed forces.[104] OCMSA was not above such "dirty tricks". In 2015, for example, Facebook users in Myanmar with links to the USDP and the Tatmadaw suggested that a British diplomat, on unpaid leave from the Foreign and Commonwealth Office to work as a liaison officer for Aung San Suu Kyi, was a British spy and thus "a danger to the country".[105] There have also been accusations that he works for MI6, and that through him the State Counsellor is being manipulated by the UK's intelligence services.[106]

Also, Myanmar now enjoys more options to collect and analyse imagery intelligence (IMINT) than ever before. There is a wide range of satellite imagery available online, both freely and through commercial arrangements. This includes high resolution photography and infra-red images.[107] In addition, the Tatmadaw is believed to operate about eleven Sky-02A surveillance drones, purchased from China. Another twenty-two have reportedly been built in Myanmar, designated the Yellow Cat A2.[108] These unmanned aerial vehicles (UAVs) carry digital colour and infra-red video cameras. Also, in 2013 or 2014 Myanmar purchased about a dozen CH-3A UAVs, also from China.[109] The CH-3A is a combat drone, but it also has an imaging capability. Data derived from all these platforms can be used for a wide range of purposes. Apart from the advantages of near or real-time imagery to operational planners conducting reconnaissance or surveillance missions, such sources can also help map-makers and those monitoring population movements, settlement patterns, land use and infrastructure developments.[110] All have obvious benefits to intelligence analysts.[111] For example, in 2017 the Bangladesh government complained that Myanmar had sent drones over the border to spy on Rohingya refugee movements.[112] The Tatmadaw has also shown some interest in the capabilities of small commercial drones, but it is not clear whether they see them as adding to their surveillance capabilities or as posing a threat to national security.[113]

In Myanmar, as elsewhere, stories about intelligence agencies and "spies" frequently feature in newspapers and magazines. Gossip about the "MI" and its supposed activities is popular fare in the country's teashops and on social media outlets like Facebook. Myanmar's intelligence apparatus has even started to feature in popular Western fiction.[114] Whenever a high profile figure dies in unexplained circumstances, there is an anonymous bombing, or an unexpected outbreak of civil unrest, the culprits are usually rumoured to be shadowy members of the intelligence world.[115] Their possible motives for disturbing the peace are the subject of much speculation.[116] Activists have been inclined to the view that such events are designed to blacken the name of EAGs, exacerbate religious tensions, heighten social concerns and help justify high levels of security oversight. Especially since 2004, there have been claims that bombings have been conducted by disgruntled former OCMI agents trying to bring home to the government and civil population the need for a strong intelligence apparatus run by professionals, as existed under General Khin Nyunt.[117] While they may seem improbable, such accusations cannot be dismissed entirely. In his book, Moe Zay Nyein alluded to disruption operations by OCMSA designed to cause fear and sow confusion among the civil population, which could be exploited by the government and armed forces.[118] However, more evidence is required before any firm conclusions can be drawn.

Despite its dark past, Myanmar's intelligence apparatus was able to survive the change of government in 2011 relatively intact. Indeed, in recent years it has probably enhanced some of its capabilities. In these circumstances, it might be expected that it would be able to protect the country from the kinds of threats to its unity, stability and sovereignty about which the military regime had so often warned. Arguably, however, this has not always been the case.

Notes

1. Todd Pitman, "In Burma, Internal Spy Network Lives on", *The Irrawaddy*, 29 July 2013, https://www.irrawaddy.com/news/burma/in-burma-internal-spy-network-lives-on.html.
2. Jared Downing, "Tatmadaw 101", *Frontier*, 10 December 2015, https://frontiermyanmar.net/en/tatmadaw-101.
3. US Department of State, "Burma 2017 Human Rights Report", Bureau of Democracy, Human Rights and Labour (Washington D.C.: US Department of State, 2018), https://www.state.gov/documents/organization/277313.pdf.

4. In 2012, there were 121,613 police officers in Myanmar. The number reportedly rose to 166,404 in 2016. The size of the Tatmadaw is not known but most estimates give its current strength as about 350,000. See Toe Wai Aung and Htoo Thant, "Police go High-Tech in Fight Against Crime", *Myanmar Times*, 19 October 2018, https://www.mmtimes.com/news/police-go-high-tech-fight-against-crime.html; and Selth, "Known Knowns and Known Unknowns".
5. *SaYaHpa* is the Burmese language abbreviation for the generic term "military intelligence organisation".
6. "Book Review: 'What is Swan Ar Shin? And Other Writings', by Moe Zay Nyein", *Kachinland News*, 4 October 2014, http://www.kachinlandnews.com/?p=24863.
7. Moe Zay Nyein, "What is *SaYaHpa*".
8. Mya Tun Oo held the position from 2014 to 2016. He was replaced in September that year by Lieutenant General Soe Htut.
9. Moe Zay Nyein, "What is *SaYaHpa*".
10. Ibid.
11. Ibid.
12. Ibid.
13. "Burma Forms New Intelligence Unit", *The Irrawaddy*, 3 May 2011, http://www2.irrawaddy.org/article.php?art_id=21223.
14. Wai Moe, "Tatmadaw Commanders Discuss Recent Ethnic Conflicts", *The Irrawaddy*, 29 June 2011, http://www2.irrawaddy.org/article.php?art_id=21593.
15. "Yangon: Regime Pours Funds into Army and Intelligence to Block Web Protests", *AsiaNews.it*, 3 September 2011, http://www.asianews.it/news-en/Yangon:-regime-pours-funds-into-army-and-intelligence-to-block-web-protests-20983.html#. See also Aung Zaw, "Burmese Spy Reveals MI's Dirty Deeds".
16. Min Lwin, "Intelligence Unit to Return to Khin Nyunt Days".
17. Priscilla Clapp, US Charge d'Affaires ad interim in Yangon from July 1999 to August 2002, quoted in Osnos, "The Burmese Spring".

18. Wai Moe, "Tatmadaw Commanders Discuss Recent Ethnic Conflicts".
19. "Yangon: Regime Pours Funds into Army and Intelligence to Block Web Protests".
20. "Old Problems Resurface on Myanmar's Road to Freedom", *The Nation*, 6 August 2013, http://www.nationmultimedia.com/opinion/Old-problems-resurface-on-Myanmars-road-to-freedom-30211936.html.
21. Tha Lun Zaung Htet, "Rangoon MPs Urge Govt to Reestablish National Intelligence Bureau", *The Irrawaddy*, 11 November 2013, https://www.irrawaddy.com/news/burma/rangoon-mps-urge-govt-reestablish-national-intelligence-bureau.html. See also Zin Linn, "Making a Dead Tiger Alive in Burma", *Asian Tribune*, 18 November 2013, http://www.asiantribune.com/node/67096.
22. "Myanmar (Burma): President's Office Denies Re-Establishing Feared NIB", *Asia News Monitor*, Bangkok, 6 January 2015.
23. Mratt Kyaw Thu, "Police Receive Orders to Reform National Intelligence Bureau", *Myanmar Times*, 9 January 2015, https://www.mmtimes.com/national-news/12757-police-receive-orders-to-reform-national-intelligence-bureau.html.
24. Interviews, Yangon and Naypyidaw, March 2014.
25. Ibid. Around this time, only about 7 per cent of SB personnel were women, a problem that was being addressed by a special recruitment drive.
26. Interview, Yangon, March 2014.
27. Personal communication from Yangon, 17 March 2017.
28. Personal communication from Yangon, 29 January 2015.
29. Htet Naing Zaw, "Activists Uneasy Over Special Branch Reshuffle", *The Irrawaddy*, 6 February 2015, https://www.irrawaddy.com/news/burma/activists-uneasy-special-branch-reshuffle.html.
30. Ibid.
31. Personal communication from Yangon, 29 January 2015.
32. Sandar Lwin, "Can't Stand Corruption? We Want to Hear About It, says BSI", *Myanmar Times*, 11 June 2012, https://www.mmtimes.

com/national-news/627-can-t-stand-corruption-we-want-to-hear-about-it-says-bsi.html.
33. Rhys Thompson, "Can Myanmar Escape Corruption?", *The Interpreter*, 7 April 2014, https://www.lowyinstitute.org/the-interpreter/can-myanmar-escape-corruption.
34. "BSI Biography", Ministry of Home Affairs, http://myanmarmoha.org/eng/index.php?option=com_content&view=article&id=92&Itemid=542&lang=en.
35. Soe Naing Oo, "Current Issues in the Investigation, Prosecution and Adjudication of Corruption Cases", text of an oral presentation in the author's possession.
36. "President's Office: Report on Pending Movement of BSI, SB is 'Groundless'", *Eleven*, 2 February 2015, http://www.elevenmyanmar.com/local/president%E2%80%99s-office-report-pending-movement-bsi-sb-%E2%80%98groundless%E2%80%99.
37. "The Anti-Money Laundering Law (The Pyidaungsu Hluttaw Law No. 11, 2014)", http://myanmarpoliceforce.org/mm/dmdocuments/Anti%20Money%20Laundering%20Law.pdf.
38. Interview, Yangon, March 2014.
39. Steve Gilmour, "Myanmar Moved off Money-Laundering Watch List", *Myanmar Times*, 27 June 2016, https://www.mmtimes.com/business/21060-myanmar-moved-off-money-laundering-watchlist.html.
40. Personal communication from Yangon, 14 December 2018.
41. See Naw Say Phaw Waa, "Activist Ye Min Oo Facing More Charges", *Myanmar Times*, 29 April 2013, https://www.mmtimes.com/national-news/6545-activist-ye-min-oo-facing-more-charges.html.
42. Naw Say Phaw Waa, "Supporters of Activist Unhappy over Arrest", *Myanmar Times*, 8 April 2013, https://www.mmtimes.com/national-news/6411-supporters-of-student-activist-unhappy-over-arrest-detention.html.
43. Personal communication from Yangon, 30 December 2013.
44. "Concern Over Five NLD Youths, Daw Pon", *Please Help Burma*, 19 January 2008, http://please-help-burma.blogspot.com/2008/01/concerns-over-5-nld-youths-daw-pon.html.

45. A Correspondent, "Major Shakeup in Myanmar's Intelligence Apparatus", p. 8.
46. "Military Junta Launches Manhunt for Informants of International News Media", *Reporters Without Borders*, 9 February 2006, https://rsf.org/en/news/military-junta-launches-manhunt-informants-international-news-media.
47. "Attacks on the Press 2006: Burma", *Committee to Protect Journalists*, 5 February 2007, https://cpj.org/2007/02/attacks-on-the-press-2006-burma.php.
48. "The Ward or Village Tract Administration Law", 2012, http://www.asianlii.org/mm/legis/laws/wovtalh2012669.pdf.
49. Htoo Thant, "'Midnight Inspection' Clause Abolished by Parliament", *Myanmar Times*, 20 September 2016, https://www.mmtimes.com/national-news/22620-midnight-inspection-clause-abolished-by-parliament.html.
50. Ye Aung Thu, "Myanmar Scraps Loathed 'Midnight Inspections' Law", *Frontier*, 20 September 2016, https://frontiermyanmar.net/en/myanmar-scraps-loathed-midnight-inspections-law.
51. Catherine Trautwein, "Mobile Operators Comply with One in Four Data Requests", *Myanmar Times*, 30 March 2016, https://www.mmtimes.com/business/technology/19721-mobile-operators-comply-with-one-in-four-data-requests.html. The Telecommunications Law was amended in 2017, but these provisions were not substantially changed.
52. See Herbert Kanale, "Internet Service Providers Overview in Myanmar", *Internet in Myanmar*, 20 December 2018, https://www.internetinmyanmar.com/isp-overview-myanmar/.
53. Catherine Trautwein, "Laws Remain Vague as Ministry Swears off Internet Shutdown", *Myanmar Times*, 4 November 2015, https://www.mmtimes.com/business/technology/17349-laws-remain-vague-as-ministry-swears-off-internet-shutdown.html.
54. *Reforming Telecommunications in Burma: Human Rights and Responsible Investment in Mobile and the Internet* (New York: Human

Rights Watch, 2013), https://www.hrw.org/sites/default/files/reports/burma0512_ForUpload.pdf.
55. "Govt Reveals Plan to Bring GAD under Civilian Control", *Frontier*, 22 December 2018, https://frontiermyanmar.net/en/govt-reveals-plan-to-bring-gad-under-civilian-control.
56. Liam Cochrane, "Myanmar: How the Military Still Controls the Country, not Aung San Suu Kyi", *ABC News*, 24 September 2017, https://www.abc.net.au/news/2017-09-24/how-military-controls-myanmar-not-aung-san-suu-kyi/8978042. See also "Myanmar Administrative Structure", *Myanmar Information Management Unit*, 4 March 2016, https://web.archive.org/web/20160304035213/http://www.themimu.info/sites/themimu.info/files/documents/Myanmar_Administrative_Structure_Aug_2015.pdf.
57. Zoltan Barany, "Burma: Suu Kyi's Missteps", *Journal of Democracy* 29, no. 1 (January 2018): 16–17.
58. See, for example, Simon Lewis and Ben Doherty, "Turmoil in Burma's Military-backed Ruling Party as Leaders are Deposed", *The Guardian*, 13 August 2015, https://www.theguardian.com/world/2015/aug/13/burmese-forces-surround-ruling-party-headquarters-and-confine-mps-report. See also Lun Lin Mang, "USDP Faces Uncertain Future After Election Annihilation", *Myanmar Times*, 19 November 2015, https://www.mmtimes.com/national-news/17702-usdp-faces-uncertain-future-after-election-annihilation.html.
59. Francis Wade, "Burma's Hard-Line Buddhists are Waging a Campaign of Hate that Nobody Can Stop", *Time*, 15 December 2015, http://time.com/4147171/burma-buddhism-islam-interfaith-intolerance-rohingya-myanmar/.
60. Andrew Selth, "Burma: The Return of the 'Vigilantes'", *The Interpreter*, 22 April 2015, https://www.lowyinstitute.org/the-interpreter/burma-return-vigilantes.
61. "Old Problems Resurface on Myanmar's Road to Freedom". See also US Department of State, "Burma 2012 Human Rights Report", Bureau of Democracy, Human Rights and Labour (Washington

D.C.: US Department of State, 2013), https://www.state.gov/documents/organization/204400.pdf.
62. Lewis Macleod, "More Press Freedom for Burma's Media", *BBC News*, 24 July 2012, https://www.bbc.com/news/world-asia-pacific-18814045.
63. See, for example, "Burma: Political Prisoners Released", *Human Rights Watch*, 13 January 2012, https://www.hrw.org/news/2012/01/13/burma-political-prisoners-released; and "Burma Regime Removed 2,000 Names From Its Blacklist, But Fears Persist", *Social Watch*, 3 September 2012, http://www.socialwatch.org/node/15308.
64. Kayleigh Long, "Myanmar's Political Exiles Return to Fight for Country's Future at Elections", *ABC News*, 2 October 2015, https://www.abc.net.au/news/2015-10-02/myanmars-political-exiles-return-home-ahead-of-election/6817804.
65. Lawi Weng, "Two Military Intelligence Officials Released, Re-Detained Amid Mass Amnesties", *The Irrawaddy*, 3 January 2014, https://www.irrawaddy.com/news/burma/two-military-intelligence-officials-released-re-detained-amid-mass-amnesties.html.
66. "Myanmar Government Removes More Than 600 Names From Official Blacklist", *Radio Free Asia*, 3 August 2016, https://www.rfa.org/english/news/myanmar/myanmar-government-removes-more-than-600-names-from-official-blacklist-08032016154050.html.
67. Nick Davies, "Myanmar's Moment of Truth", *The Guardian*, 9 March 2016, https://www.theguardian.com/world/2016/mar/09/myanmar-moment-of-truth-aung-san-suu-kyi.
68. US Department of State, "Burma 2015 Human Rights Report", Bureau of Democracy, Human Rights and Labour (Washington D.C.: Department of State, 2016), https://www.state.gov/documents/organization/252963.pdf.
69. Nick Cheesman, "Judicial Torture in Myanmar", Seminar, Department of Political and Social Change, Australian National University, Canberra, 17 September 2013.

70. See, for example, Sebastian Strangio, "Paper Tigers", *Foreign Policy*, 20 January 2012, https://foreignpolicy.com/2012/01/20/paper-tigers/.
71. Daniel Wynn, "Myanmar's Famous Blacklist Bites the Dust", *UCA News*, 31 August 2012, https://www.ucanews.com/news/myanmar-scraps-its-famous-blacklist/59329. See also Lawi Weng, "Govt Removes Names from Blacklist, But Thousands Remain", *The Irrawaddy*, 28 August 2012, https://www.irrawaddy.com/news/burma/govt-removes-names-from-blacklist-but-thousands-remain.html.
72. See, for example, *Myanmar: "All the Civilians Suffer": Conflict, Displacement and Abuse in Northern Myanmar*, AI Index ASA 16/6429/2017 (London: Amnesty International, 14 June 2017), https://www.amnesty.org/en/documents/asa16/6429/2017/en/.
73. Karin Dean, "Myanmar: Surveillance and the Turn from Authoritarianism?", *Surveillance and Society* 15, no. 3/4 (2017): 496–505.
74. "Myanmar's Police Intelligence Unit Queries Newspaper Editors", *Radio Free Asia*, 23 June 2014, https://www.rfa.org/english/news/myanmar/media-06232014193621.html.
75. See, for example, Pitman, "In Myanmar, Internal Spy Network Lives On".
76. "Despite Changes, Relic of Past Oppression Lives On in Myanmar: Internal Spy Network", *Fox News*, 29 July 2013, https://www.foxnews.com/world/despite-changes-relic-of-past-oppression-lives-on-in-myanmar-internal-spy-network. Since 2003, fuel-powered motorcycles have been banned in central Yangon, for everyone except government officials. As a result, it is widely assumed that anyone seen on a motorcycle in the city is a policeman or intelligence officer.
77. *Report of the Special Rapporteur on the Situation of Human Rights in Myanmar, Yanghee Lee*, United Nations General Assembly, Human Rights Council, A/HRC/28/72, 23 March 2015, p. 4.
78. "UN Envoy Complains of State Surveillance in Myanmar", *Al Jazeera*, 22 July 2017, https://www.aljazeera.com/news/2017/

07/envoy-complains-state-surveillance-myanmar-170722031408327.html.
79. Phil Rees, "Are Myanmar Secret Agents Still Playing 'Dirty Tricks'?", *Al Jazeera*, 28 October 2015, https://www.aljazeera.com/indepth/features/2015/10/myanmar-secret-agents-playing-dirty-tricks-151027085402365.html.
80. Larkin, *Everything is Broken*, p. 16.
81. US Department of State, "Burma 2016 Human Rights Report", Bureau of Democracy, Human Rights and Labour (Washington D.C.: US Department of State, 2017), https://www.state.gov/documents/organization/265536.pdf.
82. US Department of State, "Burma 2017 Human Rights Report".
83. See, for example, Krishnan Guru-Murthy, "Burma's Broken Dream", *SBS News*, 16 May 2017, https://www.sbs.com.au/news/dateline/story/burmas-broken-dream.
84. *"They Can Arrest You at Any Time": The Criminalisation of Peaceful Expression in Burma* (New York: Human Rights Watch, 29 June 2016), https://www.hrw.org/report/2016/06/29/they-can-arrest-you-any-time/criminalization-peaceful-expression-burma.
85. Dean, "Myanmar: Surveillance and the Turn from Authoritarianism?"
86. "Myanmar 2017/2018", *Amnesty International*, https://www.amnesty.org/en/countries/asia-and-the-pacific/myanmar/report-myanmar/.
87. Between November 2015 and November 2017, 106 criminal complaints were made under the Telecommunications Law. Of these, 95 cases (or 90 per cent) were made under the current NLD government. See *66(d): No Real Change: An Analysis of Complaints Made Before and After the 2017 Amendment* (Yangon?: Free Expression Myanmar, December 2017), p. 16, http://freeexpressionmyanmar.org/wp-content/uploads/2017/12/66d-no-real-change.pdf.
88. *Burma: Repeal Section 66(d) of the 2013 Telecommunications Law* (New York: Human Rights Watch, 29 June 2017), https://www.hrw.org/news/2017/06/29/burma-repeal-section-66d-2013-telecommunications-law.

89. "Myanmar Activist Jailed for Facebook Post Mocking Army", *Al Jazeera*, 28 December 2015, https://www.aljazeera.com/news/2015/12/myanmar-activist-jailed-facebook-post-mocking-army-151228101007793.html.

90. *Dashed Hopes: The Criminalization of Free Expression in Myanmar* (New York: Human Rights Watch, 31 January 2019), https://www.hrw.org/report/2019/01/31/dashed-hopes/criminalization-peaceful-expression-myanmar. See also Victoria Milko, "In Aung San Suu Kyi's Myanmar, Free Press Hopes Wither", *Al Jazeera*, 12 December 2018, https://www.aljazeera.com/news/2018/12/aung-san-suu-kyi-myanmar-free-press-hopes-wither-181207065931858.html.

91. Dean, "Myanmar: Surveillance and the Turn from Authoritarianism?", p. 503. See also James Coe, "A Question of Trust: Myanmar's Shadowy World of Digital Surveillance", *Frontier*, 20 December 2015, https://frontiermyanmar.net/en/features/question-trust-myanmars-shadowy-world-digital-surveillance.

92. See, for example, "Chapter 4.4, Surveillance: Lawful Interception & Other Surveillance Methods".

93. Ebara, "The Fall of Military Intelligence Under Khin Nyunt", p. 29.

94. "Mobile Phone Usage in Myanmar Increases 110 percent", *Mizzima News*, 23 May 2018, http://www.mizzima.com/business-domestic/mobile-phone-usage-myanmar-increases-110-percent.

95. "Internet Usage in Asia", *Internet World Stats*, https://www.internetworldstats.com/asia.htm#mm.

96. Ibid.

97. "Burma/Former Officer Sentenced 10 Years on Military Critical Email", *The Global Intelligence Files*, 28 August 2011, https://wikileaks.org/gifiles/docs/25/2569756_burma-former-officer-sentenced-10-years-on-military-critical.html.

98. Bill O'Toole, "Email Hacking Exposes Cybercrime in Myanmar", *Myanmar Times*, 20 February 2013, https://www.mmtimes.com/national-news/4168-email-hacking-exposes-cybercrime-in-myanmar.html.

99. Kayleigh Long, "Facebook Investigated Myanmar's Military-Linked Accounts. It Found a Covert Propaganda Campaign", *Time*, 1 September 2018, http://time.com/5383780/myanmar-facebook-propaganda-rohingya/. See also Paul Mozur, "A Genocide Incited on Facebook, With Posts From Myanmar's Military", *The New York Times*, 15 October 2018, https://www.nytimes.com/2018/10/15/technology/myanmar-facebook-genocide.html.

100. Hanna Hindstrom, "Is Myanmar's Military Behind Shadowy Cyber Attacks?", *The Diplomat*, 27 February 2016, https://thediplomat.com/2016/02/was-myanmars-military-behind-shadowy-cyber-attacks/.

101. *The Right to Privacy in Myanmar: Stakeholder Report, Universal Periodic Review, 23rd Session – Myanmar* (London: Privacy International, March 2015). See also Hanna Hindstrom, "Revealed: Domestic Surveillance Company in Talks with Burma Govt", *The Irrawaddy*, 24 July 2015, https://www.irrawaddy.com/news/burma/revealed-domestic-surveillance-company-in-talks-with-burma-govt.html; Jakub Dalek and Adam Senft, "Behind Blue Coat", *The Citizen Lab*, 9 November 2011, https://citizenlab.ca/2011/11/behind-blue-coat/; and Coe, "A Question of Trust".

102. Thomas Fuller, "E-mails of Reporters in Myanmar are Hacked", *The New York Times*, 10 February 2013, https://www.nytimes.com/2013/02/11/world/asia/journalists-e-mail-accounts-targeted-in-myanmar.html.

103. "Fox-IT has Exposed Chinese Infiltration Activities in Burmese Systems", *Fox-IT*, 13 November 2015, https://www.fox-it.com/en/insights/media/fox-discovers-espionage-activities-burmese-systems/. See also Matt Brooks, Jakub Dalek and Masashi Crete-Nishihata, "Between Hong Kong and Burma", *The Citizen Lab*, 18 April 2016, https://citizenlab.ca/2016/04/between-hong-kong-and-burma/.

104. "Myanmar Denies Hacking into At Least 12 Journalists' Email Accounts", *New York Daily News*, 11 February 2013, http://www.nydailynews.com/news/world/myanmar-denies-hacking-journalists-email-accounts-article-1.1260865.

105. Wa Lone, "'British Spy' Claim in Smear Campaign Against NLD Leader", *Myanmar Times*, 16 September 2015, https://www.mmtimes.com/national-news/16500-british-spy-claim-in-smear-campaign-against-nld-leader.html.
106. "Burmese Buddhist Monks Vs British Intelligence MI-6", *Hla Oo's Blog*, 30 September 2015, http://hlaoo1980.blogspot.com/2015/09/burmese-buddhist-monks-vs-british-mi-6.html.
107. Personal observations, Yangon, December 1999.
108. "Myanmar Air Force Uses Chinese Made UAV", *malaysiaflyingherald*, 26 June 2013, https://malaysiaflyingherald.wordpress.com/2013/06/26/myanmar-air-force-uses-chinese-made-uav/. See also "Myanmar – Air Force", *GlobalSecurity.org*, https://www.globalsecurity.org/military/world/myanmar/air-force.htm.
109. See, for example "China's Armed CH-3 Drone Spotted in Myanmar", *Defence Blog*, 31 May 2016, http://defence-blog.com/news/chinas-armed-ch-3-drone-spotted-in-myanmar.html. The Chinese drones sold to Myanmar are manufactured with the help of an Israeli firm. Judah Ari Gross, "Amid Uproar, Israel Halts Arms Sales to Myanmar – Report", *The Times of Israel*, 1 November 2017, https://www.timesofisrael.com/amid-uproar-israel-halts-arms-sales-to-myanmar-report/.
110. See, for example, Lee Mannion, "A Picture or a Thousand Words? Drone and Satellites Expose Myanmar's Pain", *zilient.org*, 1 November 2017, https://www.zilient.org/index.php/article/picture-or-thousand-words-drone-and-satellites-expose-myanmars-pain.
111. Saw Yan Naing, "Burma Army Deploying Armed Drones", *The Irrawaddy*, 13 June 2016, https://www.irrawaddy.com/news/burma/burma-army-deploying-armed-drones.html.
112. "Myanmar Sending Drones Over Bangladesh, Dhaka Says", *Radio Free Asia*, 15 September 2017, https://www.rfa.org/english/news/drones-09152017175259.html.
113. Timothy McLaughlin, "Where Flying a Drone Gets You Questioned by the Military", *Motherboard*, 13 February 2015, https://

motherboard.vice.com/en_us/article/d73kwk/in-myanmar-the-military-government-remains-suspicious-of-drones.

114. See, for example, Delphine Schrank, *Rebel of Rangoon: A Tale of Defiance and Deliverance in Burma* (New York: Nation Books, 2015); and Alison Chapman, *The Burmese Spy Adventure Book* (London: Austin Macauley Publishers, 2018).
115. See, for example, Rees, "Are Myanmar Secret Agents Still Playing 'Dirty Tricks'?"
116. Egreteau and Jagan, *Soldiers and Diplomacy in Burma*, p. 198.
117. See, for example, Seekins, *Historical Dictionary of Burma (Myanmar)*, pp. 114 and 294. See also Monique Skidmore, "Scholarship, Advocacy and the Politics of Engagement in Burma", in *Engaged Observer: Anthropology, Advocacy and Activism*, edited by Victoria Sandford and Asale Angel-Ajani (New Brunswick: Rutgers University Press, 2006), p. 44.
118. Moe Zay Nyein, "What is *SaYaHpa*".

Chapter 6

INTELLIGENCE FAILURES

> The use of intelligence depends less on the bureaucracy than on the intellects and inclinations of the authorities above it.
>
> Richard K. Betts
> "Analysis, War and Decision: Why Intelligence Failures are Inevitable" (1978)[1]

General Khin Nyunt believed that "intelligence is the state's ears and eyes".[2] In this regard, the national intelligence apparatus has faced a number of important tests since the advent of a "discipline-flourishing democracy" in Myanmar. At first sight, it does not seem to have scored particularly well, although it must be acknowledged that, in the manner of intelligence operations everywhere, failures always receive much more publicity than successes. It also needs to be recognized that, whatever their size and capabilities, intelligence agencies are not omnipotent. They cannot foresee every development or twist of fate. There will always be surprises, particularly in countries like Myanmar where unique circumstances lend themselves to unexpected developments. It can be argued, for example, that the 1988 pro-democracy uprising and the 2007 Saffron Revolution, both held up by many (including by Myanmar's ruling elite at the time) as major intelligence failures, began as largely spontaneous protests by small groups, and their dramatic escalation to national status took even their organizers by surprise. In different ways, the critical role played by key individuals in Myanmar, including its paramount leaders, has added another element of uncertainty to the local scene.

Some of the intelligence failures that have been identified in recent years relate to gaps in the government's surveillance regime and consequent problems regarding the security and stability of civil society. Others seem to have more to do with weaknesses in operational and tactical intelligence, affecting the military campaigns being waged against various insurgent groups. A few can probably be blamed on poor analysis or a failure to heed intelligence advice, bearing in mind that the regime's thinking has usually been difficult to discern.

OPERATIONAL FAILURES

In 2012 and 2013, for example, there were outbreaks of communal unrest in Rakhine State and several other parts of the country, none of which appear to have been foreseen by the authorities.[3] The results of the 2004 purge were still being felt.[4] A state of emergency was declared in Rakhine State but Naypyidaw was clearly unprepared and slow to respond. In other cases, there were accusations that the security forces deliberately waited until the violence had subsided before intervening.[5] Some observers have linked this surge of anti-Muslim violence to the relaxation of controls on speech and association after 2011, and the greater ability of extremist groups like the *MaBaTha* to organize and proselytize.[6] Under the SPDC, this was largely prevented by the country's pervasive intelligence apparatus, although on occasion there were "credible reports that military intelligence officers were involved in stirring up anti-Muslim violence".[7] Similar accusations were made in 2012–13, raising the possibility that some elements in the security forces wished to remind the new quasi-civilian administration that internal stability depended on a strong intelligence apparatus. The causes of the sectarian violence were complex, but poor intelligence and a failure to anticipate both its scale and spread must be included as factors.

In 2015, the Tatmadaw was surprised by the Myanmar National Democratic Alliance Army (MNDAA), a 3,000 strong force that was formed when the insurgent Communist Party of Burma (CPB) collapsed in 1989. In February, the MNDAA and its allies in the rebel Northern Alliance launched a major offensive in the Kokang Self-Administered Zone, bordering China.[8] Some fifty Tatmadaw soldiers were killed. President Thein Sein was forced to declare martial law in the area. Planning for the MNDAA campaign had reportedly been under way for two years, without the local OCMSA unit becoming aware of anything out of the ordinary. In Anthony Davis' view, this "total breakdown in military intelligence" stemmed from complacency after several years of relative peace, and an over-reliance by the Tatmadaw on unreliable border guard forces.[9] After an upsurge in the fighting in early 2017, the Jane's correspondent went even further, referring to "a remarkable crisis of intelligence". In his view, "The implications are obvious and stark: the Tatmadaw has little or no intelligence capability in rebel-dominated country, where enemy concentrations marshal and manoeuvre at will."[10] Imagery from the Tatmadaw's UAVs, which were employed in the area, had apparently proven of limited value.[11]

In November 2017, Anthony Davis described another example of "strikingly poor intelligence" when the Tatmadaw found itself struggling against the small but powerful Arakan Army (AA).[12] Formed at Laiza in 2009 with the assistance of the Kachin Independence Army (KIA), the AA draws mainly on the Rakhine Buddhist community for recruits. According to Davis, it has a strength of about 2,000 men, backed by a trained reserve.[13] Another observer, with experience inside the Myanmar Government at a senior level, has cited more modest numbers, writing recently that there were about 300 AA guerrillas operating along the Myanmar-India-Bangladesh border and another 200 fighting with the KIA in northern Kachin State and Shan State.[14] The AA itself claims a strength of over 10,000, including a "civilian wing", but this figure is almost certainly inflated.[15] Since 2015, the AA has also conducted operations in northern Rakhine State, extending as far south as Sittwe.[16] In late 2017, one AA ambush near Paletwa in Chin State resulted in eleven Tatmadaw soldiers killed and fourteen wounded.[17] This attack appears to have been a major factor in the dismissal of the Western Region commander, Major General Maung Maung Soe.[18] However, the historical record suggests that the Tatmadaw has always lacked reliable intelligence assets in Myanmar's far west, and is now fighting blind against a resourceful foe that enjoys a measure of local support.

There was a test of a different kind in January 2017, when the prominent Muslim lawyer Ko Ni was assassinated. A close friend of Aung San Suu Kyi, he was reputed to be working on ways to amend the 2008 constitution so that the NLD leader could become president. The MPF soon identified and arrested most of the conspirators, who appeared to be led by a former army officer.[19] No satisfactory explanation for the murder has yet been offered by the authorities, apart from "extreme patriotism".[20] However, what surprised many observers was the revelation that Ko Ni had been under surveillance by military intelligence agents when attacked. An OCMSA official responsible for the Botataung area in Yangon, where Ko Ni lived, confessed that he had been tasked with keeping a close watch on the lawyer. In a revealing admission, the official claimed that it was simply "routine surveillance of a prominent local figure".[21] OCMSA HQ received regular reports on where Ko Ni went, what he did and who he met. This high level of surveillance, however, did not prevent his murder which, once again, some local activists claimed (without evidence) was conducted by resentful military intelligence officers.[22] The government was obliged to issue a statement refuting allegations in social media that Ko Ni had been killed on the orders of the Minister for Home Affairs, former OCMSA chief Kyaw Swe, after clashing with the armed forces over constitutional issues.[23]

The greatest test for Myanmar's new intelligence system, however, came in October 2016, when a small Muslim militant group calling itself the Arakan Rohingya Salvation Army (ARSA) attacked three Border Guard Police (BGP) posts in northern Rakhine State. These actions, and a more widespread series of ARSA attacks in August 2017, provoked massive "area clearance operations" by Tatmadaw and MPF forces that, due to the widespread and systematic abuse of human rights committed, prompted an international outcry.[24] As these operations progressed, they clearly stretched local intelligence capabilities to the limit.[25]

It is not known exactly what intelligence resources the Tatmadaw and MPF were able to call upon in Rakhine State, but they appear to have started from a low base. Ever since Khin Nyunt's ouster, the intelligence apparatus in the area had been struggling to recover. The communal violence in 2012 encouraged efforts to follow developments in Rakhine State more closely, but in 2016 the impact of the 2004 purge was still apparent. Many useful intelligence sources in the Rohingya Muslim and Rakhine Buddhist communities that had been cultivated by DDSI and OCMI had been lost. There were fewer resources available to inspect letters from abroad arriving at Sittwe Post Office and to keep up lists of Rohingyas who had contacts with foreign countries.[26] This problem was compounded by the dissolution of the *NaSaKa* in 2013. While in many ways deeply flawed, it was nevertheless a powerful organization able to draw on intelligence derived from several national and provincial agencies. In Rakhine State, the *NaSaKa* commanded significant resources, particularly along the Myanmar-Bangladesh border. Through appointed agents in every Rohingya village, and a string of informers, it was able to monitor the local Muslim and Hindu populations closely.[27] The BGP, which was formed by the MPF in March 2014 in part to replace the *NaSaKa*, seems to have been much less effective in keeping tabs on local developments.

Before the first ARSA attacks in October 2016, the Special Branch and OCMSA tried to keep a close eye on both the Rakhine and Rohingya communities. In 2014, for example, there were reportedly twenty-nine SB officers and one from the CID based in Maungdaw township alone. If these numbers are typical, it suggests that intelligence officers made up more than 10 per cent of the total number of MPF personnel deployed along the Myanmar-Bangladesh border.[28] Also, the BGP maintained a string of informers in and around Rohingya villages to monitor developments and report on unauthorized movements along the border. Militants, smugglers and drug traffickers were all active in the area. The system does not appear to have been very effective.[29] As Jacques Leider observed in

2017, "The fast rise and the surprise attacks of ARSA since October 2016 reflect an extraordinary intelligence failure on the side of the security forces."[30] However, to be fair, local agents, pro-government villagers and suspected informers were identified by ARSA at an early stage of its campaign, and targeted for assassination.[31] Those who were not killed or in other ways silenced fled the area, leaving the authorities blind to many local developments.

Following the 2016 ARSA attacks, the security forces put more resources into intelligence collection and analysis in Rakhine State. This may help account for the deployment of elements of the Sagaing-based 33 LID and Meiktila-based 99 LID to the worst-affected areas shortly before the ARSA's renewed offensive in late August 2017. Senior General Min Aung Hlaing visited Rakhine State in September 2017 to appreciate the situation at first hand. While he was there, the C-in-C's Facebook page noted that he had issued instructions to local commanders "on getting timely information". This was presumably a reference to the need for better intelligence.[32] As several NGOs have demonstrated, commercial satellite imagery could also be used to monitor developments, including refugee movements and the destruction of local villages.[33] However, even after the campaign against ARSA had been going for almost a year, the lack of "security information" was a continuing concern. This "weakness" was publicly acknowledged by a "Tatmadaw True News Information Team" supposedly sent in to investigate claims of human rights abuses.[34] A vehicle ambush in January 2018 and three bombings in Sittwe in February that year suggested that there were still intelligence gaps that could be exploited by ARSA militants based in northern Rakhine State and Bangladesh.[35]

ANALYTICAL FAILURES

There is another category of intelligence failures that needs to be considered, and that relates to the analysis of data collected and assessments made about particular issues facing the government and armed forces. In countries like Myanmar, which for half a century was ruled by a military dictatorship and even now is subject to various constraints, agencies can face a range of problems. As Christopher Andrew has written:

> In all one-party states, intelligence analysis is distorted by the insistent demands of political correctness. Analysts are rarely willing to challenge the views of the political leadership ... Foreign intelligence in authoritarian regimes commonly acts as a mechanism for reinforcing rather than correcting the regimes' misconceptions of the outside world.[36]

From time to time, such factors have been evident in Myanmar. Broadly speaking, personal loyalty and political reliability have been favoured over intellectual ability and a willingness to speak truth to power. Perceived dissidence or acts of insubordination can have dire consequences. Also, as Andrew has observed, "In authoritarian regimes, particularly at times of crisis, conspiracy theory commonly degrades intelligence assessment."[37] Since Ne Win's coup in 1962 Myanmar's military leadership has often been accused of paranoia.[38] Such judgements have at times simply reflected bias or poor analysis, but on several occasions there have been grounds for believing that the regime's perspective was affected by deep-seated and not altogether justified fears for its security.

Once again, reliable information about such matters is scarce but, by drawing on a few specific examples, some broad observations can be made.

The 1990 general elections have been characterized as a massive intelligence failure on the part of the military regime.[39] They were surprisingly free and fair, and resulted in a resounding victory for those opposed to military rule. The backlash against the SLORC was eminently predictable, particularly given the tragic events of 1988. Similarly, it can be argued that, between 1988 and 2011 the generals repeatedly misread the popular mood and on several occasions were forced to respond to challenges that could have been foreseen. It has been suggested, for example, that the Saffron Revolution in 2007 could have been prevented, or at least contained, had Khin Nyunt still been running OCMI. Then again, it can be claimed that the regime was always aware of its unpopularity, hence its massive surveillance effort and constant attempts to stifle dissent. Also, it is not known to what extent the generals received sound intelligence advice, but for various reasons chose to ignore it. It would be a mistake to write them off as "woefully uninformed", as some have suggested, or lacking awareness of the likely consequences of their actions.[40] Bearing in mind the different views found in the senior officer corps, its members probably had good cause for behaving as they did, however odd or self-defeating some of their decisions may have appeared to outsiders.[41]

As Christopher Andrew has also pointed out, pseudo-scientific and faith-based systems like augury, numerology and astrology have long been seen by powerful figures as substitutes for intelligence advice.[42] It is difficult to say how such beliefs and practices may have affected developments in Myanmar, but most of its leaders have shown an interest in these matters, routinely consulting soothsayers for guidance and propitiating supernatural forces.[43] Ne Win and Than Shwe, for example, were reputed to be highly superstitious and prone to making decisions based on their belief in the occult. Khin Nyunt too was known to have a personal astrologer, although it has been suggested that he was something of a sceptic in that regard.[44] Aung San Suu Kyi claims not to subscribe to such beliefs, the result perhaps of her up-bringing outside Myanmar.[45] In any study of political culture and the behaviour of national leaders, some allowance must be made for irrational actors. There is evidence, for example, that astrology has affected the timing of important developments in Myanmar.[46] However, the government's more bizarre decisions and unexplained actions cannot simply be attributed to ignorance and superstition. Unless proven otherwise, it must be assumed that they are at least in part the outcome of rational calculations based on data and assessments supplied by its professional advisors, including the intelligence agencies.

All that said, Myanmar's intelligence analysts have been guilty of some major errors. For example, as argued elsewhere, the assessment that Myanmar faced a likely military invasion from a coalition of countries and international organizations wishing to install a democratic government in Yangon, or Naypyidaw, was fundamentally flawed.[47] Despite persistent sabre rattling in Washington and other capitals, and highly provocative remarks by some Western politicians, at no stage was military action of that kind ever seriously contemplated.[48] Nor, given China's support for the regime, could it have ever received UN Security Council endorsement. However, it can be argued that the intelligence assessment was based on a plausible interpretation of the available data. Also, as demonstrated during the Saffron Revolution, the generals did face a broad alliance of forces inside and outside Myanmar that wished to see regime change.

As Golda Meir told Henry Kissinger in 1973, "even a paranoid can have enemies".⁴⁹ To take another example, the strong response of the international community to the Tatmadaw's harsh operations against the Rohingyas, and its negative impact on Myanmar's economic development and foreign relations, was entirely foreseeable and could have been predicted by any intelligence agency tasked with making such assessments. Yet, if any warnings were sounded, they do not seem to have been heeded. Other factors were considered more important, by the Tatmadaw if not the government.

In considering such matters, it is important to bear in mind that Myanmar's military and civilian leaders have always judged the country's (and their own) interests from a unique perspective and according to a peculiar set of criteria. Indeed, as Tin Maung Maung Than has pointed out:

> Myanmars have always asserted with pride that there is a distinctive Myanmar way of accomplishing whatever tasks are at hand. Whether it be nation-building, economic development or managing conflicts, it seems that characteristic elements of 'Myanmar-ness' have been incorporated in such endeavours. As such, it may be conjectured that strategic attitudes and behaviour would also be influenced by socio-political predispositions embedded in this notion of Myanmar-ness.⁵⁰

According to this mindset, only true natives of Myanmar can understand the country's complex strategic circumstances and decide how various political, military and social challenges should be met.⁵¹ There is also the defensive nationalism of a society feeling under threat. For example, as Aung San Suu said in connection to the latest Rohingya crisis, unconsciously echoing statements made by her military predecessors:

We value the support, help and sympathy of our friends around the world ... but we must work ourselves for our country's responsibilities, because we are the ones who best understand what our country needs.[52]

Some caution thus needs to be exercised before concluding that failures of intelligence lie at the heart of what outside observers may view as policy mistakes or errors of judgement by successive Myanmar governments.

All these considerations underline the fact that, as has long been the case, the basis of official policy by Myanmar's leaders on certain issues remains something of a mystery. Inputs from the intelligence apparatus have doubtless been a factor, but the final decisions are made according to a wide range of factors, some of which are not easy to identify. In comparison, Myanmar's intelligence operations against, and liaison relationships with, foreign countries seem more straightforward.

Notes

1. Richard K. Betts, "Analysis, War and Decision: Why Intelligence Failures are Inevitable", *World Politics* 31, no. 1 (October 1978): 61.
2. Khin Nyunt, *The Experiences of My Life*.
3. *The Dark Side of Transition: Violence Against Muslims in Myanmar*, Asia Report No. 251 (Yangon/Jakarta/Brussels: International Crisis Group, 1 October 2013), https://www.crisisgroup.org/asia/south-east-asia/myanmar/dark-side-transition-violence-against-muslims-myanmar.
4. Ye Htut, "A Background to the Security Crisis in Northern Rakhine", p. 7.
5. David S. Mathieson, "Dispatches: Who Controls Burma's Police?", *Human Rights Watch*, 12 March 2015, https://www.hrw.org/

news/2015/03/12/dispatches-who-controls-burmas-police. See also US State Department, "Burma 2013 International Religious Freedom Report", Washington D.C., 2013, https://www.state.gov/documents/organization/222331.pdf.
6. See, for example, Min Zin, "Anti-Muslim Violence in Burma – Why Now?", *Social Research* 82, no. 2 (Summer 2015): 375–97.
7. "Crackdown on Burmese Muslims", Human Rights Watch Briefing Paper, July 2002, https://www.hrw.org/legacy/backgrounder/asia/burmese_muslims.pdf.
8. The Northern Alliance includes the KIA, Ta'ang National Liberation Army, MNDAA and AA. Anthony Davis, "Border Troubles Expose Myanmar Army's Intel Failures", *Jane's Defence Weekly*, 11 March 2015. See also Mong Palatino, "Refugee Crisis on the Myanmar-China Border", *The Diplomat*, 23 February 2015, https://thediplomat.com/2015/02/refugee-crisis-in-myanmar-china-border/.
9. Davis, "Border Troubles Expose Myanmar Army's Intel Failures". See also Aung Zaw, "Min Aung Hlaing's Putsch", *The Irrawaddy*, 17 February 2015, https://www.irrawaddy.com/opinion/min-aung-hlaings-putsch.html.
10. Anthony Davis, "Myanmar's Army Struggles Against a Strong New Rebel Alliance", *Nikkei Asian Review*, 6 April 2017, https://asia.nikkei.com/Politics/Myanmar-s-army-struggles-against-a-strong-new-rebel-alliance.
11. Anthony Davis, "Myanmar Military Under Pressure", *Jane's Terrorism and Insurgency Monitor*, 27 March 2017, https://www.linkedin.com/pulse/myanmar-military-under-pressure-anthony-davis. See also Ankit Panda, "Is Myanmar using Armed Chinese Drones for Counterinsurgency?", *The Diplomat*, 9 June 2016, https://thediplomat.com/2016/06/is-myanmar-using-armed-chinese-drones-for-counterinsurgency/.
12. Anthony Davis, "Myanmar's Other Rakhine Problem", *Asia Times*, 29 November 2017, http://www.atimes.com/article/myanmars-rakhine-problem/?fb_comment_id=1507345352682156_1508616409221717.

13. Ibid.
14. Ye Htut, "A Background to the Security Crisis in Northern Rakhine", p. 7.
15. "'I Want to Stress That We Are Not the Enemy'", *The Irrawaddy*, 12 June 2015, https://www.irrawaddy.com/in-person/interview/i-want-to-stress-that-we-are-not-the-enemy.html.
16. *China's Role in Myanmar's Internal Conflicts*, USIP Senior Study Group Report No. 1 (Washington D.C.: United States Institute of Peace, September 2018), p. 30, https://www.usip.org/sites/default/files/2018-09/ssg-report-chinas-role-in-myanmars-internal-conflicts.pdf.
17. Lawi Weng and Htet Naing Zaw, "Tatmadaw Troops Killed and Wounded in Arakan Army Ambush", *The Irrawaddy*, 9 November 2017, https://www.irrawaddy.com/news/tatmadaw-troops-killed-wounded-arakan-army-ambush.html.
18. Most foreign observers have seen his dismissal as the result of pressure brought to bear regarding the abuse of the Rohingyas. This may have been a factor, but it is worth bearing in mind that the Tatmadaw leadership rarely makes personnel moves in response to international opinion. Davis, "Myanmar's Other Rakhine Problem". See also Timothy McLaughlin, "Myanmar Fires General Who Led Campaign Against Rohingya", *The Washington Post*, 25 June 2018, https://www.washingtonpost.com/world/asia_pacific/myanmar-fires-general-who-led-campaign-against-rohingya/2018/06/25/9781d7c0-7567-11e8-b4b7-308400242c2e_story.html.
19. Tin Htet Paing, "Four Charged With Premeditated Murder in U Ko Ni Killing", *The Irrawaddy*, 9 February 2018, https://www.irrawaddy.com/news/four-charged-premeditated-murder-u-ko-ni-killing.html.
20. "'Patriotism' Behind U Ko Ni Assassination, says Minister", *Frontier*, 25 February 2017, https://frontiermyanmar.net/en/patriotism-behind-u-ko-ni-assassination-says-minister.
21. Wa Lone and Simon Lewis, "Surveillance and Threats: Slain Myanmar Lawyer Felt 'Targeted'", *Reuters*, 1 February 2017, https://www.reuters.com/article/us-myanmar-lawyer-idUSKBN15G4AI.

22. One of those convicted of conspiracy to murder Ko Ni was a former military intelligence officer. See Guru-Murthy, "Burma's Broken Dream".
23. Wai Moe, Mike Ives and Saw Nang, "Brazen Killing of Myanmar Lawyer Came After He Sparred With Military", *The New York Times*, 2 February 2017, https://www.nytimes.com/2017/02/02/world/asia/myanmar-ko-ni-lawyer-constitution-military.html?_r=0.
24. See, for example, *Report of the Independent International Fact-finding Mission on Myanmar*, United Nations Human Rights Council, A/HRC/39/64, Geneva, 12 September 2018, https://www.ohchr.org/Documents/HRBodies/HRCouncil/FFM-Myanmar/A_HRC_39_64.pdf.
25. The following paragraphs draw on Andrew Selth, *Myanmar's Armed Forces and the Rohingya Crisis*, Peaceworks No. 140 (Washington D.C.: United States Institute of Peace, 2018), https://www.usip.org/sites/default/files/2018-08/pw140-myanmars-armed-forces-and-the-rohingya-crisis.pdf.
26. This was standard practice before 2004. Ye Htut, "A Background to the Security Crisis in Northern Rakhine State", p. 4.
27. In 2007, there was one *NaSaKa* officer for every 100 villagers in northern Rakhine State. Also, the *NaSaKa* appointed either an ethnic Burman or Buddhist Rakhine "agent" in each village to monitor the population. "Burma's Least Wanted: The Rohingyas".
28. Asian Human Rights Commission, "Burma/Myanmar: No Rule of Law via Special Branch, Militarised Police", *Burma Partnership*, 15 March 2014, http://www.burmapartnership.org/2014/03/burmamyanmar-no-rule-of-law-via-special-branch-militarised-police/.
29. *Myanmar Tips into New Crisis after Rakhine State Attacks* (Yangon/Brussels: International Crisis Group, 27 August 2017), https://www.crisisgroup.org/asia/south-east-asia/myanmar/myanmar-tips-new-crisis-after-rakhine-state-attacks.
30. Sangeeta Barooah Pisharoty, "The Frictions in the Rakhine State Are Less About Islamophobia Than Rohingya-Phobia", *The Wire*,

30 September 2017, https://thewire.in/182611/frictions-rakhine-state-less-islamophobia-rohingya-phobia/. See also Subir Bhaumik, "Myanmar has a New Insurgency to Worry About", *South China Morning Post*, 1 September 2017, https://www.scmp.com/week-asia/geopolitics/article/2109386/myanmar-has-new-insurgency-worry-about.

31. Wa Lone and Anton Slodkowski, "'And Then They Exploded': How Rohingya Insurgents Built Support for Assault", *Reuters*, 7 September 2017, https://www.reuters.com/article/us-myanmar-rohingya-insurgents-insight/and-then-they-exploded-how-rohingya-insurgents-built-support-for-assault-idUSKCN1BI06J.

32. *Myanmar: "My World is Finished". Rohingya Targeted in Crimes Against Humanity in Myanmar*, AI Index ASA 16/7288/2017 (London: Amnesty International, 18 October 2017), p. 41.

33. See, for example, "UNOSAT Analysis of Destruction and Other Developments in Rakhine State, Myanmar" (Geneva: United Nations Institute for Training and Research, 7 September 2018), https://www.ohchr.org/Documents/HRBodies/HRCouncil/FFM-Myanmar/UNOSATReportMyanmar_20180912.pdf.

34. In November 2017, a Tatmadaw True News Information Team conducted an investigation into claims made against the armed forces. It found no evidence of atrocities, but conceded that there had been "weaknesses in doing management and acquiring security information". See "Military Release Findings on Security Force Reaction to Aug 25 Rakhine Terrorist Attacks", *Mizzzima News*, 13 November 2017, http://www.mizzima.com/news-domestic/military-release-findings-security-force-reaction-aug-25-rakhine-terrorist-attacks.

35. Katie Hunt, "Rakhine Ambush Could Mark New Phase for Rohingya Insurgency", *CNN*, 11 January 2018, https://edition.cnn.com/2018/01/10/asia/myanmar-rohingya-militants-arsa-intl/index.html.

36. Andrew, *The Secret World*, p. 594.

37. Ibid., p. 326.

38. See, for example, Mikael Gravers, *Nationalism as Political Paranoia in Burma: An Essay on the Historical Practice of Power*, NIAS Report No. 11 (Copenhagen: Nordic Institute of Asian Studies, 1993); and Larry Jagan, "Paranoia Drives Myanmar's Generals", *South China Morning Post*, 6 August 2005, https://www.scmp.com/article/511106/paranoia-drives-myanmars-generals.
39. Seekins, *Historical Dictionary of Burma (Myanmar)*, p. 349. See also Andrew Selth, "Even Paranoids Have Enemies: Cyclone Nargis and Myanmar's Fears of Invasion", *Contemporary Southeast Asia* 30, no. 3 (2008): 379–402.
40. Alexander Dukalskis and Christopher D. Raymond, "Failure of Authoritarian Learning: Explaining Burma/Myanmar's Electoral System", *Democratization* 25, no. 3 (November 2017): 546.
41. Activists have been fond of portraying Myanmar's military leaders as oafs in uniform, ignorant peasants unschooled in international diplomacy and determined to cling to power by any means to safeguard their ill-gotten gains and escape retribution for past actions. Such descriptions should be recognized as the caricatures they are. See Harn Lay, *Defiant Humour: The Best of Harn Lay's Cartoons from 'The Irrawaddy'* (Chiang Mai: Irrawaddy Publishing Group, 2006).
42. Andrew, *The Secret World*, pp. 27–53.
43. Andrew Selth, "Burma's 'Superstitious' Leaders", *The Interpreter*, 22 October 2009, https://archive.lowyinstitute.org/the-interpreter/burma-uperstitious-leaders.
44. Shenon, "Mutual Need Ties Dictator and Dissident in Myanmar". See also James Pringle, "Political Voodoo comes to Superstitious Burma", *The New York Times*, 30 May 2002, https://www.nytimes.com/2002/05/30/opinion/IHT-political-voodoo-comes-to-superstitious-burma.html.
45. Sudha Ramachandran and Swe Win, "Instant Karma in Myanmar", *Asia Times*, 18 June 2009, http://www.atimes.com/atimes/Southeast_Asia/KF18Ae02.html.

46. For example, the precise time of the declaration of Myanmar's independence, at 0420 on 4 January 1948, was decided on the basis of astrological readings. The timing of the transfer of the capital from Yangon to Naypyidaw at 0637 on 6 November 2005 was reportedly determined by Than Shwe's personal astrologer. See, for example, Damien McElroy, "Burma: Welcome to Naypyidaw – the Home of Kings – and the World's Weirdest City", *The Telegraph*, 18 November 2011, https://www.telegraph.co.uk/news/worldnews/asia/burmamyanmar/8900217/Burma-welcome-to-Naypyidaw-the-home-of-kings-and-the-worlds-weirdest-capital-city.html.
47. Andrew Selth, *Burma and the Threat of Invasion: Regime Fantasy or Strategic Reality?*, Regional Outlook No. 17 (Brisbane: Griffith Asia Institute, Griffith University, 2008).
48. For example, soon after the 1988 uprising a US Congressman promised military aid to anti-regime student groups on the Thai-Myanmar border. Also, when the regime refused to allow foreign aid to be delivered directly to the victims of Cyclone Nargis in 2008, Australian Prime Minister Kevin Rudd talked of "kicking the doors down". See "Rohrabacher Goes Into Burma Illegally, Vows to Aid Students", *Los Angeles Times*, 16 November 1988, http://articles.latimes.com/1988-11-16/news/mn-41_1_dana-rohrabacher; and "Behind the News", *ABC News*, http://www.abc.net.au/btn/story/s2241750.htm.
49. Kissinger liked the expression so much that he later claimed it as his own. See Jerrold Schechter, "His Legacy: Realism and Allure", *Time*, 24 January 1977, p. 28.
50. Tin Maung Maung Than, "Myanmar: Myanmar-ness and Realism in Historical Perspective", in *Strategic Cultures in the Asia-Pacific Region*, edited by Ken Booth and Russell Trood (London: Macmillan, 1999), pp. 165–81.
51. See, for example, David I. Steinberg, "Legitimacy in Burma/Myanmar: Concepts and Implications", in *Myanmar: State, Society and Ethnicity*, edited by N. Ganesan and Kyaw Yin Hlaing (Singapore: Institute of Southeast Asian Studies, 2007), pp. 117–21.

52. "Myanmar's Aung San Suu Kyi Thanks People, Deflects Criticism of Her Year-Old Government", *Radio Free Asia*, 31 March 2018, https://www.rfa.org/english/news/myanmar/myanmars-aung-san-suu-kyi-thanks-people-deflects-criticism-of-her-year-old-government-03312017152622.html.

Chapter 7

FOREIGN RELATIONSHIPS

> The Myanmar language word for the term security is *lon-choan yei*. Its connotation implies a sense of safety through an enveloping impermeability. For various reasons associated with Myanmar's historical experience with colonialism, World War II, the civil war (in the first decade of independence) and Cold War, as well as the multi-ethnic nature of its polity (officially identified as 135 nationalities in eight major ethnic groups), successive Myanmar governments have always adopted a state-centric national security approach with much emphasis on national sovereignty, territorial integrity and national unity (of all ethnic nationalities).
>
> Tin Maung Maung Than
> "Tatmadaw and Myanmar's Security Challenges"[1]

Ever since Myanmar regained its independence from the United Kingdom in 1948, successive governments have been preoccupied with the preservation of the country's stability, unity and sovereignty, as they have been perceived at the time. After 1988, these goals were adopted by the new government as the "three national causes". They were later enshrined in the 2008 constitution. Despite their appearance on billboards around the country, and daily reiteration in the news media, they were not just propaganda slogans. They reflected deeply-held beliefs and shared commitments, not only on the part of the military regime but also the two quasi-civilian governments that have been in power since 2011. In large part, they derived from what Timothy Garton Ash once called Myanmar's "fiendishly complex" internal problems, many of which still defy solution.[2] However, they also reflected an intense nationalism and a related wariness of foreigners and foreign commitments. The country's isolation under Ne Win was not just the result of one man's youthful experiences and suspicions of the outside world.[3] One consequence of this mindset has been that, for seventy years, the overwhelming focus of Myanmar's intelligence effort has been on domestic issues. That said, there has always been a need for intelligence from and about other countries, and their attitudes towards Myanmar.

FOREIGN OPERATIONS

Prime Minister U Nu once described Myanmar as being "hemmed in like a tender gourd among the cactus", a reference to its powerful and potentially hostile neighbours, China and India.[4] President Thein Sein made the same point to Hillary Clinton during her visit to Naypyidaw as US Secretary of State in 2011.[5] At different times, both countries have been considered Myanmar's "number one enemy", an accusation that has occasionally also been levelled at Thailand. More distant powers have posed different kinds of threats, but in some cases they have been treated no less seriously. Such concerns have contributed to the regime's need for timely and accurate intelligence about the policies, plans and capabilities of Myanmar's perceived enemies and their supporters.

Myanmar has faced a range of foreign threats. During the Cold War, for example, Myanmar was a cockpit for great power rivalry, played out in part through US and Taiwanese support for Nationalist Chinese (*Kuomintang*, or KMT) forces based in northern Myanmar.[6] Also, after the 1988 uprising Myanmar became a pariah state, an "outpost of tyranny", shunned by most of the Western world for its egregious abuses of universal human rights.[7] For decades, the military regime was subject to a suite of diplomatic pressures, economic sanctions, arms embargoes and travel bans. It was condemned in public fora, including the United Nations. Opposition figures and groups were openly supported by governments, semi-official agencies and privately-funded organizations.[8] As a result, the regime's already exaggerated suspicions of the outside world became even more pronounced. This extended to the not altogether unjustified perception that it faced a possible military invasion. The Tatmadaw leadership was also convinced that, in other ways, external forces were engaged in a concerted campaign to force it to surrender power to a democratic government led by Aung San Suu Kyi. After Cyclone Nargis in 2008, the regime was pressured to accept foreign aid, which it believed would bring with it the risk of subversion and "contamination" of the country by outsiders.[9]

At the same time, many of Myanmar's internal problems overflowed its borders, or were exacerbated by the activities of governments and groups in neighbouring countries. Over the years, various political, ethnic, religious, ideological and economic "insurgents" have used China, Thailand, Laos, India and Bangladesh as sanctuaries in which to rest and regroup, evade official controls or from which to conduct activities hostile to Myanmar's central government. Some of these groups have had foreign help, ranging from a begrudging acceptance of their presence on foreign territory through to the provision of training, funds and arms.[10] Thus, when they have looked over their borders, Myanmar's military leaders have seen a legion of enemy combatants, terrorists, spies, subversives, propagandists, black marketeers, narcotics smugglers, people traffickers, arms dealers, money launderers and refugees. To their minds, these diverse threats have required responses ranging from the passive monitoring of developments in the frontier areas, to the collection of intelligence, and even direct action.[11]

Given the large number of people opposed to Myanmar's central government who were resident in or operated from Thailand, it is not surprising that Myanmar's eastern neighbour has always been a particular focus of attention. Under Khin Nyunt, DDSI and OCMI made it a major target. In June 2001, for example, an article in the *Bangkok Post* claimed:

> Over 1,000 Burmese Military Intelligence Service agents have infiltrated Thai border towns, spying on and sometimes assassinating anti-Rangoon elements, reporting on Thai military movements and, inevitably, supplementing their meagre incomes with drug money.[12]

A senior member of the Royal Thai Police's Special Branch was quoted as saying "Our country is flooded with MIS agents ... Some of them sneak into the country as illegal immigrants or as job seekers or enter legally as businessmen. But their main objective is the same: spy work."[13] In the same newspaper article, unnamed Thai security officials were quoted as saying that Myanmar's spies were also engaged in illegal businesses, such as drug trafficking.[14] At the time, this story was criticized by the Thai Foreign Minister as harmful to relations between Bangkok and Yangon, and the figures quoted cannot be confirmed.[15] However, the Thai-Myanmar border was undoubtedly a major operational area for DDSI/

OSS/OCMI, and is reportedly still an important target for OCMSA.[16]

Arguably, all these activities, although conducted in another country, were related to Myanmar's domestic security, which was always given the highest priority. Other kinds of foreign intelligence collection also seemed to reflect the regime's immediate security concerns. As already noted, intelligence officers were posted abroad, usually to Myanmar's major diplomatic missions.[17] However, their remit appears to have been primarily to observe and report on the activities of expatriates and activist groups.[18] Refugee communities were another target, even in countries as far away as the United States, United Kingdom, Canada, Germany and Australia.[19] Some agents sent abroad were actively engaged in operations against exile organizations and prominent dissidents, but from the limited evidence available the mission of most was simply to observe and report on individuals and groups constituting a real or potential threat to the central government.[20] Gathering strategic intelligence seems to have been given a low priority. Broadly speaking, the task of following external developments and reporting on international attitudes toward Myanmar was left to the Ministry of Foreign Affairs, guided from 1994 to 2004 by the OSS.[21]

OCMSA has an economics intelligence branch, but under Khin Nyunt Myanmar's intelligence apparatus does not appear to have given much attention to economic espionage, or to the clandestine promotion of its own commercial interests. This is hardly surprising, given the parlous state of the country's economy for many years, its low level of technological development and its limited contacts with the outside world. In one volume of his memoirs, written after his release from house arrest in January 2012, Khin Nyunt observed that:

> Nowadays, famous intelligence agencies such as the CIA, KGB and Mossad travel around the world and used funds extravagantly and used various techniques to develop the economy of their countries. They used every means possible to advance and improve their respective country. But our country's intelligence differs from them and is used only in the motherland (sic).[22]

Khin Nyunt's comment seems to confirm the resource constraints faced by Myanmar's intelligence apparatus and its strong focus on domestic political issues.[23] As noted above, however, his last claim is not entirely true. DDSI, OCMI and OCMSA have all had branches that were responsible for foreign intelligence and the conduct of operations "abroad". As far as is known, Myanmar has never had a dedicated foreign intelligence agency operating along the lines of the UK's Secret Intelligence Service (MI6), France's General Directorate for External Security (DGSE) or India's Research and Analysis Wing (RAW). This too seems to have been confirmed by the former CI.

COUNTERESPIONAGE CONCERNS

Myanmar's intelligence apparatus has also been employed to guard against the hostile activities of foreign services, including those with a physical presence in the country. These were serious concerns for successive governments, prompting the development of counter-espionage capabilities in both the military intelligence organization and police force. Indeed, David Steinberg has suggested that the large number of suspected foreign spies in Yangon and the continued leak of official information contributed to the decision to transfer Myanmar's capital to Naypyidaw.[24] This view is supported by

Maung Aung Myoe, who has also highlighted the regime's concerns about the interception of its classified communications traffic.[25] It was apparently felt that these problems could be resolved, at least in part, if the seat of Myanmar's government was upcountry, and public servants were more isolated. There were other factors involved, particularly when Myanmar faced more serious threats from insurgents and dacoits, but similar concerns were believed to lie behind the restrictions imposed on internal travel by resident diplomats.[26]

These measures may have struck some observers as evidence of the regime's paranoia, but it cannot be denied that there have been sufficient historical examples of hostile intelligence operations, and enough news media reports of foreign interference in Myanmar's internal affairs, to warrant a degree of vigilance on the part of the country's security agencies.

Hard evidence of clandestine intelligence operations by foreign countries in Myanmar is difficult to obtain, but over the years there have been some credible reports. For example, there seems to have been a CIA station in Yangon since the US Embassy opened there in 1948.[27] Together with Taiwan's intelligence services, notably the Intelligence Bureau of the Ministry of National Defence (IBMND, or *Ch'ing pao chu*), the Agency supported the KMT remnants based in northern Myanmar.[28] In the 1980s, it sponsored secret commando raids from Thailand against narcotics warlords in the Shan States.[29] Taiwan was found to be running agents in Myanmar as recently as 2010.[30] The Soviet Union's embassy in Yangon was always a major intelligence gathering post, harbouring representatives of both the KGB and the military intelligence service known as the GRU.[31] According to a GRU officer who defected in 1959, the Tatmadaw was a prime target of both agencies.[32] In 1973, the KGB's budget for Myanmar was higher than that for any other Southeast Asian country, except Indonesia.[33] Possibly at a lower level, these activities are doubtless continuing.[34] During the 1950s, there was a MI6 station in Yangon.[35] Later, an officer from the UK's Security Service (known as MI5) was posted to Yangon and doubled as the MI6 representative, even running an agent inside SB.[36] More recently, MI6 has reportedly been keeping a close eye on Myanmar's drug barons.[37] Australia was accused of having an intelligence officer based in its Yangon embassy during the 1960s, although his focus seems to have been China and the insurgent CPB rather than Myanmar's government or armed forces.[38]

Just as dangerous to Myanmar, if not much more so, were the activities of its near neighbours. China's intelligence services (both civilian and military) have long paid "particular attention" to Myanmar.[39] This included support for the CPB, until the group's collapse in 1989.[40] As might be expected, other groups opposing the military regime have been monitored closely by Beijing.[41] Given their geographical positions, and the tensions which have periodically occurred along their common borders, it can be assumed that India, Bangladesh and Thailand too view Myanmar as a high priority target, and routinely post intelligence officers to their Yangon embassies.[42] All three countries are believed to have run hostile operations against Myanmar. For example, India's RAW secretly funded pro-democracy activists during and after the 1988 uprising, has provided support to the KIA and Rakhine State-based insurgents, and worked with the CIA to limit Chinese influence in northern Myanmar.[43] According to Desmond Ball, who made a special study of regional SIGINT operations, Bangkok routinely monitored Myanmar's communications.[44] The CIA-sponsored raids into Myanmar during the 1980s were conducted by Royal Thai Army special forces.⁴⁵ In 2002, OCMI accused Thailand of supporting Karen insurgents, even providing them with arms.⁴⁶ In 2005, Thailand was reported to be assisting the United States and Australia to operate both mobile and fixed facilities aimed at gathering intelligence about Myanmar's shadowy relations with North Korea, including Naypyidaw's interest in acquiring nuclear and missile technologies.⁴⁷

Myanmar is reported to be the target of other SIGINT collection operations, including by members of the "Five Eyes" intelligence community, comprising the United States, United Kingdom, Canada, Australia and New Zealand.⁴⁸ In 2013, for example, Tom Kean published a story in the *Myanmar Times* claiming that Myanmar's international communications were being intercepted by Australia, with the help of Singapore. He wrote that, according to material leaked by US National Security Agency (NSA) contractor Edward Snowden, these two countries were tapping the SEA-ME-WE-3 undersea cable that connected Europe to Asia and Australia. According to Kean, "almost all of Myanmar's internet traffic is funnelled through this one cable".⁴⁹ The same year, there were reports in the international news media that the US Embassy in Yangon was hosting a Special Collection Service SIGINT facility jointly operated by the CIA and NSA.⁵⁰ In 2015, New Zealand was reported to be collecting terrorism-related SIGINT on Myanmar, on behalf of its allies in the Five Eyes community.⁵¹ If all this was true, these Western countries were not alone in paying Myanmar attention. For example, the Soviet Embassy in Yangon conducted SIGINT operations against China and regional countries, possibly with the agreement of the Myanmar Government.⁵² It can safely be assumed that the

Russian Federation's embassy in Yangon also targets Myanmar's communications, as does that of China.[53]

In addition to threats from foreign agencies operating from, or with the help of embassies in Yangon, Myanmar's intelligence services were also alert to the suspected activities of "spies" operating independently, or under cover of international organizations and private groups. At various times, visiting consultants, teachers, journalists, academics, businessmen and even tourists have been accused by the regime of being the agents of foreign powers. As the Asia Society has noted, "the government tends to see foreign—especially Western—aid workers as spies" and watches them closely.[54] In 2009, an eccentric American tourist who swam across Yangon's Inya Lake to make an unauthorized visit to Aung San Suu Kyi's lakeside home, was accused by Myanmar officials of being a "spy", or "secret agent".[55] In 2011, two volunteer teachers at a Yangon school were accused of being undercover CIA officers.[56] In 2014, when two local journalists published a story about a suspected chemical weapons plant, they were charged under a law that covered acts of espionage.[57] In 2018, two local stringers for the Reuters news agency were sentenced to seven years in gaol after they were accused of being "spies" and breaching the 1923 Official Secrets Act. Although they revealed nothing new, "confidential" documents found in the journalists' possession were deemed to be useful to "enemies of the state and terrorist organisations".[58]

COOPERATIVE ARRANGEMENTS

As is the nature of the intelligence business, at the same time as Myanmar's security apparatus was trying to protect the country against espionage, and other activities by foreign agents, it was also developing liaison relationships with many of the services accused of conducting operations against it.

Both formal and informal exchanges have taken place with counterpart agencies in neighbouring countries, as dictated by their mutual interests.[59] Desmond Ball overstates the case in describing China as Myanmar's only "major intelligence partner".[60] This comment seems to be based on the mistaken belief that China was operating a large SIGINT station on Myanmar's Coco Islands.[61] However, since 1988 Myanmar and China have developed a close relationship and there have been several reports of intelligence sharing arrangements, at both the strategic and operational levels.[62] For many years, Thailand has engaged in talks with Myanmar's intelligence officials on a wide range of issues relating to their shared border, and groups based on either side of it.[63] The Indian Government has long been concerned about Naga, Assamese and Manipuri insurgents based in northwestern Myanmar, problems which have prompted a series of intelligence exchanges.[64] New Delhi has recently called for real-time intelligence sharing with Myanmar on the Rohingya problem.[65] There has also been a chequered history of exchanges between Myanmar and Bangladesh on border security and related matters.[66] Russia has a wide-ranging defence cooperation agreement with Myanmar which probably includes an intelligence component.[67]

Western countries like the United States, the members of the European Union and Australia have been more circumspect in developing bilateral intelligence ties. Such relationships have tended to arouse the opposition of human rights campaigners and other activist groups, to which democratic governments have felt the need publicly to respond.[68] However, these countries have been able openly to engage Myanmar on contemporary problems like international terrorism, narcotics and people trafficking, and money laundering, where a strong case can always be made for cooperative links, including the sharing of relevant intelligence.[69] During Khin Nyunt's term as CI, discussions on these subjects were usually conducted through Myanmar's intelligence agencies which, in close cooperation with the MPF, have taken the lead in such matters.[70] There have also been other contacts. For example, in 2012 a team from OCMI visited Hawaii to discuss the recovery of the remains of US servicemen left behind from the Second World War.[71] Other attempts to develop relations were not always as successful. In his memoirs, for example, Floyd Paseman describes one disastrous attempt in 1994 to arrange bilateral discussions between the CIA and DDSI.[72] Other countries, like Singapore and Israel, reputedly enjoy strong intelligence ties with Myanmar, but invariably deny them.[73]

The extent to which foreign agencies have helped to train Myanmar's military intelligence personnel is not known, but over the years several appear to have done so. During the 1950s, for example, officers from Myanmar attended courses at US and UK institutions.[74] In the 1960s, the United States provided DDSI with training and advice, mainly under its Security Assistance Program.[75] Mya Maung has suggested that, to help balance these Western contacts, Myanmar also received intelligence training from Yugoslavia, the Soviet Union and possibly the GDR.[76] In his memoirs, Khin Nyunt revealed that after becoming CI in 1983 he sent an unspecified number of intelligence officers abroad to "learn the trade" from foreign experts.[77] He did not say which countries were involved, but it has been claimed that the CIA trained dozens of DDSI officers, presumably before the 1988 uprising when relations between

Myanmar and the United States took a sharp downwards turn.⁷⁸ Israel has denied such links, but there have been several unconfirmed reports of Mossad (or former Mossad) agents helping to train intelligence officers in Myanmar.⁷⁹ It has also been claimed that China and Russia have provided assistance of various kinds, but few details are available.⁸⁰ The specialist surveillance equipment sold to Myanmar by these and other countries was presumably accompanied by training packages.⁸¹

Myanmar's police forces have also benefited from foreign intelligence expertise. Following Myanmar's independence in 1948, for example, police officers received specialist training in the United Kingdom. As described by Kin Oung:

> Burma sent promising young men to Britain to receive instruction from not only the Criminal Investigation Department of London's Metropolitan Police Force (Scotland Yard) but also MI6, the British Secret Service. Most of this training took place at the Sheffield Police Academy, and a selected few went to a much more secretive intelligence school called Shetmead.⁸²

Particularly since the mid-1990s, when the PPF underwent a far-reaching administrative review conducted by Khin Nyunt (and in 1995 was renamed the MPF), Myanmar's police forces have been receptive to foreign expertise and intelligence sharing arrangements.⁸³ Hundreds of "secret police" have reputedly attended courses in Singapore.⁸⁴ MPF officers have also received training in China and the United States.⁸⁵ Russia has admitted to providing training in "investigation techniques" but related that to international anti-terrorism and anti-narcotics efforts.⁸⁶ Australia has helped MPF officers attend intelligence-related courses at the Jakarta Centre for

Law Enforcement Cooperation.[87] The UN Office on Drugs and Crime has also given the MPF training in data collection and analysis.[88] These courses have been justified by the need to strengthen Myanmar's ability to tackle transnational crime but have implications for its intelligence agencies, something criticized by foreign activist groups.

After 2011, and the advent of a quasi-civilian administration, Myanmar's international security relations blossomed as it became easier for foreign governments to venture into areas of bilateral cooperation that had once been considered off-limits. Since he assumed his position as the Tatmadaw's C-in-C in March 2011, Senior General Min Aung Hlaing has made forty-six trips abroad to twenty-three different countries.[89] Probably as part of this campaign of defence diplomacy, Myanmar's intelligence agencies appear to have reached out more to their foreign counterparts, both in the region and further afield. There have also been efforts to stimulate multilateral cooperation, prompted in large part by transnational problems. For example, the Tatmadaw participates in the ASEAN Military Intelligence Informal Meeting (AMIIM) forum, which sponsors high level discussions and analyst level exchanges, mainly on non-traditional security threats.[90] In 2014, Myanmar hosted the 11th annual AMIIM meeting.[91] In 2016, the ASEAN Regional Forum (ARF) undertook to increase intelligence exchanges on international terrorism, and the global trafficking of arms, narcotics, people and funds. This effectively linked the intelligence efforts of the ten ASEAN member states with those of its fourteen ARF partners.[92] The MPF's Financial Intelligence Division has memoranda of understanding (MOU) with several regional financial intelligence units, and maintains informal contacts with its counterparts in a number of other countries.[93] Myanmar's intelligence apparatus stands to benefit substantially from all these links and exchanges.

A cloud now hangs over some of these relationships, however, as a result of the latest Rohingya crisis and the international outcry over the Tatmadaw's brutal area clearance operations, which the UN has labelled ethnic cleansing, if not genocide.[94] Naypyidaw is now facing the prospect of a return to international isolation and punitive sanctions. Already a number of Western countries have reduced or cancelled nascent military-to-military exchanges.[95] While they are rarely conducted openly, or are subject to public scrutiny, another casualty of Myanmar's renewed pariah status may be any developing intelligence contacts.[96] However, the bilateral relationships already forged with intelligence agencies in Myanmar's immediate neighbours and the major ASEAN states will doubtless survive any international measures taken against Myanmar's government and armed forces. As seen so often in the past, including in the three decades since the 1988 uprising, sanctions and boycotts are rarely very successful. Mutual self-interest will always trump concerns about universal human rights or internationally acceptable standards of behaviour.

Notes

1. Tin Maung Maung Than, "Tatmadaw and Myanmar's Security Challenges", in *Asia Pacific Countries' Security Outlook and its Implications for the Defence Sector* (Tokyo: National Institute for Defence Studies, 2010), pp. 124–25.
2. Timothy Garton Ash, "Beauty and the Beast in Burma", *New York Review of Books*, 25 May 2000, http://www.ibiblio.org/obl/docs/Beauty_and_the_Beast_in_Burma.htm.

3. See, for example, Robert H. Taylor, *General Ne Win: A Political Biography* (Singapore: Institute of Southeast Asian Studies, 2015).
4. U Nu, speech delivered in the Union Parliament, 5 September 1950, in *From Peace to Stability: Selected Speeches*, by U Nu (Rangoon: Government of Burma, 1951), pp. 95–105.
5. Hillary R. Clinton, *Hard Choices* (London: Simon and Schuster, 2014), p. 116.
6. Matthew Foley, *The Cold War and National Assertion in Southeast Asia: Britain, the United States and Burma, 1948-1962* (London: Routledge, 2010). See also Richard J. Aldrich, *The Hidden Hand: Britain, America and Cold War Secret Intelligence* (Woodstock: Overlook Press, 2001), pp. 293–314.
7. The original "axis of evil" named by President George W. Bush in his 2002 State of the Union speech was effectively expanded in 2005 by Secretary of State Condoleeza Rice, who added four "outposts of tyranny", one of which was Myanmar. See "Axis of Evil: Rice Adds Four More States", *Irish Times*, 20 January 2005, https://www.irishtimes.com/news/axis-of-evil-rice-adds-four-more-states-1.407741.
8. For example, the National Endowment for Democracy, which receives an annual allocation from the US Congress, provided funds to a range of anti-regime groups. The Open Society Institute, which did the same, was founded by billionaire philanthropist George Soros in 1993.
9. Selth, "Even Paranoids Have Enemies".
10. See, for example, *Intelligence Report: Peking and the Burmese Communists: The Perils and Profits of Insurgency* (Langley: Central Intelligence Agency, July 1971), approved for public release on May 2007, https://www.cia.gov/library/readingroom/docs/esau-52.pdf.
11. See, for example, "Burmese Spy Arrested by Bangladesh Army", *Defence Update Bangladesh*, 18 September 2017, https://medium.com/@DefenseUpdateBangladesh/breaking-burmese-spy-arrested-by-bangladesh-army-12fac9845ea5.

12. "Burmese Spies are Everywhere". See also Phil Thornton, "'Big Brain' on the Border", in *Insurgent Intellectual: Essays in Honour of Professor Desmond Ball*, edited by Brendan Taylor, Nicholas Farrelly and Sheryn Lee (Singapore: Institute of Southeast Asian Studies, 2012), pp. 152–53.
13. "Burmese Spies are Everywhere".
14. Ibid. See also "Agents under Arrest", *Bangkok Post*, 10 June 2001, http://www.burmalibrary.org/reg.burma/archives/200106/msg00053.html.
15. "Foreign Minister Says Thailand Eager to Mend Myanmar Ties", *Burma Related News*, 10 June 2001, http://www.burmalibrary.org/TinKyi/archives/2001-06/msg00009.html.
16. Min Lwin, "Junta's Spies Active Among Ethnic, Exiled Groups", *The Irrawaddy*, 19 February 2009, http://www2.irrawaddy.com/article.php?art_id=15149.
17. See, for example, "Thai Spy Story", *Naeo Na*, 21 July 1994 (in Thai), http://www.burmalibrary.org/reg.burma/archives/199407/msg00119.html; "Background to Thai Spy Story", *Naeo Na*, 8 August 1994 (in Thai), http://www.burmalibrary.org/reg.burma/archives/199408/msg00024.html; and Aung Zaw, "SLORC's Spies Keep Close Watch on Junta's Foes at Home and Abroad", *The Nation*, 2 September 1994, http://www.burmalibrary.org/reg.burma/archives/199409/msg00004.html.
18. Selth, "Burma's Intelligence Apparatus" (1998), pp. 42–44 and 54. See also Research and Information Services Section, Refugee Review Tribunal Australia, RRT Research Response No. MMR33916, Burma, 14 November 2008, https://www.refworld.org/pdfid/4f42078a2.pdf.
19. See, for example, Sandra H. Dudley, *Materialising Exile: Material Culture and Embodied Experience Among Karenni Refugees in Thailand* (New York: Berghahn Books, 2010), pp. 72–73.
20. See, for example, Richard Horsey's description of "a situation of blatant entrapment by the military intelligence service". Richard Horsey, *Ending Forced Labour in Myanmar: Engaging a Pariah Regime*

(London: Routledge, 2011), p. 112. See also Charles Miranda, "Burmese Spies Slip Past ASIO", *The Daily Telegraph*, 6 January 1997, http://www.burmalibrary.org/reg.burma/archives/199701/msg00041.html; "Burma Intelligence to Conduct Propaganda Training, Send Agents to Thailand", *Democratic Voice of Burma*, 24 August 2000; and Bell, "Burma's Dissidents in Fear of Regime's Assassins".
21. Interview, Canberra, October 2013.
22. Khin Nyunt, *I, the Military Intelligence, SLORC and SPDC*.
23. Maxmilian Wechsler has claimed that Khin Nyunt created a sophisticated spying network, "stretching even around the world". It is not clear what he means by this, but it is presumably a reference to Myanmar's network of defence attachés and other agents under diplomatic cover, and the informants embedded in expatriate communities. Maxmilian Wechsler, "The Downfall of Gen Khin Nyunt", *Bangkok Post*, 31 October 2004.
24. David I. Steinberg, *Burma/Myanmar: What Everyone Needs to Know* (Oxford: Oxford University Press, 2013), p. 135.
25. Maung Aung Myoe, *The Road to Naypyitaw: Making Sense of the Myanmar Government's Decision to Move its Capital*, Working Paper Series No. 79 (Singapore: Asia Research Institute, National University of Singapore, November 2006), http://www.ari.nus.edu.sg/wps/wps06_079.pdf. Maung Aung Myoe has gone further, suggesting that the regime's concerns about the constant leaks of military secrets and other classified information contributed to the choice of the title of the new military intelligence agency, namely the Office of the Chief of Military Affairs Security (OCMAS).
26. See, for example, Wilson, *Eyewitness to Early Reform in Myanmar*, p. 46.
27. David Wise and Thomas B. Ross, *The Invisible Government* (London: Jonathan Cape, 1964), pp. 128–35. See also Joseph Allchin, "How the CIA bedded down in Burma – OpEd", *Democratic Voice of Burma*, 28 August 2010, http://www.eurasiareview.com/28082010-how-the-cia-bedded-down-in-burma-oped/. Carleton Ames, the

father of CIA traitor Aldrich Ames, was posted to Yangon as a CIA officer from 1953–55. At the time, there was reported to be over 100 CIA "operatives" working in Burma. See James Adams, *Sellout: Aldrich Ames and the Corruption of the CIA* (New York: Viking, 1995), p. 21.
28. Richard M. Gibson with Wenhua Chen, *The Secret Army: Chiang Kai-shek and the Drug Warlords of the Golden Triangle* (Singapore: John Wiley and Sons, 2011), pp. 265ff.
29. Kenton Clymer, *A Delicate Relationship: The United States and Burma/Myanmar Since 1945* (Ithaca: Cornell University Press, 2015), p. 253.
30. Wai Moe, "Taiwanese Spies on Burmese Soil?", *The Irrawaddy*, 11 September 2010, http://www2.irrawaddy.com/article.php?art_id=19447&page=1.
31. The GRU agent Dmitri Polyakov, who for thirty years worked secretly for the CIA, was posted to the Soviet Embassy in Myanmar from 1965 to 1969. Eva Dillon, *Spies in the Family: An American Spymaster, his Russian Crown Jewel, and the Friendship That Helped End the Cold War* (New York: Harper, 2017), pp. 115–23.
32. Aleksandr Kaznacheev, *Inside a Soviet Embassy: Experiences of a Russian Diplomat in Burma* (Philadelphia: Lippincott, 1962), pp. 172–202.
33. Christopher Andrew and Vasili Mitrokhin, *The World Was Going Our Way: The KGB and the Battle for the Third World* (New York: Basic Books, 2005), p. 557, note 44.
34. "Desmond Ball Unbound", *The Irrawaddy*, 12 October 2016, https://www.irrawaddy.com/from-the-archive/desmond-ball-unbound.html.
35. "Allan Rowley", *The Times*, 13 October 2014, https://share.trin.cam.ac.uk/sites/public/Alumni/obituaries/Martin_Mays-Smith.pdf.
36. Calder Walton, *Empire of Secrets: British Intelligence, the Cold War and the Twilight of Empire* (London: Harper Press, 2013), pp. 340–41.

See also Keith Jeffrey, *MI6: The History of the Secret Intelligence Service, 1909-1949* (London: Bloomsbury, 2010), pp. 704–5.
37. Steve Crawshaw and Matthew Chance, "Secret Agents go to War on Drug Barons", *The Independent*, 29 August 1997, https://www.independent.co.uk/news/secret-agents-go-to-war-on-drug-barons-1247732.html.
38. Brian Toohey and William Pinwill, *Oyster: The Story of the Australian Secret Intelligence Service* (Melbourne: William Heinemann, 1989), pp. 114–17.
39. Richard Deacon, *A History of the Chinese Secret Service* (London: Frederick Muller, 1974), p. 382; and Nicholas Eftimiades, *Chinese Intelligence Operations* (Annapolis: Naval Institute Press, 1994), pp. 76 and 99. See also "Myanmar Army Holds Three Chinese Nationals on Suspicion of Spying", *Radio Free Asia*, 14 May 2015, https://www.rfa.org/english/news/china/myanmar-china-05142015125627.html.
40. Bertil Lintner, *The Rise and Fall of the Communist Party of Burma (CPB)* (Ithaca: Southeast Asia Program, Cornell University, 1990).
41. Julia Bader, *China's Foreign Relations and the Survival of Autocracies* (London: Routledge, 2015), p. 42.
42. For example, since its creation in 1968 India's Research and Analysis Wing (RAW) has had a "Burma Branch" to run clandestine operations against, and prepare intelligence analyses about, Myanmar. See Special Correspondent, "A Kao-boy till the end", *The Hindu*, 7 June 2016, https://www.thehindu.com/news/national/a-kaoboy-till-the-end/article4820697.ece.
43. Jayshree Bajoria, "RAW: India's External Intelligence Agency", *Council on Foreign Relations*, 7 November 2008, https://www.cfr.org/backgrounder/raw-indias-external-intelligence-agency; and Raman, *The Kaoboys of R&AW*, pp. 20–22. Also relevant is Nandita Haksar, *Rogue Agent: How India's Military Intelligence Betrayed the Burmese Resistance* (New Delhi: Penguin, 2009); and Randeep Ramesh, "Burmese Rebels Accuse India of Betrayal", *The Guardian*, 8 October

2007, https://www.theguardian.com/world/2007/oct/08/india.
burma.
44. "Desmond Ball Unbound".
45. Clymer, *A Delicate Relationship*, p. 253.
46. In 2002, OCMI's Colonel San Pwint accused the Thais of giving the KNU weapons "left over" from the annual US-Thailand Cobra Gold military exercises. "FM invited to Burma in bid to Defuse Tension", *The Nation*, 1 August 2002, http://www.burmalibrary.org/TinKyi/archives/2002-08/msg00000.html.
47. Kavi Chongkittavorn, "Spy Me, Spy You, Sa-bai Thailand", *The Nation*, 4 November 2013, http://www.nationmultimedia.com/opinion/Spy-me-spy-you-sa-bai-Thailand-30218613.html.
48. See, for example, Kate Grayson, "After 40 Years, Five-Eyes is Out in the Open", *The Interpreter*, 11 March 2016, http://lowyinstitute.org/the-interpreter/after-40-years-five-eyes-out-open.
49. Tom Kean, "Australia, Singapore Accused of Monitoring Communications Line", *Myanmar Times*, 1 December 2013, https://www.mmtimes.com/national-news/8921-australia-singapore-accused-of-monitoring-communications-line.html.
50. Tim McLaughlin and Nyan Lynn Aung, "US Embassy in Yangon a Secret Listening Post: Snowden", *Myanmar Times*, 31 October 2013, https://www.mmtimes.com/national-news/8646-us-embassy-in-yangon-a-secret-listening-post-snowden.html.
51. Nicky Hager and Ryan Gallagher, "Secret Documents Shine Light on GCSB Spying on Bangladesh", *New Zealand Herald*, 16 April 2015, https://www.nzherald.co.nz/nz/news/article.cfm?c_id=1&objectid=11433216.
52. Dillon, *Spies in the Family*, p. 116.
53. "Desmond Ball Unbound".
54. *Current Realities and Future Possibilities in Burma/Myanmar: Options for U.S. Policy*, Asia Society Task Force Report (New York: Asia Society, March 2010), p. 36, http://www2.jiia.or.jp/pdf/report/201003/BurmaMyanmar_TaskForceReport2.pdf.

55. Yeni, "Burmese FM Says Yettaw Visit Part of Opposition Plot", *The Irrawaddy*, 22 May 2009, http://www2.irrawaddy.com/opinion_story.php?art_id=15715.
56. Wai Moe, "Burma Arrests Two Foreigners for Spying: Sources", *The Irrawaddy*, 28 February 2011, http://www2.irrawaddy.com/article.php?art_id=20845.
57. Andrew Selth, "Burma: A Critical Look at Those Chemical Weapons Claims", *The Interpreter*, 25 February 2014, https://www.lowyinstitute.org/the-interpreter/burma-critical-look-those-chemical-weapons-claims.
58. The documents had been given to them by a police officer, and contained information that had already appeared in the news media. Shoon Naing and Aye Min Thant, "Myanmar Court Jails Reuters Reporters for Seven Years in Landmark Secrets Case", *Reuters*, 3 September 2018, https://www.reuters.com/article/us-myanmar-journalists/myanmar-court-jails-reuters-reporters-for-seven-years-in-landmark-secrets-case-idUSKCN1LJ09E.
59. See, for example, *Anti-Money Laundering and Counter-Terrorist Financing Measures: Myanmar: Mutual Evaluation Report* (Bangkok: Asia/Pacific Group on Money Laundering, September 2018), pp. 107–12.
60. Bert, "Burma, China and the USA", p. 273.
61. China's relationship with Myanmar has been the subject of many exaggerated claims. As Li Chenyang has stated, there are no Chinese military bases in Myanmar. He has also claimed that there is no formal intelligence sharing agreement between the two countries. However, even if this is the case (and it is a disputed point), it does not exclude informal exchanges which, given the long shared border, are inevitable. Li Chenyang, "The Policies of China and India toward Myanmar", in *Myanmar/Burma: Inside Challenges, Outside Interests*, edited by Lex Rieffel (Washington D.C.: Brookings Institution Press, 2010), p. 120.

62. See, for example, "Sino-Burmese Pact", *Far Eastern Economic Review*, 30 January 1997, p. 12; Rowan Callick, "China and Burma Strengthen Ties with Military Agreement", *Australian Financial Review*, 24 January 1997; and "China, Myanmar to Deepen Law Enforcement, Security Cooperation", *Xinhua*, 4 July 2018, http://eng.chinamil.com.cn/view/2018-07/04/content_8079359.htm.
63. See, for example, Desmond Ball, *Security Developments in the Thailand-Burma Borderlands*, Working Paper No. 9 (Sydney: Australian Mekong Resource Centre, University of Sydney, October 2003).
64. See, for example, Aung Zaw, "India Courts Myanmar", *The Irrawaddy*, 20 July 2017, https://www.irrawaddy.com/opinion/commentary/india-courts-myanmar.html; Iftikhar Gilani, "Strengthening Intelligence Sharing Mechanism to be Discussed with Myanmar Next Week", *Tehelka*, 24 December 2010; and "India, Burma Officials to Focus Talks on Intelligence Sharing, Counter-Terrorism", *PTI News Agency*, 18 January 2010.
65. "Indian Official Calls for Real-Time Intelligence Sharing", *Mizzima News*, 10 November 2017, http://mizzima.com/development-news/indian-official-calls-real-time-intelligence-sharing.
66. See, for example, "3 Armies, 2 Spies of Burma Arrested in Border Area", *Kaladan News*, 22 March 2009, http://www.kaladanpress.org/index.php/news/100-news-2009/march-2009/1867-3-armies-2-spies-of-burma-arrested-in-border-area.html.
67. While intelligence is not specifically mentioned in any public statements, it is widely assumed that it is included in the references to "other promising spheres of military cooperation". "Russia and Myanmar Sign Agreement on Military Cooperation", *Tass*, 16 June 2016, http://tass.com/defense/882419.
68. Cameron Hill, *Defence Cooperation with Myanmar — Australia and Other Countries: A Quick Guide*, Research Paper Series, 2017–18 (Canberra: Parliamentary Library, Parliament of Australia, 13 October 2017), http://apo.org.au/system/files/114236/apo-nid114236-450741.pdf.

69. "Commissioner Signs Policing Pact with Myanmar", *Australian Federal Police*, 14 June 2016, https://www.afp.gov.au/news-media/media-releases/commissioner-signs-policing-pact-myanmar.
70. See, for example, "Burma: US Bilateral Initiatives Victim of Post-Khin Nyunt Purge"; and "EAP DAS Daley Meets With SPDC Secretary One General Khin Nyunt — Discussion on Counter Terrorism, Political Dialogue and Prisoner Releases Show Some Result", Cable from the US Embassy, Rangoon, 7 May 2003, *Public Library of US Diplomacy*, https://wikileaks.org/plusd/cables/03RANGOON554_a.html.
71. Jason Szep and Andrew R.C. Marshall, "U.S. to invite Myanmar to Joint Military Exercises", *Reuters*, 19 October 2012, https://www.reuters.com/article/usa-myanmar-military/exclusive-u-s-to-invite-myanmar-to-joint-military-exercises-idINDEE89I02620121019.
72. See Paseman, *A Spy's Journey*, pp. 174–75.
73. See, for example, Selth, *Burma's Secret Military Partners*.
74. The training provided by the United Kingdom was given in both Myanmar and the United Kingdom. The training provided by the United States was partly in Myanmar, but also at a secret CIA facility on the Pacific island of Saipan, which had as its cover name the "Naval Technical Training Unit". The facility conducted courses in intelligence tradecraft, communications, counter-intelligence and psychological warfare. Myanmar officers may have also attended training courses on Okinawa.
75. Callahan, *Making Enemies*, p. 198. See also Mya Maung, *The Burma Road to Poverty* (New York: Praeger, 1991), p. 199.
76. Mya Maung, *Totalitarianism in Burma: Prospects for Economic Development* (New York: Paragon House, 1992), pp. 36–39; and interview, Canberra, July 1998.
77. Khin Nyunt, *Secretary One*. See also Aung Zaw, "The Spring before Khin Nyunt's Fall".
78. Aung Zaw, "How Should the US Engage Myanmar?", *The Irrawaddy*, 9 February 2018, https://www.irrawaddy.com/opinion/commentary/us-engage-myanmar.html.

79. Selth, *Burma's Secret Military Partners*, pp. 51–52. See also Yossi Melman, "Israel's Censored Arms Deals", *The Jerusalem Post*, 18 November 2017, https://www.jpost.com/Jerusalem-Report/Censored-Arms-Deals-513187. While most reports cite Mossad as the Israeli intelligence agency involved, former members of the Israeli Defence Force and the internal security service known as Shin Bet may have also participated in such programmes.
80. Larkin, *Finding George Orwell in Burma*, pp. 57–58. See also Bert, "Burma, China and the USA", p. 273; and Steinberg, *Burma: The State of Myanmar*, p. 226.
81. Under US Public Law 110-286-July 29, 2008, the State Department was required to report all foreign intelligence assistance to Myanmar. It issued public versions of its annual reports for 2009, 2010 and 2011, but they were very cryptic, and revealed little information of value, as was doubtless intended. See *Tom Lantos Block Burmese JADE (Junta's Anti-Democratic Efforts) Act of 2008*, https://www.congress.gov/110/plaws/publ286/PLAW-110publ286.pdf; and "Report to Congress Per PL 110-286 on Military and Intelligence Aid to Burma", US Department of State, https://www.state.gov/s/inr/rls/burmareport/.
82. Kin Oung, *Who Killed Aung San?* (Bangkok: White Lotus, 1996), p. 81.
83. Andrew Selth, *Police Reform in Burma (Myanmar): Aims, Obstacles and Outcomes*, Regional Outlook No. 44 (Brisbane: Griffith Asia Institute, Griffith University, 2013).
84. Chee Soon Juan, *To Be Free: Stories from Asia's Struggle Against Oppression* (Clayton: Monash Asia Institute, 1999), pp. 83–84.
85. Interview, Yangon, March 2014.
86. "Russian Ambassador Talks Myanmar Relations, Security and 'Asia's Century'", *Mizzima*, 30 January 2016, http://mizzima.com/latest-news-politics-news-opinion-opinion/russian-ambassador.
87. Marian Sawer, Norman Abjorensen and Philip Larkin, *Australia: The State of Democracy* (Sydney: Federation Press, 2009), p. 292. See

also Craig Skehan, "We Trained Burmese Officers, Police Admit", *Sydney Morning Herald*, 5 October 2007, https://www.smh.com.au/national/we-trained-burmese-officers-police-admit-20071005-gdr9ov.html.

88. "Training on Data Collection Strengthens Myanmar's Borders", *UN Office on Drugs and Crime*, 29 March 2016, https://www.unodc.org/southeastasiaandpacific/en/myanmar/2016/03/border-data-training/story.html. See also "Myanmar Front-line Officers Strengthen Capacities to Track Cross-Border Criminals", *UN Office on Drugs and Crime*, 12 August 2016, https://www.unodc.org/southeastasiaandpacific/en/myanmar/2016/08/blo-data-training/story.html.
89. "Senr-Gen Min Aung Hlaing Ushers in Period of Close Ties Between Myanmar and Thai Defence Forces", *The Irrawaddy*, 10 August 2018, https://www.irrawaddy.com/news/snr-gen-min-aung-hlaing-ushers-period-close-ties-myanmar-thai-defence-forces.html.
90. "Enhancing ASEAN Military Intelligence Cooperation for ASEAN Community Building: The Way Forward", Defence Intelligence Staff Division, Ministry of Defence, Malaysia, http://mod.gov.la/10thADMM/assets/paper_13-amiim_12-mac-16.pdf.
91. "Myanmar Hosts the 11th ASEAN Chief of Defence Forces Informal Meeting", Ministry of Defence, Brunei Darussalam, 5 March 2014, http://www.mindef.gov.bn/Lists/News/DispForm.aspx?ID=1885.
92. "ASEAN, Partners Agree to Boost Intelligence Sharing", *ASEAN Regional Forum*, http://aseanregionalforum.asean.org/news-21895/13-asean-partners-agree-to-boost-intelligence-sharing.html.
93. Feng Yingqui, "Myanmar Steps Up Fight Against Money-Laundering", *Xinhua*, 22 March 2017, http://www.xinhuanet.com//english/2017-03/22/c_136149093.htm.
94. "Report of the Independent International Fact-finding Mission on Myanmar".

95. See, for example, Roland Oliphant and Neil Connor, "Britain to Stop Training Burmese Military Until Rohingya Crisis is Resolved", *The Telegraph*, 19 September 2017, https://www.telegraph.co.uk/news/2017/09/19/britain-stop-training-burmese-military-rohingya-crisis-resolved/; and Michael Peel and John Reed, "EU to Scale Back Relations with Myanmar's Military", *Financial Times*, 17 October 2017, https://www.ft.com/content/cf0b94f6-b25d-11e7-a398-73d59db9e399.
96. Hill, *Defence Cooperation with Myanmar*.

Chapter 8

QUESTIONS OF ACCOUNTABILITY

> True democracies do not allow impunity to flourish, as it does, and has always done, in Myanmar. Responsible democracies do not engage in systematic violations of their peoples' rights or mass atrocities. Rule of law involves all, regardless of their position, being answerable to fair laws that are impartially applied. Accountability is necessary to ensure that impunity ends and Myanmar's transition to real democracy continues; respecting human rights is integral for democracy.
>
> Yanghee Lee and Georgia Drake,
> *Time*, 26 September 2018[1]

When Aung San Suu Kyi and the NLD took office in March 2016, after a landslide election victory the previous year, a wave of euphoria swept over Myanmar, shared by many people in other parts of the world. At the time, there was a rather naive belief that everything in Myanmar would suddenly be transformed. It was widely assumed, for example, that the key components of the repressive old regime would be dismantled, and the government that had effectively ruled Myanmar for the past half century—the most durable military dictatorship in the modern world—would soon become a bad memory.[2] Clearly, that has not happened and, as several Myanmar-watchers predicted at the time, was never going to happen.

It might have helped everyone to keep in mind Robert Taylor's observation that "Military intelligence has served as a means of social control throughout the existence of independent Burma", and to ask if and how the NLD government planned to depart from this pattern, and whether the armed forces would actually allow this to happen.[3] As expected, Aung San Suu Kyi has faced the same challenges as the military regime but, to the surprise of many, she seems to be relying on the same kinds of mechanisms and methods to tackle them.

Indeed, eight years after the armed forces stepped back from direct rule, and despite promises of sweeping reforms, there are few indications that Myanmar's basic approach to security matters has significantly changed. The vast intelligence apparatus that underpinned military rule still seems to be in place. It is no longer dominated by a large military intelligence organization, as it was under General Khin Nyunt, but either directly or indirectly it still answers to the Tatmadaw's commander-in-chief. Also, there may have been some noticeable changes in the way that the intelligence agencies operate, but there seems to have been a greater shift in manner and style, than in substance. Below the surface, the same agencies still display many of the same characteristics that made the intelligence apparatus a powerful and feared arm of the military government, before Aung San Suu Kyi took office. In some areas of the country, such as Rakhine State, Kachin State and Shan State, the main intelligence agencies have demonstrated a continuing commitment to the Tatmadaw's narrow and uncompromising vision of a unitary, compliant and independent Myanmar, dominated by ethnic Burman Buddhists.[4]

Foreign observers always find it difficult to know exactly what is happening behind the scenes in Myanmar, but State

Counsellor Aung San Suu Kyi's relationship with the armed forces and the national intelligence apparatus is a complicated one.

She is the de facto leader of Myanmar and acts "above the president", but Aung San Suu Kyi appears to have little control over the country's intelligence apparatus, almost all elements of which are answerable, directly or indirectly, to Min Aung Hlaing, as the Tatmadaw's C-in-C. Under the terms of the 2008 constitution, he appoints the Ministers for Defence and Home Affairs, in whose portfolios OCMSA, SB, CID and BSI fall.[5] He also appoints the Minister for Border Affairs, who manages other intelligence assets. Aung San Suu Kyi is the Minister for Foreign Affairs, and is thus responsible for Myanmar's diplomatic missions. This gives her a role in the collection and analysis of OSINT, but defence attachés are appointed and controlled by the armed forces. When Khin Nyunt was CI, this was done through a Military Attachés Office within DDSI, and later OCMI. Such appointments now appear to be made by Tatmadaw HQ, although OCMSA is doubtless consulted. Nor has the MFA any real control over their intelligence-related activities, which are managed by OCMSA and, possibly in some areas, SB. Other agents operating abroad, even if they were under diplomatic cover, would also fall outside Aung San Suu Kyi's normal span of control. That being the case, she cannot be held directly responsible for the supervision or behaviour of Myanmar's intelligence apparatus, or any of its individual agencies.

Indeed, rather than dealing directly with the intelligence apparatus, Aung San Suu Kyi seems to have adopted a strategy of bypassing it as much as possible and avoiding any circumstances in which she can be held directly responsible for its behaviour. Even in terms of briefings, it appears that she has tried to put some distance between herself and the intelligence agencies.⁶ It is not known what intelligence product she routinely receives as the State Counsellor, but she has made it clear that she wants to tap into independent sources of information and advice. The appointment of a career diplomat as her national security advisor in January 2017, for example, seems to be in part at least an attempt to reduce her reliance on the military-dominated national intelligence apparatus. His responsibility is "to advise the President and the Union Government on internal and external threats, by assessing situations from a strategic point of view".⁷ It is not clear how this role differs from those of other ministers, or government agencies like the MFA and OCMSA.⁸ Also, while Aung San Suu Kyi has held numerous meetings with key members of the NDSC, it appears that she has yet to call a formal meeting of that body.⁹ It used to meet almost weekly under Thein Sein. Aung San Suu Kyi is a member of the council, as the Minister for Foreign Affairs, but seven of the council's eleven members answer first to the C-in-C, effectively putting it beyond her ability to control.

Also, despite her repeated calls for the observation of universal human rights and the rule of law when she was a prisoner of conscience, Aung San Suu Kyi has shown no obvious inclination to curb the excesses of the intelligence apparatus or to change the way that Myanmar's laws are being misused to silence dissent. Nor does the NLD seem to have given serious consideration to restructuring the intelligence system to make it more efficient and accountable, and thus reflective of the transition to a more democratic form of government. For example, in the new Myanmar, it might be expected that responsibility for the investigation of political crimes—those which relate primarily to domestic, and certain aspects of external, security—would fall exclusively to the MPF, or to a dedicated civilian agency, as occurs in most democratic countries.[10] There has been some progress in "civilianising" the management of internal security in recent years, but these responsibilities are still shared between the police and the armed forces.[11] This is likely to continue for the foreseeable future.

Formally, SB has responsibility for the collection and assessment of political intelligence. OCMSA is supposed to concern itself only with defence related matters.[12] However, given the Tatmadaw's self-appointed guardianship role and the power wielded by military intelligence agencies in the past, it is unlikely that the armed forces would be prepared to give up its ability independently to monitor domestic and possibly also international developments. Not only do the generals distrust the NLD government and civilian agencies but the Tatmadaw has always preferred to rely on its own resources when it comes to national security, a term with a very wide meaning in Myanmar. This will remain the case as long as the military leadership perceives continuing threats to the country—and itself—from a wide range of foreign governments and international organizations, political activists and ethnic armed groups.[13] There is thus the potential for the continued duplication of functions, with the attendant jurisdictional disputes, professional jealousies and competition for scarce resources.

There are probably some in Myanmar who view the more open political environment since 2011 with unease, if not concern, and thus deserving of close attention by official agencies. However, an entirely new security system seems unlikely. Whether or not there is a restructuring of the national intelligence apparatus, it will need a clearly defined mission that fully takes into account Aung San Suu Kyi's reformist agenda and the more liberal atmosphere that now prevails in the country. That guidance currently seems to be lacking, or if it does exists it appears to be poorly enforced. Also, a strong argument can be mounted for a rationalization and redistribution of intelligence roles. This would not only increase the level of cooperation between agencies and better exploit their limited resources, but it would also provide a clearer delineation of their responsibilities, in particular the separation of military and civilian functions. This in turn could aid in the future oversight of intelligence operations in Myanmar by a genuinely elected and fully civilian government, should that ever eventuate.[14]

Notes

1. Yanghee Lee and Georgia Drake, "There Can Be No Peace for Myanmar Without Justice", *Time*, 26 September 2018, http://time.com/5404328/myanmar-accountability-yanghee-lee/.
2. "Despite Changes, Relic of Past Oppression Lives on in Myanmar: Internal Spy Network".
3. Robert H. Taylor, "The Military in Myanmar (Burma): What Scope for a New Role?", in *The Military, the State, and Development in Asia and the Pacific*, edited by Viberto Selochan (Boulder: Westview Press, 1991), p. 145.
4. See, for example, Gavin Kelleher, "Beyond the Rohingya: Myanmar's Other Crises", *The Diplomat*, 8 February 2018, https://thediplomat.com/2018/02/beyond-the-rohingya-myanmars-other-crises/.
5. Arguably, OCMSA falls under the C-in-C's jurisdiction, as a formal distinction is drawn between the Defence Services and the Defence Ministry.

6. Yuichi Nitta, "Tension Builds Between Suu Kyi and Military over Refugee Probe", *Nikkei Asian Review*, 26 June 2018, https://asia.nikkei.com/Politics/International-Relations/Tension-builds-between-Suu-Kyi-and-military-over-Myanmar-refugee-probe. See, however, John Geddie and Fathin Ungku, "Myanmar's Suu Kyi says Relations with Military 'Not That Bad'", *Reuters*, 21 August 2018, https://www.reuters.com/article/us-singapore-myanmar-suukyi/myanmars-suu-kyi-says-relations-with-military-not-that-bad-idUSKCN1L60OP.
7. Prashanth Parawesmaran, "What's Behind Myanmar's New National Security Adviser Post?", *The Diplomat*, 11 January 2017, https://thediplomat.com/2017/01/whats-behind-myanmars-new-national-security-adviser-post/.
8. "The National Security Advisor Post Created", *Myanmar Insider*, February 2017, http://www.myanmarinsider.com/the-national-security-advisor-post-created/.
9. These meetings have at times included the Chief of OCMSA. See, for example, Anthony Davis, "Myanmar's Military Ordered to 'Crush' Rakhine Rebels", *Janes 360*, 10 January 2019, https://www.janes.com/article/85627/myanmar-s-military-ordered-to-crush-rakhine-rebels.
10. The FBI has provided training to the MPF, but this seems to have been confined to helping the CID improve its investigation skills. See Thu Thu Aung, "FBI Conducts Police Training in Myanmar", *Myanmar Times*, 28 October 2016, https://www.mmtimes.com/national-news/yangon/23367-fbi-conducts-police-training-in-myanmar.html.
11. Andrew Selth, "Police Reform and the 'Civilianisation' of Security in Myanmar", in *Law, Society and Transition in Myanmar*, edited by Melissa Crouch and Tim Lindsey (Oxford: Hart Publishing, 2014), pp. 271–88.
12. Interview, Naypyidaw, February 2013.

13. Andrew Selth, "All Going According to Plan? The Armed Forces and Government in Myanmar", *Contemporary Southeast Asia* 40, no. 1 (April 2018): 1–26.
14. Selth, "Myanmar's Coercive Apparatus", pp. 13–36.

Chapter 9

CONCLUSION

> Every state gets the intelligence service it deserves.
> Wesley K. Wark
> *Security and Intelligence in a Changing World* (1991)[1]

Over the past 200 years, Myanmar (known before 1989 as Burma) has experienced almost every major system of government. After the monarchy was conquered and the kingdom annexed in three stages by the British in the nineteenth century, it endured various forms of colonial rule and military administration before it regained its independence and became a parliamentary democracy in 1948. From 1958 to 1960, the country was managed by an unelected "caretaker" government, led by General Ne Win. The military dictatorship he installed in 1962 morphed into an authoritarian one-party state when a new constitution was promulgated in 1974. An abortive pro-democracy uprising in 1988 was followed by another military regime. Finally, under a carefully managed seven-step road map, a "discipline-flourishing democracy" was allowed to emerge in 2011 under mixed civilian-military rule.[2] For almost all of this period, but particularly between 1962 and 2011, Myanmar's government was supported by a powerful national intelligence apparatus. Much of it remains under Aung San Suu Kyi's NLD government. Indeed, rather than being "the textbook example of a police state", as it was once called, Myanmar could be described instead as a classic "intelligence state".[3]

Looking back over the seventy years since 1948, it is possible to identify five features that have marked the intelligence state.[4] First, the apparatus has been dominated by the armed forces, in one way or another. Second, the primary focus of the national intelligence effort has always been on domestic security. Third, Myanmar's intelligence apparatus has been characterized by an uncompromising commitment to the preservation of the Union, in particular its unity, stability and sovereignty, as perceived by the government of the day. Fourth, due largely to Myanmar's isolation and persistent economic problems, its security agencies have relied heavily on human intelligence rather than technical sources, although this is now changing as the electronic revolution makes a greater impact on the country. Fifth, in terms of intelligence management, there has always been a tension in Myanmar between the imperative to have a single person or organization to guide and direct the vast national intelligence apparatus, and the wish to create multiple agencies under different managers, each performing specialized functions, and to safeguard their independence. Over the years, blunt responses to this dilemma have contributed to some notable intelligence failures.

In another way too, there has been a measure of continuity, albeit not one that has been readily acknowledged by successive Myanmar governments.

For decades, Myanmar's leaders have denigrated the country's former colonial rulers. The reputed arrogance, brutality and greed of the British between 1824 and 1948 have become an essential part of the nationalist narrative that is taught in schools, civil service academies and military training institutions. It has been referred to in countless official speeches and endlessly repeated in books and state propaganda outlets like the (English language) *Global New Light of Myanmar* (formerly the *Working People's Daily*) and (Burmese language) *Kyemon* ("The Mirror").[5] According to this view, the British administration constituted a privileged elite that denied Myanmar its rightful place in the world, repressed its people and exploited its natural riches.[6] The colonialists imposed their rule on the country and enforced their draconian laws through the army, a large paramilitary police force and an alien judicial system. Challenges to colonial rule by patriots and others were met with administrative and, on many occasions, physical force. The British enjoyed a monopoly of coercive power that could be directed against the civil population in large part because of a nation-wide intelligence apparatus that monitored everyone and everything, compiled and collated vast amounts of data and reported any signs of dissent.

In portraying the British colonial administration in this way, it seems never to have occurred to Myanmar's military rulers after 1962 that they presided over a series of governments that in many ways fitted the same pattern. To take just one aspect, there are strong similarities in the way that the British colonial administration and the Tatmadaw viewed the role of intelligence. There are also some obvious differences, but both considered the mastery of information a vital component in the ability of a self-appointed minority to rule a large country with a diverse population made up of many different and often competing ethnic, religious and cultural groups, at various stages of political, economic and social development. Although their fears were often exaggerated, colonial and post-colonial Myanmar also faced pressures from neighbouring countries, which needed to be closely monitored. Throughout its modern history, the national intelligence apparatus has tried to give the central government the information it needed to anticipate problems and respond in a timely manner. Before and after Myanmar's independence, intelligence failures led to costly and sometimes dangerous breakdowns in law and order. They also put the country's sovereignty at risk.

Since independence, the structure and inner dynamics of Myanmar's intelligence agencies have always been difficult to determine. Even now, after the lifting of many controls on political, economic and social life, the apparatus remains "enigmatic and secretive".[7] Also, given developments in and around the country, such as the growing popular dissatisfaction with the NLD government and the potential for further religious violence following the latest Rohingya crisis, the agencies will most likely attempt to update their modus operandi and demand greater resources. HUMINT will doubtless continue to play a dominant role in intelligence collection, both within Myanmar and in neighbouring countries, but there is bound to be an increased emphasis on technical intelligence. This would probably be through improved organic capabilities (such as the acquisition of more modern SIGINT equipment) and a more sophisticated use of commercial options (for example, with regard to IMINT). Whether the system is better able to analyse and assess all the data collected remains to be seen, and of course it will always be up to the government to accept or reject the intelligence advice it receives.

Despite some movement along the road towards a genuine democracy, and the rule of law, it is unlikely that the government's dependence on the national intelligence apparatus will diminish. Even though Myanmar is currently facing a number of new external challenges, from both national and transnational threats, the priority currently given to internal security is unlikely to change. Both Aung San Suu Kyi's quasi-civilian government and the armed forces leadership know that their survival—and, in their view, the country's survival—is threatened more by disunity and domestic instability than by any foreign developments. Myanmar has weathered international pressures in the past and is confident that it can do so again. It will be assisted by countries such as China and Russia, which will be quick to exploit any opportunities flowing from renewed Western sanctions. Despite misgivings about some of Myanmar's policies, ASEAN is unlikely to do anything to jeopardize its regional links. The greatest threats to Naypyidaw will come from within the country. This will ensure that the national intelligence apparatus will continue to occupy an important place in the Myanmar government's thinking. Also, from all the indications available, it will remain firmly under the control of the armed forces, as it has always been.

Notes

1. Wesley K. Wark, "Introduction", in *Security and Intelligence in a Changing World: New Perspectives for the 1990s*, edited by A. Stuart Farson, David Stafford and Wesley K. Wark (London: Frank Cass and Co., 1991), p. 9.
2. Selth, "All Going According to Plan?"
3. The "police state" description is by Brad Adams, Head of Human Rights Watch's Asia Division, cited in Neil A. Englehart, *Sovereignty, State Failure and Human Rights: Petty Despots and Exemplary Villains* (London: Routledge, 2017), p. 104.
4. Andrew Selth, "Myanmar: An Enduring Intelligence State, or a State Enduring Intelligence?", in *Handbook of Asian Intelligence Communities*, edited by Bob de Graaff (Boulder: Lynne Rienner, 2019).

5. See, for example, *Cruel and Vicious Repression of Myanmar Peoples by Imperialists and Fascists and the True Story About the Plunder of the Royal Jewels* (Yangon: Ministry of Information, Government of the Union of Myanmar, 1991); and Yadanasi Sayadaw (Loilem), "Row in Harmony and Unison", *Global New Light of Myanmar*, 8 May 2005, http://www.ibiblio.org/obl/docs2/NLM2005-05-08.pdf.
6. See, for example, "Greetings of Commander-in-Chief of Defence Services Senior General Min Aung Hlaing at the Second Anniversary of the Nationwide Ceasefire Agreement – NCA", Republic of the Union of Myanmar, President Office, Nay Pyi Taw, 16 October 2017, http://www.president-office.gov.mm/en/?q=issues/peace/id-7778.
7. Andrew Buncombe, "Burma: the Misery, the Fear and the Secrecy", *The Independent*, 16 May 2008, https://www.independent.co.uk/news/world/asia/burma-the-misery-the-fear-and-the-secrecy-829747.html.

SELECT BIBLIOGRAPHY[1]

Official Publications

A Resident of Kayin State. *Whither KNU?* Rangoon: News and Periodicals Enterprise, 1995.

"A Review of the Annual Report for the Year 2000 of the Reporters Sans Frontiers". *The Truth* 7 (16 May 2000).

Burma Communist Party's Conspiracy to take over State Power. Rangoon: News and Periodicals Enterprise, 1989.

"Complete Explanation on the Developments in the Country given by General Thura Shwe Mann, member of the State Peace and Development Council and Lt. General Soe Win, Prime Minister, at Zeya Thiri Hall on October 24, 2004 and Explanation by Secretary-1, Lt. General Thein Sein, Chairman of the National Convention Convening Commission on October 22, 2004". Supplement to the *Global New Light of Myanmar*, 7 November 2004.

Constitution of the Republic of the Union of Myanmar (2008). Nay Pyi Taw: Ministry of Information, 2008.

Country of Origin Information (COI) Report: Burma (Myanmar). London: UK Border Agency, Home Office, 2 February 2012.

Country of Origin Information Report: Burma (Union of Myanmar). London: UK Border Agency, Home Office, 23 July 2010.

Criminal Investigation Department Manual, Part 1. Rangoon: Central Press, 1964.

Criminal Investigation Department Manual, Part 3. Rangoon: Superintendent of Government Printing?, 1922?

---

[1] Online addresses for most of the references listed below, and for other sources mentioned in the book, have not been included in this bibliography, but details can be found in the endnotes. An exception has been made, however, for the US diplomatic cables (as claimed) that were released by Wikileaks.

Cruel and Vicious Repression of Myanmar Peoples by Imperialists and Fascists and the True Story About the Plunder of the Royal Jewels. Yangon: Ministry of Information, Government of the Union of Myanmar, 1991.

Daw Suu Kyi, the NLD Party and Our Ray of Hope and Selected Articles. Yangon: News and Periodicals Enterprise, 2003.

Hla Min. *Political Situation of Myanmar and its Role in the Region.* Yangon: Office of Strategic Studies, Ministry of Defence, 1997.

"How Some Western Powers Have Been Aiding and Abetting Terrorism Committed by Certain Organisations Operating Under the Guise of Democracy and Human Rights by Giving Them Assistance in Both Cash and Kind". Special news briefing by the Secretary-1 of the State Law and Order Restoration Council, Lt-Gen Khin Nyunt, in the Defence Services Assembly Hall, Rangoon, 27 June 1997.

Human Resource Development and Nation Building in Myanmar: Papers Presented at the International Business Centre, from 18th to 20th November 1997. Yangon: Office of Strategic Studies, Ministry of Defence, 1998.

Intelligence Report: Peking and the Burmese Communists: The Perils and Profits of Insurgency. Langley: Central Intelligence Agency, July 1971.

Is Trust Vindicated? A Chronicle of the Various Accomplishments of the Government headed by General Ne Win during the Period of Tenure from November, 1958 to February 6, 1960. Rangoon: Director of Information, Government of the Union of Burma, 1960.

Military Terms. Yangon: Directorate of Training, Ministry of Defence, 2007 (in Burmese).

"Myanmar (Burma): Whether the Military Intelligence Force in Myanmar has been Fully or Partially Disbanded and Who is Carrying out their Duties (2004–February 2008)". Ottawa: Research Directorate, Immigration and Refugee Board, 25 February 2008.

Research and Information Services Section, Refugee Review Tribunal Australia, RRT Research Response No. MMR33916, Burma, 14 November 2008.

Skyful of Lies: BBC, VOA: Their Broadcasts and Rebuttals to Disinformation. Rangoon: News and Periodicals Enterprise, Ministry of Information, August 1988.

Staff Duty. Yangon: Directorate of Training, Ministry of Defence, 1989 (in Burmese).

Symposium on Socio-Economic Factors Contributing to National Consolidation: Papers and Discussions Presented at the Symposium Held at the International Business Centre, 6 1/2 Miles, Yangon, from 9th to 11th October 1996. Yangon: Office of Strategic Studies, Ministry of Defence, 1996.

The Conspiracy of Treasonous Minions Within the Myanmar Naing-Ngan and Traitorous Cohorts Abroad. Rangoon: Ministry of Information, October 1989.

The Infantry Battalion. Yangon: Directorate of Training, Ministry of Defence, 2000 (in Burmese).

U Nu. *From Peace to Stability: Selected Speeches.* Rangoon: Government of Burma, 1951.

US Army Intelligence and Security Command (INSCOM). "Directorate of Defence Services Intelligence (DDSI) Influence in Burma", 12 January 1973.

US Department of State. "Burma: Human Rights Practices 1993". Washington D.C.: Department of State, 31 January 1994.

——. "Burma". 2004 Country Reports on Human Rights Practices, Bureau of Democracy, Human Rights and Labour. Washington D.C.: Department of State, 28 February 2005.

——. "Burma 2015 Human Rights Report". Bureau of Democracy, Human Rights and Labour. Washington D.C.: Department of State, 2016.

——. "Burma 2016 Human Rights Report". Bureau of Democracy, Human Rights and Labour. Washington D.C.: Department of State, 2017.

——. "Burma 2017 Human Rights Report". Bureau of Democracy, Human Rights and Labour. Washington D.C.: Department of State, 2018.

(Leaked) Diplomatic Cables

"An Overview of Northern Thailand-based Burmese Media Organisations". Cable from the US Consulate General, Chiang Mai, 14 February 2007. *Public Library of US Diplomacy*. https://wikileaks.org/plusd/cables/07CHIANGMAI33_a.html.

"Arakan Rohingya National Organisation Contacts with Al Qaeda and with Burmese Insurgent Groups on the Thai Border". Cable from the US Embassy, Rangoon, 10 October 2002. *Public Library of US Diplomacy*. https://wikileaks.org/plusd/cables/02RANGOON1310_a.html.

"Australia Sees Grim Burma Getting Grimmer". Cable from the US Embassy, Rangoon, 14 September 2005. *Public Library of US Diplomacy*. https://wikileaks.org/plusd/cables/05RANGOON1054_a.html.

"Burma: 2004 Annual Terrorism Report". Cable from the US Embassy, Rangoon, 23 December 2004. *Public Library of US Diplomacy*. https://wikileaks.org/plusd/cables/04RANGOON1627_a.html.

"Burma: Khin Nyunt's Cronies Feeling the Squeeze". Cable from the US Embassy, Rangoon, 30 November 2004. *Public Library of US Diplomacy*. https://wikileaks.org/plusd/cables/04RANGOON1518_a.html.

"Burma: Khin Nyunt's Gone, But Big Brother's Still Watching". Cable from the US Embassy, Rangoon, 1 December 2004. *Public Library of US Diplomacy*. https://wikileaks.org/plusd/cables/04RANGOON1522_a.html.

"Burma: New Secret Police Special Units". Cable from the US Embassy, Rangoon, 8 November 2001. *Public Library of US Diplomacy*. https://wikileaks.org/plusd/cables/03RANGOON1326_a.html.

"Burma: Tatmadaw Takes Away M.I.'s Keys". Cable from the US Embassy, Rangoon, 24 November 2004. *Public Library of US Diplomacy*. https://wikileaks.org/plusd/cables/04RANGOON1503_a.html.

"Burma: US Bilateral Initiatives Victim of Post-Khin Nyunt Purge". Cable from the US Embassy, Rangoon, 14 January 2005. *Public Library of US Diplomacy*. https://wikileaks.org/plusd/cables/05RANGOON104_a.html.

Select Bibliography

"Burma: Views From Military Intelligence". Cable from the US Embassy, Rangoon, 30 April 2004. *Public Library of US Diplomacy.* https://wikileaks.org/plusd/cables/04RANGOON545_a.html.

"Burma: Who's Who in the Regime". Cable from the US Embassy, Rangoon, 7 December 2007. *Public Library of US Diplomacy.* https://wikileaks.org/plusd/cables/07RANGOON1170_a.html.

"Burma's Generals Promote Themselves". Cable from the US Embassy, Rangoon, 30 March 1993. *Public Library of US Diplomacy.* https://wikileaks.org/plusd/cables/93RANGOON1836_a.html.

"Burma's Grunts vs MI: Round One?" Cable from the US Embassy, Rangoon, 14 October 2004. *Public Library of US Diplomacy.* https://wikileaks.org/plusd/cables/04RANGOON1345_a.html.

"Burma's Least Wanted: The Rohingyas". Cable from the US Embassy, Rangoon, 22 February 2007. *Public Library of US Diplomacy.* https://wikileaks.org/plusd/cables/07RANGOON181_a.html.

"Burmese General Khin Nyunt as Prime Minister: Promotion or Demotion?" Cable from the US Embassy, Rangoon, 26 August 2003. *Public Library of US Diplomacy.* https://wikileaks.org/plusd/cables/03RANGOON1029_a.html.

"Burmese Regime Begins Release of 4,000 Prisoners". Cable from the US Embassy, Rangoon, 19 November 2004. *Public Library of US Diplomacy.* https://wikileaks.org/plusd/cables/04RANGOON1488_a.html.

"Burmese Regime Recalls Foreign Envoys for 'Reorientation'". Cable from the US Embassy, Rangoon, 1 December 2004. *Public Library of US Diplomacy.* https://wikileaks.org/plusd/cables/04RANGOON1524_a.html.

"EAP DAS Daley Meets With SPDC Secretary One General Khin Nyunt – Discussion on Counter Terrorism, Political Dialogue and Prisoner Releases Show Some Result". Cable from the US Embassy, Rangoon, 7 May 2003. *Public Library of US Diplomacy.* https://wikileaks.org/plusd/cables/03RANGOON554_a.html.

"Economic Tensions in the Burmese Military". Cable from the US Embassy, Rangoon, 30 July 2004. *Public Library of US Diplomacy.* https://wikileaks.org/plusd/cables/04RANGOON967_a.html.

"Is the Burmese Regime Coming Unglued?" Cable from the US Embassy, Rangoon, 28 January 2005. *Public Library of US Diplomacy.* https://wikileaks.org/plusd/cables/05RANGOON121_a.htm.

"Khin Nyunt's Ouster: One Week Later". Cable from the US Embassy, Rangoon, 26 October 2004. *Public Library of US Diplomacy.* https://wikileaks.org/plusd/cables/04RANGOON1401_a.html.

"Lee Kuan Yew on Burma's 'Stupid' Generals and the 'Gambler' Chen Shui-Bian". Cable from the US Embassy, Singapore, 19 October 2007. *Public Library of US Diplomacy.* https://wikileaks.org/plusd/cables/07SINGAPORE1932_a.html.

"Military Intelligence-Affiliated Media Shut Down". Cable from the US Embassy, Rangoon, 20 October 2004. *Public Library of US Diplomacy.* https://wikileaks.org/plusd/cables/04RANGOON1366_a.html.

"NLD in Central Burma: Treading Water". Cable from the US Embassy, Rangoon, 6 July 2006. *Public Library of US Diplomacy.* https://wikileaks.org/plusd/cables/06RANGOON946_a.html.

"No Big Power Struggle Behind Customs Arrests". Cable from the US Embassy, Rangoon, 16 January 2007. *Public Library of US Diplomacy.* https://wikileaks.org/plusd/cables/07RANGOON52_a.html.

"Parting Thoughts on Burma". Cable from the US Embassy, Rangoon, 4 August 2005. *Public Library of US Diplomacy.* https://wikileaks.org/plusd/cables/05RANGOON901_a.html.

"Rangoon Incidents/Anomalies". Cable from the US Embassy, Rangoon, 25 November 2013. *Public Library of US Diplomacy.* https://wikileaks.org/plusd/cables/03RANGOON1519_a.html.

"Scenesetter for Codel Webb to Burma". Cable from the US Embassy, Rangoon, 5 August 2009. *Public Library of US Diplomacy.* https://wikileaks.org/plusd/cables/09RANGOON494_a.html.

"The Burmese Regime Airs its Dirty Laundry: Former PM 'Corrupt and Insubordinate'". Cable from the US Embassy, Rangoon, 12 November 2004. *Public Library of US Diplomacy.* https://wikileaks.org/plusd/cables/04RANGOON1462_a.html.

Books, Reports and Research Monographs

66(d): No Real Change: An Analysis of Complaints Made Before and After the 2017 Amendment. Yangon?: Free Expression Myanmar, December 2017.

A Choice for China: Ending the Destruction of Burma's Northern Frontier Forests. A Briefing Document by Global Witness, Bangkok, October 2005.

Adams, James. *Sellout: Aldrich Ames and the Corruption of the CIA*. New York: Viking, 1995.

Aldrich, Richard J. *The Hidden Hand: Britain, America and Cold War Secret Intelligence*. Woodstock: Overlook Press, 2001.

Andrew, Christopher. *The Secret World: A History of Intelligence*. London: Allen Lane, 2018.

Andrew, Christopher and Visili Mitrokhin. *The World Was Going Our Way: The KGB and the Battle for the Third World*. New York: Basic Books, 2005.

Anti-Money Laundering and Counter-Terrorist Financing Measures: Myanmar: Mutual Evaluation Report. Bangkok: Asia/Pacific Group on Money Laundering, September 2018.

Aung San Suu Kyi. *Letters from Burma*. London: Penguin, 1996.

Bader, Julia. *China's Foreign Relations and the Survival of Autocracies*. London: Routledge, 2015.

Ball, Desmond. *Burma's Military Secrets: Signals Intelligence (SIGINT) from 1941 to Cyber Warfare*. Bangkok: White Lotus, 1998.

———. *Security Developments in the Thailand-Burma Borderlands*. Working Paper No. 9. Sydney: Australian Mekong Resource Centre, University of Sydney, October 2003.

Bo Tun Kyi (Monywa). *My Experiences Over Fifty Years*. Yangon: Moe Ywae, 2010 (in Burmese).

Bullets in the Alms Bowl: An Analysis of the Brutal SPDC Suppression of the September 2007 Saffron Revolution. Washington D.C.?: NCGUB, March 2008.

Burma: Human Rights Yearbook 2008. Washington D.C.: Human Rights Documentation Unit, National Coalition Government of the Union of Burma, 2009.

Burma: Repeal Section 66(d) of the 2013 Telecommunications Law. New York: Human Rights Watch, 29 June 2017.

Burma's Prisons and Labour Camps: Silent Killing Fields. Mae Sot: Assistance Association for Political Prisoners (Burma), 2009?

Burmese Women's Union and Assistance Association for Political Prisoners (Burma). *Women Political Prisoners in Burma*, September 2004.

Butwell, Richard. *U Nu of Burma.* Stanford: Stanford University Press, 1963.

Callahan, Mary P. *Making Enemies: War and State Building in Burma.* Ithaca: Cornell University Press, 2003.

Chapman, Alison. *The Burmese Spy Adventure Book.* London: Austin Macauley Publishers, 2018.

Charney, Michael W. *A History of Modern Burma.* Cambridge: Cambridge University Press, 2009.

Chee Soon Juan. *To Be Free: Stories from Asia's Struggle Against Oppression.* Clayton: Monash Asia Institute, 1999.

Cheesman, Nicholas. *Opposing the Rule of Law: How Myanmar's Courts Make Law and Order.* Cambridge: Cambridge University Press, 2015.

China's Role in Myanmar's Internal Conflicts. USIP Senior Study Group Report No. 1. Washington D.C.: United States Institute of Peace, September 2018.

Clinton, Hillary R. *Hard Choices.* London: Simon and Schuster, 2014.

Clymer, Kenton. *A Delicate Relationship: The United States and Burma/Myanmar Since 1945.* Ithaca: Cornell University Press, 2015.

Cockett, Richard. *Blood, Dreams and Gold: The Changing Face of Burma.* New Haven: Yale University Press, 2015.

Crackdown: Repression of the 2007 Protests in Burma. New York: Human Rights Watch, 22 September 2009.

Crimes in Burma: A Report by the International Human Rights Clinic at the Harvard Law School. Cambridge: Harvard Law School, 2009.

Current Realities and Future Possibilities in Burma/Myanmar: Options for U.S. Policy. Asia Society Task Force Report. New York: Asia Society, March 2010.

Dahlberg, Keith. *Bridge Ahead: A Medical Memoir.* New York: iUniverse, 2008.

Dashed Hopes: The Criminalization of Free Expression in Myanmar. New York: Human Rights Watch, 31 January 2019.

Deacon, Richard. *A History of the Chinese Secret Service.* London: Frederick Muller, 1974.

Decobert, Anne. *The Politics of Aid to Burma: A Humanitarian Struggle on the Thai-Burmese Border.* Oxford: Routledge, 2016.

Delang, Claudio O., ed. *Suffering in Silence: The Human Rights Nightmare of the Karen People of Burma.* Parkland: Universal Publishers and Karen Human Rights Group, 2000.

Dillon, Eva. *Spies in the Family: An American Spymaster, his Russian Crown Jewel, and the Friendship That Helped End the Cold War.* New York: Harper, 2017.

Dudley, Sandra H. *Materialising Exile: Material Culture and Embodied Experience Among Karenni Refugees in Thailand.* New York: Berghahn Books, 2010.

Eftimiades, Nicholas. *Chinese Intelligence Operations.* Annapolis: Naval Institute Press, 1994.

Egreteau, Renaud and Larry Jagan. *Soldiers and Diplomacy in Burma: Understanding the Foreign Relations of the Praetorian State.* Singapore: NUS Press/IRASEC, 2013.

Englehart, Neil A. *Sovereignty, State Failure and Human Rights: Petty Despots and Exemplary Villains.* London: Routledge, 2017.

Falco, Mathea. *Burma: Time for a Change: Report of an Independent Task Force Sponsored by the Council on Foreign Relations.* New York: Council on Foreign Relations Press, 2003.

Falla, Jonathan. *True Love and Bartholomew: Rebels on the Burmese Border.* Cambridge: Cambridge University Press, 1991.

Fink, Christina. *Living Silence in Burma: Surviving under Military Rule*, 2nd ed. London: Zed Books, 2009.

Foley, Matthew. *The Cold War and National Assertion in Southeast Asia: Britain, the United States and Burma, 1948-1962*. London: Routledge, 2010.

Gibson, Richard M. with Wenhua Chen. *The Secret Army: Chiang Kai-shek and the Drug Warlords of the Golden Triangle*. Singapore: John Wiley and Sons, 2011.

Gravers, Mikael. *Nationalism as Political Paranoia in Burma: An Essay on the Historical Practice of Power*. NIAS Report No. 11. Copenhagen: Nordic Institute of Asian Studies, 1993.

Haksar, Nandita. *Rogue Agent: How India's Military Intelligence Betrayed the Burmese Resistance*. New Delhi: Penguin, 2009.

Harn Lay. *Defiant Humour: The Best of Harn Lay's Cartoons from 'The Irrawaddy'*. Chiang Mai: Irrawaddy Publishing Group, 2006.

Hill, Cameron. *Defence Cooperation with Myanmar – Australia and Other Countries: A Quick Guide*. Research Paper Series, 2017-18. Canberra: Parliamentary Library, Parliament of Australia, 13 October 2017.

Horsey, Richard. *Ending Forced Labour in Myanmar: Engaging a Pariah Regime*. London: Routledge, 2011.

Horton, Guy. *Dying Alive: A Legal Assessment of Human Rights Violations in Burma*. Chiang Mai: Images Asia and the Netherlands Ministry for Development Cooperation, April 2005.

James, Helen. *Security and Sustainable Development in Myanmar*. London: Routledge, 2006.

Jeffrey, Keith. *MI6: The History of the Secret Intelligence Service, 1909-1949*. London: Bloomsbury, 2010.

Kaznacheev, Aleksandr. *Inside a Soviet Embassy: Experiences of a Russian Diplomat in Burma*. Philadelphia: Lippincott, 1962.

Khin Nyunt. *The Experiences of My Life*, volume 1. Yangon: Daw Maw Maw, 2015 (in Burmese).

———. *The Experiences of My Life*, volume 2. Yangon: Daw Maw Maw, 2016 (in Burmese).

———. *I, the Military Intelligence, SLORC and SPDC*. Yangon: Daw Maw Maw, 2017 (in Burmese).

———. *Secretary One*. Yangon: Daw Maw Maw, 2018 (in Burmese).

Kin Oung. *Who Killed Aung San?* Bangkok: White Lotus, 1996.

Kipgen, Nehginpao. *Democratisation of Myanmar*. New Delhi: Routledge, 2016.

Kipling, Rudyard. *Kim*. London: Penguin, 1989.

Kyi Pyar Chit Saw and Matthew Arnold. "Administering the State in Myanmar: An Overview of the General Administration Department". Discussion Paper No. 6. Yangon: Asia Foundation, October 2014.

Kyi Win Sein. *Me and the Generals of the Revolutionary Council: Memoirs of Turbulent Times in Myanmar*. Whitley Bay: Consilience Media, 2015.

Larkin, Emma. *Everything is Broken: A Tale of Catastrophe in Burma*. New York: Penguin, 2010.

———. *Finding George Orwell in Burma*. London: Granta, 2011.

Lee, Terence. *Defect or Defend: Military Responses to Popular Protests in Authoritarian Asia*. Baltimore: Johns Hopkins University Press, 2015.

Len, Christopher and Johan Alvin. *Burma/Myanmar's Ailments: Searching for the Right Remedy*. Silk Road Paper. Washington D.C.: Central Asia – Caucasus Institute and Silk Road Studies Program, March 2007.

Lintner, Bertil. *The Rise and Fall of the Communist Party of Burma (CPB)*. Ithaca: Southeast Asia Program, Cornell University, 1990.

———. *The Resistance of the Monks: Buddhism and Activism in Burma*. New York: Human Rights Watch, 22 September 2009.

Lowenthal, Mark M. *Intelligence: From Secrets to Policy*. Los Angeles: Sage, 2012.

Marshall, Andrew. *The Trouser People: A Story of Burma – In the Shadow of Empire*. Washington D.C.: Counterpoint, 2002.

Maung Aung Myoe. *The Road to Naypyitaw: Making Sense of the Myanmar Government's Decision to Move its Capital*. Working Paper Series No. 79. Singapore: Asia Research Institute, National University of Singapore, November 2006.

———. *Building the Tatmadaw: Myanmar Armed Forces Since 1948*. Singapore: Institute of Southeast Asian Studies, 2009.

Maung Maung. *The 1988 Uprising in Burma*. Monograph No. 49. New Haven: Yale Southeast Asia Studies, 1999.

McCargo, Duncan and Ukrist Pathmanand. *The Thaksinization of Thailand*. Copenhagen: NIAS Press, 2005.

McClelland, Mac. *For Us Surrender is Out of the Question: A Story from Burma's Never-ending War*. Berkeley: Soft Skull Press, 2010.

Midnight Intrusions: Ending Guest Registration and Household Inspections in Myanmar. Bangkok: Fortify Rights, March 2015.

Moe Zay Nyein. *What's Swann Ar Shin and Other Articles*. Yangon: Ma Hla Hla Win, 2014 (in Burmese).

Mya Maung. *The Burma Road to Poverty*. New York: Praeger, 1991.

———. *Totalitarianism in Burma: Prospects for Economic Development*. New York: Paragon House, 1992.

Myanmar: "All the Civilians Suffer": Conflict, Displacement and Abuse in Northern Myanmar. AI Index ASA 16/6429/2017. London: Amnesty International, 14 June 2017.

Myanmar: "In the National Interest": Prisoners of Conscience, Torture, Summary Trials under Martial Law. AI Index ASA 16/101/1990. London: Amnesty International, 1990.

Myanmar: Justice on Trial. AI Index ASA 16/019/2003. London: Amnesty International, 2003.

Myanmar: "My World is Finished". Rohingya Targeted in Crimes Against Humanity in Myanmar. AI Index ASA 16/7288/2017. London: Amnesty International, 18 October 2017.

Myanmar: The Administration of Justice – Grave and Abiding Concerns. AI Index ASA 16/001/2004. London: Amnesty International, 2004.

Myanmar: The Military Regime's View of the World. Asia Report No. 28. Yangon/Brussels: International Crisis Group, 7 December 2001.

Myanmar Tips into New Crisis after Rakhine State Attacks. Yangon/Brussels: International Crisis Group, 27 August 2017.

Myanmar's "Nasaka": Disbanding an Abusive Agency. Yangon/Brussels: International Crisis Group, 16 July 2013.

Nanda, Prakash. *Rediscovering Asia: Evolution of India's Look-East Policy*. New Delhi: Lancer Publications, 2003.

Nang Zing La. *Life in Burma Military Prisons: Memoir of Pro-Democracy Advocate Nang Zing La*. Pittsburgh: RoseDog Books, 2005.

Paseman, Floyd L. *A Spy's Journey*. St. Paul: Zenith Press, 2004.

Pedersen, Morten B. *Promoting Human Rights in Burma: A Critique of Western Sanctions Policy*. Lanham: Rowman and Littlefield, 2008.

Popham, Peter. *Perfect Hostage: A Life of Aung San Suu Kyi*. London: Hutchinson, 2007.

———. *The Lady and the Peacock: The Life of Aung San Suu Kyi*. London: Rider, 2011.

Preliminary Report of the Ad hoc Commission on Depayin Massacre (Burma), July 4, 2003. Bangkok: National Council of the Union of Burma and the Burma Lawyers' Council, 2004.

Pye, Lucian W. *The Spirit of Burmese Politics: A Preliminary Survey of a Politics of Fear and Charisma*. Cambridge: Centre for International Studies, Massachusetts Institute of Technology, 1959.

Raman, Bahukutumbi. *The Kaoboys of R&AW: Down Memory Lane*. New Delhi: Lancer Publications, 2007.

Rand, Nelson. *Conflict: Journeys Through War and Terror in Southeast Asia*. Dunboyne: Maverick House, 2009.

Reforming Telecommunications in Burma: Human Rights and Responsible Investment in Mobile and the Internet. New York: Human Rights Watch, 2013.

Report of the Independent International Fact-finding Mission on Myanmar. United Nations Human Rights Council, A/HRC/39/64, Geneva, 12 September 2018.

Report of the Special Rapporteur on the Situation of Human Rights in Myanmar, Yanghee Lee. United Nations General Assembly, Human Rights Council, A/HRC/28/72, Geneva, 23 March 2015.

Roberts, T.D. et al. *Area Handbook for Burma*. Washington D.C.: US Government Printing Office, June 1968.

Rogers, Benedict. *Than Shwe: Unmasking Burma's Tyrant*. Chiang Mai: Silkworm Books, 2010.

———. *Burma: A Nation at the Crossroads*. London: Ebury Publishing, 2015.

Sawer, Marian, Norman Abjorensen, and Philip Larkin. *Australia: The State of Democracy*. Sydney: Federation Press, 2009.

Schrank, Delphine. *Rebel of Rangoon: A Tale of Defiance and Deliverance in Burma*. New York: Nation Books, 2015.

Seekins, Donald M. *Historical Dictionary of Burma (Myanmar)*. Lanham: Scarecrow Press, 2006.

Selth, Andrew. *Burma's Intelligence Apparatus*. Working Paper No. 308. Canberra: Strategic and Defence Studies Centre, Australian National University, 1997.

———. *Burma's Secret Military Partners*. Canberra Papers on Strategy and Defence No. 136. Canberra: Strategic and Defence Studies Centre, Australian National University, 2000.

———. *Burma's Armed Forces: Power Without Glory*. Norwalk: EastBridge, 2002.

———. *Burma and the Threat of Invasion: Regime Fantasy or Strategic Reality?* Regional Outlook No. 17. Brisbane: Griffith Asia Institute, Griffith University, 2008.

———. *Burma's Coco Islands: Rumours and Realities in the Indian Ocean*. Working Paper No. 101. Hong Kong: Southeast Asia Research Centre, City University of Hong Kong, November 2008.

———. *Police Reform in Burma (Myanmar): Aims, Obstacles and Outcomes*. Regional Outlook No. 44. Brisbane: Griffith Asia Institute, Griffith University, 2013.

———. *Myanmar's Armed Forces and the Rohingya Crisis*. Peaceworks No. 140. Washington D.C.: United States Institute of Peace, 2018.

Skidmore, Monique. *Karaoke Fascism: Burma and the Politics of Fear*. Philadelphia: University of Pennsylvania Press, 2004.

Smith, Martin. *State of Fear: Censorship in Burma (Myanmar)*. An Article 19 Country Report. London: Article 19, December 1991.

Steinberg, David I. *Burma: The State of Myanmar*. Washington D.C.: Georgetown University Press, 2001.

———. *Turmoil in Burma: Contested Legitimacies in Myanmar*. Norwalk: EastBridge, 2006.

———. *Burma/Myanmar: What Everyone Needs to Know*. Oxford: Oxford University Press, 2013.

Taylor, Robert H. *General Ne Win: A Political Biography*. Singapore: Institute of Southeast Asian Studies, 2015.

The Dark Side of Transition: Violence Against Muslims in Myanmar. Asia Report No. 251. Yangon/Jakarta/Brussels: International Crisis Group, 1 October 2013.

The Darkness We See: Torture in Burma's Interrogation Centres and Prisons. Mae Sot: Assistance Association for Political Prisoners (Burma), 2005.

The Myanmar Elections: Results and Implications. Asia Briefing No. 147. Yangon/Brussels: International Crisis Group, 9 December 2015.

The Right to Privacy in Myanmar: Stakeholder Report, Universal Periodic Review, 23rd Session – Myanmar. London: Privacy International, March 2015.

The White Shirts: How the USDA Will Become the New Face of Burma's Dictatorship. Mae Sot: Network for Democracy and Development, May 2006.

"They Can Arrest You at Any Time": The Criminalisation of Peaceful Expression in Burma. New York: Human Rights Watch, 29 June 2016.

Thornton, Phil. *Restless Souls: Rebels, Refugees, Medics and Misfits on the Thai-Burma Border*. Bangkok: Asia Books, 2006.

Tinker, Hugh. *The Union of Burma: A Study of the First Years of Independence*. London: Oxford University Press, 1957.

Tinsa Maw-Naing and Y.M.V. Han. *A Burmese Heart*. US: Y.M.V. Han, 2015.

Todd, Paul and Jonathan Bloch. *Global Intelligence: The World's Secret Services Today*. Bangkok: White Lotus, 2003.

Toohey, Brian and William Pinwill. *Oyster: The Story of the Australian Secret Intelligence Service*. Melbourne: William Heinemann, 1989.

Tortured Voices: Personal Accounts of Burma's Interrogation Centres. Bangkok: All Burma Students' Democratic Front, 1998.

Valentine, Douglas. *The Phoenix Program*. New York: Morrow, 1990.

Victor, Barbara. *The Lady: Aung San Suu Kyi, Nobel Laureate and Burma's Prisoner*. Chiang Mai: Silkworm Books, 1998.

Vote to Nowhere: The May 2008 Constitutional Referendum in Burma. New York: Human Rights Watch, 30 April 2008.

Wallechinsky, David. *Tyrants: The World's 20 Worst Living Dictators*. New York: Regan, 2006.

Walton, Calder. *Empire of Secrets: British Intelligence, the Cold War and the Twilight of Empire*. London: Harper Press, 2013.

Wilson, Trevor. *Eyewitness to Early Reform in Myanmar*. Canberra: Australian National University Press, 2016.

Wise, David and Thomas B. Ross. *The Invisible Government*. London: Jonathan Cape, 1964.

Ye Htut. "A Background to the Security Crisis in Northern Rakhine". *ISEAS Perspective*, no. 2017/79, 23 October 2017.

Zollner, Hans-Bernd and Rodion Ebbighausen. *The Daughter: A Political Biography of Aung San Suu Kyi*. Chiang Mai: Silkworm, 2018.

Book Chapters and Major Articles

Aung-Thwin, Maureen. "Burma: Plus ça Change". In *Asian Security Handbook: Terrorism and the New Security Environment*, edited by William M. Carpenter and David G. Wiencek. London: M.E. Sharpe, 2005.

Barany, Zoltan. "Burma: Suu Kyi's Missteps". *Journal of Democracy* 29, no. 1 (January 2018).

Bert, Wayne. "Burma, China and the USA". *Pacific Affairs* 77, no. 2 (Summer 2004).

Betts, Richard K. "Analysis, War and Decision: Why Intelligence Failures are Inevitable". *World Politics* 31, no. 1 (October 1978).

Callahan, Mary P. "Junta Dreams or Nightmares? Observations of Burma's Military since 1988". *Bulletin of Concerned Asian Scholars* 31, no. 3 (1999).

"Chapter 4.4, Surveillance: Lawful Interception & Other Surveillance Methods". *ICT Sector-Wide Impact Assessment*. Yangon: Myanmar Centre for Responsible Business, 24 September 2015.

Clapp, Priscilla A. "Burma: Poster Child for Entrenched Repression". In *Worst of the Worst: Dealing with Repressive and Rogue Nations*, edited by Robert I. Rotberg. Cambridge and Washington D.C.: World Peace Foundation and Brookings Institution, 2007.

Dean, Karin. "Myanmar: Surveillance and the Turn from Authoritarianism?" *Surveillance and Society* 15, no. 3/4 (2017).

Dukalskis, Alexander and Christopher D. Raymond. "Failure of Authoritarian Learning: Explaining Burma/Myanmar's Electoral System". *Democratization* 25, no. 3 (November 2017).

Englehart, Neil A. "Two Cheers for Burma's Rigged Election". *Political Science Faculty Publications* 1 (2012).

Guyot, James T. and John Badgley. "Myanmar in 1989: Tatmadaw V". *Asian Survey* 30, no. 2 (February 1990).

Hariharan, R. "Burma (Myanmar): Why the Prime Minister was Sacked?" *South Asia Analysis Group*, Paper No. 1150, 25 October 2004.

Houtman, Gustaaf. "Remaking Myanmar and Human Origins". *Anthropology Today* 15, no. 4 (August 1999).

Jagan, Larry. "Myanmar Looks to ASEAN First for Its Future". In *Myanmar: Reintegrating into the International Community*, edited by Li Chenyang, Chaw Chaw Sein and Zhu Xianghui. Singapore: World Scientific Publishing, 2016.

James, Helen. "Myanmar in 2005: In a Holding Pattern". *Asian Survey* 46, no. 1 (January/February 2006).

Kyaw Yin Hlaing. "Myanmar in 2004: Why Military Rule Continues". In *Southeast Asian Affairs 2005*, edited by Daljit Singh and Liak Teng Kiat. Singapore: Institute of Southeast Asian Studies, 2005.

———. "Challenging the Authoritarian State: Buddhist Monks and Peaceful Protests in Burma". *The Fletcher Forum of World Affairs* 38, no. 1 (Winter 2008).

———. "The State of the Pro-Democracy Movement in Authoritarian Myanmar/Burma". In *Myanmar/Burma: Challenges and Perspectives*, edited by Xiaolin Guo. Stockholm: Institute for Security and Development Policy, 2008.

Leehey, Jennifer. "Writing in a Crazy Way: Literary Life in Contemporary Urban Burma". In *Burma at the Turn of the 21st Century*, edited by Monique Skidmore. Honolulu: University of Hawaii Press, 2005.

Li Chenyang. "The Policies of China and India toward Myanmar". In *Myanmar/Burma: Inside Challenges, Outside Interests*, edited by Lex Rieffel. Washington D.C.: Brookings Institution Press, 2010.

Mathieson, David S. "The Burma Road to Nowhere: The Failure of the Developmental State in Myanmar". *Policy, Organisation and Society* 17, no. 7 (1999).

Matthews, Bruce. "Burma/Myanmar: Government *A La Mode* – From SLORC to SPDC: A Change of Public Dress-Up and Manner?" *The Round Table* 349 (January 1999).

McCarthy, Stephen. "Burma and ASEAN: Estranged Bedfellows". *Asian Survey* 48, no. 6 (November/December 2008).

Min Zin. "Anti-Muslim Violence in Burma – Why Now?" *Social Research* 82, no. 2 (Summer 2015).

Seekins, Donald M. "Burma in 1998: Little to Celebrate". *Asian Survey* 39, no. 1 (1999).

Selth, Andrew. "SLORC's 'Intel-Net': Burma's Intelligence Apparatus". *Burma Debate* 4, no. 4 (October 1997).

———. "Burma's Intelligence Apparatus". *Intelligence and National Security* 13, no. 4 (Winter 1998).

———. "Burma, China and the Myth of Military Bases". *Asian Security* 3, no. 3 (2007).

———. "Burma's 'Saffron Revolution' and the Limits of International Influence". *Australian Journal of International Affairs* 62, no. 3 (September 2008).

———. "Even Paranoids Have Enemies: Cyclone Nargis and Myanmar's Fears of Invasion". *Contemporary Southeast Asia* 30, no. 3 (2008).

———. "Known Knowns and Known Unknowns: Measuring Myanmar's Military Capabilities". *Contemporary Southeast Asia* 31, no. 2 (August 2009).

———. "Police Reform and the 'Civilianisation' of Security in Myanmar". In *Law, Society and Transition in Myanmar*, edited by Melissa Crouch and Tim Lindsey. Oxford: Hart Publishing, 2014.

———. "Myanmar's Coercive Apparatus: The Long Road to Reform". In *Myanmar: The Dynamics of an Evolving Polity*, edited by David I. Steinberg. Boulder: Lynne Rienner, 2015.

———. "All Going According to Plan? The Armed Forces and Government in Myanmar". *Contemporary Southeast Asia* 40, no. 1 (April 2018).

———. "Myanmar: An Enduring Intelligence State, or a State Enduring Intelligence?" In *Handbook of Asian Intelligence Communities*, edited by Bob de Graaff. Boulder: Lynne Rienner, 2019.

Skidmore, Monique. "Scholarship, Advocacy and the Politics of Engagement in Burma". In *Engaged Observer: Anthropology, Advocacy and Activism*, edited by Victoria Sandford and Asale Angel-Ajani. New Brunswick: Rutgers University Press, 2006.

Smith, Martin. "Army Politics as a Historical Legacy: The Experience of Burma". In *Political Armies: The Military and National Building in the Age of Democracy*, edited by Kees Koonings and Dirk Kruijt. London: Zed, 2002.

Steinberg, David I. "Legitimacy in Burma/Myanmar: Concepts and Implications". In *Myanmar: State, Society and Ethnicity*, edited by N. Ganesan and Kyaw Yin Hlaing. Singapore: Institute of Southeast Asian Studies, 2007.

Taylor, Robert H. "The Military in Myanmar (Burma): What Scope for a New Role?" In *The Military, the State, and Development in Asia and the Pacific*, edited by Viberto Selochan. Boulder: Westview Press, 1991.

———. "'One Day, One Fathom, Bagan Won't Move': On the Myanmar Road to a Constitution". In *Myanmar's Long Road to National Reconciliation*, edited by Trevor Wilson. Singapore: Institute of Southeast Asian Studies, 2006.

Thompson, Rhys. "'Underground Banking' and Myanmar's Changing Hundi System". *Journal of Money Laundering Control* 22, no. 2 (2019).

Thornton, Phil. "'Big Brain' on the Border". In *Insurgent Intellectual: Essays in Honour of Professor Desmond Ball*, edited by Brendan Taylor, Nicholas Farrelly and Sheryn Lee. Singapore: Institute of Southeast Asian Studies, 2012.

Tin Maung Maung Than. "Burma in 1983: From Recovery to Growth?" In *Southeast Asian Affairs 1984*, edited by Pushpa Thambipillai. Singapore: Institute of Southeast Asian Studies, 1984.

———. "Myanmar: Myanmar-ness and Realism in Historical Perspective". In *Strategic Cultures in the Asia-Pacific Region*, edited by Ken Booth and Russell Trood. London: Macmillan, 1999.

———. "Tatmadaw and Myanmar's Security Challenges". In *Asia Pacific Countries' Security Outlook and its Implications for the Defence Sector*. Tokyo: National Institute for Defence Studies, 2010.

Turnell, Sean. "Banking and Financial Regulation and Reform in Myanmar". *Journal of Southeast Asian Economies* 31, no. 2 (August 2014).

Walinsky, Louis J. "The Rise and Fall of U Nu". *Pacific Affairs* 38, no. 3/4 (Autumn 1965–Winter 1965–66).

Wark, Wesley K. "Introduction". In *Security and Intelligence in a Changing World: New Perspectives for the 1990s*, edited by A. Stuart Farson, David Stafford and Wesley K. Wark. London: Frank Cass and Co., 1991.

Win Min. "Internal Dynamics of the Burmese Military: Before, During and After the 2007 Demonstrations". In *Dictatorship, Disorder and Decline in Myanmar*, edited by Monique Skidmore and Trevor Wilson. Canberra: ANU E Press, 2008.

———. "Looking Inside the Burmese Military". *Asian Survey* 48, no. 6 (November/December 2008).

Unpublished Sources

Ebara, Miki. "The Fall of Military Intelligence Under Khin Nyunt: An Analysis of Power Dynamics in Myanmar". Thesis submitted in partial fulfilment of the requirements for the Degree of Master of Arts Program in Southeast Asian Studies (Inter-Department), Graduate School, Chulalongkorn University, Bangkok, 2005.

Ei Ei Zaw. "A Study on the Changing Role of Myanmar Police Force". Unpublished thesis submitted to Yangon University for the degree of MRes in History, History Department, Yangon, 31 May 2002.

McAndrew, James. "From Combat to Karaoke: Burmese Military Intelligence, 1948–2006". Unclassified thesis submitted to the faculty of the National Defence College in partial fulfilment of the requirements for the degree of Master of Science of Strategic Intelligence, Washington D.C., March 2007.

INDEX

Note: Page numbers followed by "n" refer to endnotes.

A
accountability, 197–202
Action Committee Against Corruption in 2013, 125
agents provocateurs, 117
AIU, 22
Amnesty International, 14, 20, 104n21, 130, 134
amphetamine, 124
analytical failures, 158–62
Andrew, Christopher, 158, 159
Anti-Corruption Act, 51n119, 125
Anti-Corruption Commission, 125
Anti-Money Laundering Law, 125–26, 141n37
anti-Muslim violence, 152–57
anti-narcotics operations, 26, 182
anti-Rangoon activists, 14–15
Arakan Army (AA), 153, 154, 163n8
Arakan Rohingya Salvation Army (ARSA), 155–57
archaeological excavations, 42n52
ASEAN meeting, 41n44
ASEAN Military Intelligence Informal Meeting (AMIIM) forum, 183
ASEAN Regional Forum (ARF), 41n44, 183
Asia Foundation, 31
Asia-Pacific Defence Reporter, 127
Asia Society, 179
Association of Southeast Asian Nations (ASEAN), 3, 15, 41n44, 121, 183, 184, 209
Assistance Association for Political Prisoners, 14
Aung San Suu Kyi
  biography of, 20
  briefings, 199–200
  challenges, 198
  country's surveillance network, 121
  country's survival, 209
  foreign operations, 172
  guest checks, 33
  house arrest of, 99, 110n86
  landslide election victory, 197

233

NLD administration, 113, 205
Nobel Peace Prize, 37n9
office in March 2016, 197–98
"personal" theory, 63
police surveillance and monitoring, 133
"policy" theory, 62
political crimes, 200–201
reformist agenda, 202
relationship with armed forces, 199
Rohingya crisis, 161
surveillance of the opposition NLD, 11
unauthorized visit, 179
USDA militia members attacking, 70
Australia, 174, 177, 178, 180, 182
Australian ambassador, in Yangon, 69, 79n73

B

Bagan Cybertech, 18, 86–87
Ball, Desmond, 45n78, 177, 180
Bangladesh, 19, 38n17, 88, 101, 137, 154, 156, 157, 172, 177, 180
Baw Bi Doh, 46n79
blacklist, 3, 13, 131, 144n66
black market deals, 64
bomb attacks, 112n102
  after high profile figure death, 137–38
  in former capital, 121
  in population centres, 117
  in Sittwe, 157
  at Thai trade fair, 92
  against visiting South Korean president, 2
Border Area Immigration Control Command, 32
Border Area Trade Directorate, 88
Border Commerce, 105n28
Border Guard Police (BGP), 155, 156
British colonial administration, 207
Bureau of Special Investigation (BSI), 20, 27, 28, 30, 51n119, 67, 96, 100, 119, 121, 125, 199
Burma Branch, 189n42
Burma Lawyers Council, 103n8
Burma Socialist Programme Party (BSPP), xiii, 32, 103n9

C

Callahan, Mary, 5n8, 16–17
Canada, 174, 178
"caretaker" government, 32, 205
ceasefires, 16, 61, 85–86, 99, 116
Central Control Board on Money Laundering, 94
Central Executive Committee (CEC), 94
Central Intelligence Agency (CIA), 4, 20, 55n156, 92, 175, 176, 177, 178, 179, 181, 188n27, 188n31, 193n74

Charge d'Affaires, 71, 80n83, 139n17
Chief of Intelligence (CI), 2, 5n6, 8, 14, 25, 26, 30, 57, 65, 84, 85, 98, 103n9, 125, 175, 181, 199
Chin, 132
China, 3, 6n12, 15, 19, 56, 59, 62, 68, 85, 136, 137, 153, 160, 171, 172, 177, 178, 179, 180, 182, 191n61, 209
China's intelligence services, 177
civilian agencies, 2, 201
civilianization, 114
civilian-military rule, 205
Clinton, Hillary, 171
colonial-era manuals, 50n109
communications intelligence (COMINT), 135
Communist Party of Burma (CPB), 153, 177
Computer Science Development Law (1996), 18
Control of Money Laundering Law (2002), 93
counterespionage concerns, 175–79
Counterintelligence Department, 117
counter-intelligence group, 74n20
Criminal Investigation Department (CID)
  manuals, 50n109
  responsibilities, 26–27
  during turbulent period, 124

cyber attack, 101
cyber-crime unit, Russian-trained, 43n63
Cyber Warfare Centre, 18, 22
Cyclone Nargis, in 2008, 118, 168n48, 172

D

Dam Byan Byaut Kya, 20, 45n78
"data thief" project, 101
death squad, 20
Defence Services Academy (DSA), 63, 75n34
Defence Services Computer Directorate, 43n62
Defence Services Intelligence Bureau (DSIB), 21–22
Defence Services Intelligence Collection Training School, 21
Defence Services Intelligence Support Depot, 21
Defence Services (Army) Officer Training School (OTS), 63
Democratic Karen Buddhist Army (DKBA), 86
Democratic Voice of Burma (DVB), 1, 93, 120
Depayin massacre, 70
diplomatic missions, 2, 38n17, 171–75, 176–79, 180–83, 199
Directorate of Defence Services Intelligence (DDSI), 8–9, 35n2, 82

armed forces, 12
brutal methods, 14
ceasefire groups, 86
coercive muscle, 18
combat power, 24
domestic servants, 12
headquarters, 9–10
hit squad, 14
information warfare, 19
intercept capabilities, 43n61
investigation, 13–14
involvement in arrests, 13–14
IT training, 18
Ministry of Defence, 35n2
Myanmar Army's Signal Corsps, 18
National League for Democracy, 11
paramilitary operations, 20
"pillage" theory, 64
plain clothes operations, 6n10
Research and Information Unit, 21
surveillance capabilities, 29
surveillance operations, 39n25
training centre, 9
discipline-flourishing democracy, 48n94, 57, 89, 102, 151, 205
domestic servants, 12
double agents, 117

E

Ebara, Miki, 23, 36n8
economic crimes, 69, 78n57
Einsatzgruppen death squads, 45n78
Eleven Media, 122
Emma Larkin, 68, 133
"enemies of the state", 3
Essential Services and Supply Act (1947), 51n119
ethnic armed groups (EAGs), 10, 16, 62, 63, 85, 87, 92, 99, 137, 201
ethnic minorities, 11
  Chin, 132
  Kachin, 132
  Karen, 92, 132, 178
  Rohingya, 33, 39n25, 75n35, 132, 137, 156, 161, 164n18
  Shan, 132
European Union, 180
Export and Import Supervision (Temporary) Act (1948), 51n119

F

Federal Bureau of Investigation (FBI), 4, 203n10
fibre-optic military communications network, 100, 111n92
Financial Action Task Force, 126
Financial Intelligence Division, 126
Foreign Exchange Regulation Act (1948), 51n119

foreign observers, 12, 164n18, 198–99
foreign operations, 171–75
foreign relationships
  counterespionage concerns, 175–79
  foreign operations, 171–75
  intelligence cooperation, 179–84
Forum for Democracy, 96
Freedom of Information Act, 6n10

G

General Administration Department (GAD), 31, 129
General Directorate for External Security, 175
German Democratic Republic's (GDR) notorious secret police, 35
Germany, 55n155, 174
Gestapo, 34–35, 55n155
Global New Light of Myanmar, 19, 44n73, 57, 207
GRU, 176

H

hackers, 135–36
hit squad, 14
Home Affairs Minister, 121
Houtman, Gustaaf, 13
Htane Chan Mhu, 53n142
Htein Chan Hmu, 32

human intelligence (HUMINT), 134–35, 208
human rights violations, 131–38
Human Rights Watch, 31, 95–96, 128, 130

I

imagery intelligence (IMINT), 6n12, 136, 208
India, 6n12, 38n17, 88, 101, 154, 171, 172, 177
India's Research and Analysis Wing (RAW), 175, 177, 189n42
Indonesia, 67, 177
information warfare, 3
informers, 89, 96, 117
  around Rohingya villages, 156
  in neighbouring countries, 3
  paid, 11, 23
  recruitment, 99
  unpaid, 2, 6n14, 11, 23
Inland Security Ministry, 102
Insein Gaol, 12–13
intelligence agencies, 25–30, 98, 151
  brutal methods, 14
  concerns and capabilities of, 12
  cooperation with MPF, 181
  development, 3
  Maung Aye, 24
  Min Aung Hlaing, 119
  Moe Zay Nyein, 118

private, 74n20
stories about, 137
structure and inner dynamics of, 208
transnational crime, 183
unpaid informers, 6n14
Intelligence Branch (IB), 26
Intelligence Bureau of the Ministry of National Defence (IBMND), 176
intelligence cooperation, 179–84
intelligence developments
    behavioural changes, 130–38
    Thein Sein's quasi-civilian government, 113
intelligence failures, 152
    analytical failures, 158–62
    operational failures, 152–57
intelligence state, 206
Internal Department, 116
internal security, 114, 122
International Crisis Group (ICG), 15–17
international radio services, 1
international terrorism, 39n25, 181, 183
investigation techniques, 182
investigative units, 2, 8, 28
Israel, 3, 19, 181, 182

J

journalists
    chemical weapons plant, 179
    drawn up by intelligence agents, 13
    freedoms, 134
    telephone tapping, 101
    Thai, 121
    visiting Myanmar, 12, 70, 136

K

Kachin, 61, 132
Kachin Independence Army (KIA), 153, 154, 163n8, 177
Karen, 11, 15, 20, 37n15, 92, 132, 178
Karen Human Rights Group, 20
Karen National Liberation Army (KNLA), 20
Karen National Union (KNU), 15, 20, 92, 190n46
KGB, 4, 35, 55n156, 175
    budget, 176–77
Khin Nyunt, 2, 5n6, 8–9
    apology for arrogance and disrespect, 75n32
    archaeological excavations, 42n52
    arrest, 20–21, 62, 66–68, 107n58
    ceasefires, 16, 85–86
    corruption at Pang Hpak Man checkpoint, 59
    discipline-flourishing democracy, 48n94, 89
    economic espionage, 174
    insubordination, 63, 68

intelligence agency, 98
intelligence empire, destroying, 82
IT training, 18
journals and magazines licence, 86
Muse corruption case, 60–61, 64–65
Ne Win's arrest and death, 59
OCMSA's influence, 91
offences committed by, 57–58
Office of Strategic Studies, 15
operational capabilities, 30
OSS, 17
personal astrologer, 160
"personal" theory, 63
"pillage" theory, 64
"policy" theory, 62
"power" theory, 62–63
press briefing in 1997, 12
promotion, 25, 41n42
retirement, 56–57
rumours after arrest, 87–88
secret shadow organization, 24
Special Branch, 26
special tribunal, 68
successor as Prime Minister, 85
Kim (Kipling), 13
Ko Ni, 154–55, 165n22
Kuomintang, 171
Kyaw Swe, 95, 120, 155
Kyaw Win, 25, 69
Kyaw Yin Hlaing, 64, 83, 97, 98
Kyemon, 207

L
Laos, 172
Larkin, Emma, 50n110
Law and Order Restoration Councils (LORCs), 31
Levin, Burton, 80n82
Light Infantry Division (LID), 2, 10, 157

M
MaBaTha, 130, 152
mafia-like operation, 64
Maung Aung Myoe, 176, 187n25
Maung Aye, 24, 59, 75n34, 95
 appointment of, 85
 destroying Khin Nyunt's intelligence empire, 82
 "personal" theory, 63–64
 "policy" theory, 62
 secret intelligence group, 60
Maung Lwin, 103n9
Maung Maung Soe, 154
Maung Yin Hmaing, 44n73
MaWaTa, 52n135
MaYaKa, 52n135
McAndrew, James, 22, 23, 36n4
memoranda of understanding (MOU), 183
midnight inspections law, 127
Military Affairs Security (MAS), 82, 90, 99, 120
military communications systems, 118

military development budget, 2, 5n7
military dictatorship, 205
Military Intelligence (MI), xvi, 4, 6n11, 14, 83, 86, 87, 88, 118, 127, 153, 198
Military Intelligence Sections, 9, 35n2
Military Intelligence Service (MIS). See Directorate of Defence Services Intelligence (DDSI)
Military Operation Commands. See Operation Control Commands (OCC)
military regime, ix, xiii, 12, 17, 33, 72, 80n82, 95, 97, 98, 132–34, 138, 159, 170, 172, 177, 198, 205
Military Security Affairs (MSA). See Office of the Chief of Military Security Affairs (OCMSA)
Military Security Force, 127
military-to-military exchanges, 184
Min Aung Hlaing, 119, 157, 183, 199
Ministry of Defence, 35n2
Ministry of Foreign Affairs (MFA), 15, 28
  Detectives Department, 29
  Special Branch, 51n125
Ministry of Home Affairs, 122, 124, 125

Ministry of Planning and Finance, 54n146
Ministry of Posts and Telecommunications (MPT), 29, 30
Mitchell, Derek, 80n82
Moe Zay Nyein, 115
  bombs in population centres, 117
  External Department, 118–19
  Technology Department, 117–18
money-laundering, 125–26
monk-led protests, 97
Mossad, 4, 194n79
MRTV, 56, 82
Myanmar
  foreigners visiting, 12
  independence, declaration of, 168
  information warfare, 3
  intelligence state, 206
  intelligence system. See intelligence agencies
  journalists visiting, 12
  military development budget, 2, 5n7
  North Korea constructing underground facilities in, 100
  satellite imagery, 3
  training provided by United Kingdom, 193n74

Index

Myanmar Army's Intelligence Corps, 83
Myanmar Army's Signal Corps, 18, 87
Myanmar Financial Intelligence Unit (MFIU), 93–94, 125–26
Myanmar Maternal and Child Welfare Association, 67
Myanmar National Democratic Alliance Army (MNDAA), 153, 163n8
Myanmar Police Force (MPF), 14, 43n62
  bomb attacks, 92
  Financial Intelligence Division, 126, 183
  importance of, 114
  intelligence agencies cooperation with, 181
  new military intelligence organization, 91–92
  NIB re-establishment, 122
  OCMI dismantling, 90
  Russian-trained cyber-crime unit, 43n63
  size and role of, 122
Myanmar Times, 19, 86, 122, 126, 178
Myanmar Women's Affairs Federation, 67
Mya Tun Oo, 115
Myint Hlaing, 59, 60
Myint Swe, 90, 95

N

Naga Min Operation, 75n35
narcotics, 116, 124, 176, 181
NaKaTha, 88
NaSaKa, 32–33, 54n147, 59–60
  dissolution of, 156
  Muse corruption case, 60–61
  "policy" theory, 62
  rumours after Khin Nyunt's arrest, 87–88
  smugglers, 86
NaSaYa, 33, 54n147
National Coalition Government of the Union of Burma (NCGUB), 41n39, 92
National Defence and Security Council (NDSC), 121, 200
National Defence and Security Force, 121
National Endowment for Democracy, 185n8
national financial intelligence units, 94
National Intelligence Bureau (NIB), 26, 52n130
  abolition, 83–84
  formal status, 29–30
  re-establishment, 120–22
National Intelligence Bureau Act, 14, 29, 30, 84
National League for Democracy (NLD), x, xiv, 11, 15, 20, 37n9, 41n39, 45, 70, 87, 94, 95, 100, 113, 129, 130, 134,

154, 197, 198, 200, 201, 205, 208
Naval Technical Training Unit, 193n74
NaWaTa, 52n135
Ne Win, 26, 78n60
   analytical failures, 159–60
   caretaker government, 32, 205
   country's isolation under, 171
   coup, 158
   under house arrest, 23, 59, 73n12
   Revolutionary Council, 29
   self-imposed isolation, 71
new security system, 120, 201
New Zealand, 178
NIU, 22
nuclear weapons programme, 100, 111n91

O

Office of Strategic Studies (OSS), 15–17
   academic seminars, 19
   archaeological excavations, 42n52
   ceasefire groups, 86
   combat power, 24
   Democratic Voice of Burma, 44n72
   information warfare, 19
   paramilitary operations, 20
   "pillage" theory, 64
   publicity-conscious, 42n55
   Truth, The, 20

Office of the Chief of Military Affairs Security (OCMAS). *See* Office of the Chief of Military Security Affairs (OCMSA)
Office of the Chief of Military Intelligence (OCMI), 22–23, 49n102, 82–83, 85
   agency's operational responsibilities, 115
   Bagan Cybertech, 86–87
   bombings, 138
   ceasefire groups, 86
   characterizing, 34–35
   collapsing BSI jurisdiction, 125
   combat power, 24
   control of information flows, 62
   "data thief" project, 101
   dismantling Myanmar Police Force, 90
   dismantling of, 89–90
   front trading company, 86
   in illegal economic activities, 57
   International Relations Department, 86
   Khin Nyunt's arrest, 69–70
   new military intelligence organization, 91
   "pillage" theory, 64
   surveillance capabilities, 29
   team visiting Hawaii, 181

Office of the Chief of Military Security Affairs (OCMSA), 90–91, 187n25
   agency's operational responsibilities, 115
   bomb attacks, 92
   bombs in population centres, 117
   disruption operations, 138
   economics intelligence branch, 174
   house arrest of Aung San Suu Kyi, 99
   Human Rights Watch, 95–96
   influence Khin Nyunt, 91
   Kyaw Swe, 120
   monitoring electronic coverage, 118
   Myint Swe replacement, 95
   narcotics production and distribution, 124
   new military intelligence organization, 91–92
   surveillance by new recruits, 93
Official Secrets Act, 179
Open Society organisation, 96
open source intelligence (OSINT), 28, 54n152, 199
operational failures, 152–57
Operation Control Commands (OCC), 10, 36n6
opiates, 124
Organisation of the Islamic Conference (OIC), 127

P

Padoh Mahn Shah, 15
patriotism, 154
PaWaTa, 52n135
Peace and Development Councils (PDCs), 31
People's Property Protection Police, 27
People's Police Force (PPF), 26, 50n109, 182
People's Property Protection Police, 27
People's Reporter system, 32
Phoenix Program, 20, 45n78
"pillage" theory, 64
Police Special Branch, 90
"policy" theory, 62
political crimes, 200–201
political police, 26
Political Situation of Myanmar and Its Role in the Region, 19
"power" theory, 62–63
Press Scrutiny Board, 86
preventative police, 126
Provincial Reconnaissance Units, 45n78
Public Properties Protection Act (1947), 51n119

R

Radio Free Asia, 1
real-time intelligence, 180
Regional Control Commands (RCC), 10, 36n6

regional military commands (RMC), 9, 10, 20, 36n5, 47n92, 76n40
Reporters Without Borders (RSF), 127
resident diplomats, 11, 176
Revolutionary Council, 29
Rohingya, x, 12, 33, 39n25, 75n35, 132, 135, 137, 156, 164n18, 180
Rohingya crisis, 161, 184, 208
Royal Thai Police, 14–15, 173
Russian-trained cyber-crime unit, 43n63
Russia, 180, 209
  training in investigation techniques, 182

S

Saffron Revolution, 2007, 98–99, 102, 118, 128, 151, 159, 160
San Pwint, 190n46
SaSaSa, 46n80
satellite imagery, 3
Sa Thon Lon unit, 20
SaYaKha, 115
SaYaHpa, 115, 127
Science and Technology Department, 22
Secret Intelligence Service (MI6), 4
sectarian violence, 153
Security Assistance Program, 181
Shan, 132

Shin Bet, 194
Shin Corp, 18
Shwe Mann, 56, 57, 82, 84
Signal Corps, 18
signals intelligence (SIGINT), 19, 135, 177–78, 180, 208
Singapore, 19, 60, 67, 178, 181, 182
Sino-Burmese Pact, 192n62
Skyful of Lies, 18
Snowden, Edward, 178
Soe Win, 56, 57, 70, 85
Sonny Swe, 86, 103n14
South Asia, 3
Special Branch (SB), 12, 26, 89–90, 120
  investigation and documentation centres, 123
  in MFA, 51n125
  Minister for Home Affairs, 125
  Royal Thai Police's, 173
  SB2, 26, 50n111
  strength, 123
Special Intelligence Department (SID), 26
speech crimes, 97
Stasi, 35
State Law and Order Restoration Council (SLORC), xiii, 15–17, 25, 26, 28, 30, 31, 33, 39n24, 70, 159
State Peace and Development Council (SPDC), 13, 57

anti-Khin Nyunt campaign, 62
arrest warrants, 69
Cyclone Nargis in 2008, 118
destroying Khin Nyunt's
     intelligence empire, 82–83
Human Rights Watch, 31
import licences, 85
Military Security Affairs, 90
report and press briefing, 97
restoring country's intelligence
     capabilities, 89
Secretary-1, 59
strength, 27
Steinberg, David, 65, 175
"stool pigeons", 117
Strategic and Defence Studies
     Centre, xvii
surveillance machine, 101

T

Taiwan, 171, 176
TaLaYa-Naing, 126, 127
targeted killings, 14, 20
Tatmadaw, 1
     combat-related intelligence, 116
     Commander-in-Chief, 119, 124
     Defence Services Computer
          Directorate, 43n62
     foreign operations, 172
     Khin Nyunt's dismissal, 58
     Military Intelligence Sections,
          35n2
     Muse corruption case, 60
     new generation officers, 16

nomenclature of, 47n93
Peace and Development
     Councils, 31
"pillage" theory, 64
regional military command
     structure, 20
resource constraints, 76n40
self-appointed guardianship
     role, 201
training and staff manuals, 9
True News Information Team,
     166n34
UAVs, 153
underground facilities, 100
Technology Department, 117–18
Telecommunications Law, 128,
     134, 142n51, 146n87
telephone tapping, 6n11, 13, 101
Thailand, 5n7, 6n13, 15, 19, 68,
     85, 86, 88, 92, 101, 171, 172,
     173, 176, 177, 178, 180
Thailand's National Security
     Council, 2
Thaksin Shinawatra, 18
Thanom Watcharaphut, 5n7
Than Shwe, 59, 60, 62, 90
     analytical failures, 159–60
     appointment of, 85
     destroying Khin Nyunt's
          intelligence empire, 82
     Khin Nyunt's arrest, 67–69
     Muse corruption case, 64–65
     Saffron Revolution, 98–99
Thein Sein, 88

Anti-Corruption Commission, 125
foreign operations, 171
intelligence developments, 113
level of overt oppression, 130
martial law, 153
midnight inspections law, 127
new intelligence agency, 119
vigilante gangs, 130
Ward or Village Tract Administration Law, 2012, 127
Thein Swe, 86
Tin Maung Maung Than, 30
Tin Oo, 103
Tomorrow News, 122
Towns Act (1907), 33
Trade Policy Council, 88
transnational crime, 183
Treaty of Amity and Cooperation, 41n44
Truth, The, 20
Tun Kyi, 63

U
UK's Security Service (MI5), 48n95, 177
Union Solidarity Development Association (USDA), 32
branches, 53n144
local intelligence branches, 94
militia members attacking Aung San Suu Kyi, 70
Union Solidarity Development Party (USDP), xiv, 32, 129, 136
United Kingdom (UK), xii, 15, 170, 174, 178, 182, 193n74
United States (US), 18, 38n17, 39n25, 80n76, 80n82, 97, 171, 174, 178, 180, 181, 182, 193n74
United Wa State Army (UWSA), 86
unmanned aerial vehicles (UAVs), 137, 153
U Nu, 21, 27, 171
US Army Intelligence and Security Command (INSCOM), 6n10
US Embassy in Yangon, 12, 34, 41n42, 62, 87, 88
US National Security Agency (NSA), 178
US State Department, 61, 71, 88, 194n81

V
Vientiane, 19
Village Act (1907), 33
visa restrictions, 131
Voice Daily, 122

W
Ward or Village Tract Administration Law (2012), 127

What's Swann Ar Shin and Other Articles, 115
"White Shirts", 32, 53n141, 53n143
Working People's Daily, 19

Y

Yanghee Lee, 132–33

YaWaTa, 52n135
YaYaKa, 33, 52n135
Ye Kyi Aing detention centre, 21
Ye Min Oo, 126–27
Ye Myint, 95, 99

Z

zero-sum game, 65

ABOUT THE AUTHOR

Andrew Selth is an Adjunct Professor at the Griffith Asia Institute, Griffith University, Brisbane, Australia. He has been studying international security issues and Asian affairs for forty-five years, as a diplomat, strategic intelligence analyst and research scholar. Dr Selth has published seven books and more than fifty peer-reviewed works, most of them about Myanmar (Burma) and related subjects. His latest major publications include *Myanmar's Armed Forces and the Rohingya Crisis* (2018) and *Burma (Myanmar) Since the 1988 Uprising: A Select Bibliography*, 3rd ed. (2018).

www.ingramcontent.com/pod-product-compliance
Lightning Source LLC
Chambersburg PA
CBHW070243230426
43664CB00014B/2389